THE BIG BAD WOLF

BOOK 1: BLOOD

13 PITCH BLACK CATS

Copyright © 2022 by 13 Pitch Black Cats

All rights reserved.

No part of this book may be reproduced in any form or by any electronic or mechanical means, including information storage and retrieval systems, without written permission from the author, except for the use of brief quotations in a book review.

ACKNOWLEDGMENTS

Thank you, Royal Road, for giving me a place to work up the courage to do this monumental task of writing this book.
Thank you to everyone who read the rough—and I mean very rough—first iteration of this book. I have taken your feedback to heart, and I hope that work is truly something you enjoy.
To my family: thank you for being a voice that said "Do it." Even among all the voices that said that what I was doing wasn't a good idea, your voice helped keep things moving forward.
To my editor: thank you for your patience. Your guidance has helped me learn so much and fix all the mistakes.
To my coach, I have "embraced the suck" and wrote the story I have always wanted to write. If it weren't for your lessons, this story wouldn't be a fraction as good as it is now.
To the person I never gave enough credit to, myself. You did it!

1

WE'RE NOT IN KANSAS ANYMORE

An unending flood of pain drowned my existence, radiating from everywhere and continuing for eternity. The pain abruptly dissipated. *Wow, what just happened? I can't feel anything and I can't see anything. There's no light and all I see is darkness. Did I just die? It's good to know that dying is exceedingly boring. Where's that light at the end of the tunnel? You know, the one that everyone always references?*

"Is that what you were hoping for? It's too late for me to change things, so you get to have the default experience." An odd-sounding voice rang out from everywhere, assaulting senses I thought were long gone. "Sorry, I'll dial it back a bit for you. There, is that better?" The voice sounded extremely generic, androgynous even.

Who...? I attempted to look for the source of the voice but came to the most disturbing realization yet. *I don't have a body!*

"Calm down, please. Yes, you are dead. No, you don't have a body yet. No, I am not God. I will not send you back. I have a job for you. My name is too difficult for you to pronounce, let alone understand, so you can call me 'The Voice' if that helps you. I believe that answers all the usual questions." The Voice sounded almost melancholic as they listed off answers to unasked questions.

Wait, what did she mean "yet?" A job? Do I get any say? Am I going to be paid? Or am I going to be given another life and, in recompense, I do whatever "The Voice" wants? I have more questions that she, or he, hasn't answered. I guess The Voice is a woman; it's kinda hard to tell with how androgynous they sound.

"I can read your mind. No, I am not a 'she.' Your archaic pronouns are insufficient to describe me properly. If you must use one, 'it' is the closest one in your limited vocabulary." Its voice sounded almost tired. But the liveliness from earlier returned as it continued. "You're surprisingly quick on the uptake and taking this rather well." A short giggle escaped from the void. "You are correct. You'll be given a new life and the job will be tied to your new life. Don't worry, I won't have you go through the whole experience of being born again. I learned my lesson the first time I tried that. The individual went completely insane and everything was counterproductive to what I needed. But I've found that starting you off young is quite helpful and can speed things along nicely without leaving you unprepared."

My metaphorical jaw plummeted into the unending abyss below me. *This not-God supreme being talking to me must be insane. Can I please get a new one, maybe someone with all of their marbles?*

"Well, that's just rude!" The Voice's volume shook my entire existence and left me wishing I had eardrums so they would burst.

I forgot you can read my thoughts. I guess that makes sense, considering I have no other way of communicating. I'm sorry. Please don't do anything rash.

"I guess I can forgive you. It is your first offense, after all." The tone of its words left me feeling more insignificant than ever.

"However, before I can send you off to your new life, there are some rules I need to observe. Yes, even I have rules, although I don't have to bore you with them. Just answer some simple questions for me." The pause made me dread the checklist of questions it was about to ask. "First question, do you remember your death? If you do, please describe what you can for me."

I guess I haven't thought about it yet. I remember tornado sirens going off, and suddenly the wind picked up. I ran to the bathroom of my house since I didn't have a basement. The memory played out in my nonexistent head. Tornados were rare where I lived, but apparently I'd won the lottery and had one strike my house. The sirens never quit and my house groaned with the increasing wind speeds that howled even louder as I hid in my bathtub. Then, suddenly, a loud cracking and a bang erupted, then the next thing I knew was pain, followed by this bizarre situation I found myself in. *So I guess the tornado killed me, fantastic.*

"You're correct, but at least it was quick."

As if that's supposed to make me feel better now that I'm dead. But you're right, there are far worse ways to go. I should take any victory I can when I can, no matter how small.

"Alright, second question: What's your name?"

Oh no, I don't like where this is going. Wait, what is *my name? Why can't I remember my name? I know I was a male, but that's all I remember. What happened to my body when I died that made it so I can't remember my name?*

"Well, what part of your body are you asking about? There are four pieces spread across the county. If you could name the part, I could narrow it down for you." A giggle followed the morbid sentence.

Now I don't want to know. Good grief, that sounds horrible. I did not need to know that.

"But you asked," The Voice said with a sadistic tone.

Just because someone asks for something doesn't mean you need to give them the gory details. You could have just said, "You don't want to know" and I could have left it at that. What if I asked what the answer to life, the universe and everything is? Would you answer that?

"You don't want to know."

You're toying with me now, aren't you? I'm also going to guess that you aren't going to tell me why I don't know my name.

"Nope. Now to the next question: Do you remember your family?"

Nothing, no memories there either. I know I had a family, but I don't know if I had any siblings, a wife, or children. I know I had a mother and a father because I know how babies are made. But I know nothing about them. I don't even know how old I was.

"Good, I'm getting better at this." The Voice sounded self-satisfied and peppy, which shook me to my core.

Wait just one minute. Good? This was intended? I'm not allowed to remember who I am or who my family was? I can remember the things I learned in school, but not where I went to school or who taught me. Oh, I see. I'm not allowed to remember details about real people. Weird rules, but I imagine there's a reason. I'm getting dizzy from all these special rules. Why does dying have to be so complicated?

"I told you, rules are rules. Now that that has been covered, we can get to your job description. Please understand that I know that this is a cliché and is a story that has been told an uncountable number of times in your world. But, spoiler alert: you won't be in your world anymore. You will be in a "fantasy world" your authors write so much about. I won't tell you much about it because that's one of the benefits of starting off as a child. You get to learn about the world organically."

You sound way too happy to be saying that. But that does make sense. Kids need to learn about the world one way or another. Do I have to go back to school again? Weren't the years of school I had in one life enough? Will any of it be practical?

"I won't spoil it for you. Back to the topic at hand: there's a demon king trying to invade the world, and he will eventually succeed. I don't know when, but I do know that he is close. Your job is to defeat him when he arrives. You'll have time to grow up, get strong and gain allies. All that fun stuff you can do to give yourself a chance. Don't worry, I'm sending you to replace the last person I sent. He's going to retire soon, so you will take his post. Don't worry, the same thing could happen to you. The king may never invade while you're there, and you can live your life. I will send another replacement for you, like I've been doing."

Practical. I guess this Voice isn't all bad. How long have you been doing this?

"And what measurement of time would you like that in?"

Nevermind. It's not worth it. The voice tried and failed to hold back its giggling.

"Don't worry about trying to explain anything about me or the fact that I reincarnated you. Nobody will believe you anyway. Now, as to why people will act like you've had a change in personality—"

Personality change?

"I'll leave that to you to figure out, but it'll be obvious. So, before I send you to your new life, any questions on your mind?"

Have we made it to the end of this little exchange? My biggest concern is that if this demon king is so powerful, how will I have the strength to defeat him?

"Figuring that out is mostly up to you. I will tell you that magic is real in this world. You'll have the opportunity to learn it if that's what you choose. Other than that, you'll be physically better in all aspects than a regular person. So long as you keep up your training and don't just laze around, you will have every opportunity to succeed in this task. Don't fret."

That sounds like it almost cares for me. If I didn't know I was just another person sent on this lifelong job, I would have believed that. But if I were to, by chance, confront the demon king, what would happen if I defeated him? What would happen if I lost?

"If you lose, then a lot of people are going to die and many more will suffer. I have a plan in place should that happen, but I really don't want to use it. And you aren't allowed to know it—just in case, you understand. If you defeat him in the material realm, then he will be banished for four hundred and twenty years and will be unable to enter the world in the same manner as before. Don't even think about fighting him in the demon realm. You will be significantly weaker while he will be even stronger. That is, unless you find a way to become almost godlike in your power. But that isn't going to happen. Though that is the only way to kill him permanently."

So guard duty it is. Wait, can I refuse?

"You can, but you won't," The Voice teasingly purred.

I guess since it's been reading my thoughts, it should know by this point I'm too curious to decline. As scary of a prospect as this is, at least I'm not a guinea pig and this is a semi-refined process. But for the sake of argument, what will happen to me if I refuse?

"I can't tell you that." It sounded disappointed. "Now, before you ask why, the most important reason is you are here and I'm giving you an option. You can choose not to take the job and continue as you were supposed to, or you can get another life and have fun."

I sense a "but" coming.

"So long as you do the job," The Voice added as almost an afterthought.

Ah, there it is.

"The deal is this. You can take this chance at a new life, and maybe or maybe not have to fight the demon king. Or you can face the unknown of what the majority of souls, those that don't get opportunities like this, face after they die. In the end, it's your choice. Since you hadn't objected, I was going to take that as consent. Nobody ever takes option two." All emotion disappeared from The Voice. "So what will it be?"

I wasn't really planning on dying the first time. But since you're offering, I'll take option one. And since I can't think of any more questions, I guess I'm as ready as I'll ever be. Oh wait, I got one. If I die again, what will happen to me? Let me guess, you can't tell me. Because rules are rules.

"That's right. You catch on quickly. Since we're going with the reincarnation route, it's time to send you on your way. Also, I just wanted to let you know: Good luck. We are all counting on you."

We? Who's we?

"Please remain calm and keep your arms and legs inside the ride at all times." The Voice returned to an almost mechanical tone.

Thanks to a tornado, I don't even have arms, legs, a torso, or even a head. Why did you say that?

"Because it's fun to see everyone's reaction to me saying that. Just remember, good luck. We are all counting on you." Its playful tone was more annoying than its answer.

This sounds familiar, but I can't put my finger on it, and it isn't because I don't have a finger. But is this going to be a jarring experience or something?

"More than any past or future experiences. Bye-bye now." The entity I was conversing with seemed to be yanked away, or maybe I was the one pulled away; I didn't have a frame of reference.

Everything started to spin with color and motion. Colors I didn't know existed blended into a psychedelic pattern that any drug addict would sell their soul to see. *It wasn't kidding about this being a wild experience.*

Beginning with the return of the sensation of movement, everything felt wrong. I never really gave credit to all the things that my body used to feel, until all feeling was stripped away then returned without a warning. Everything came back with a vengeance, and my vision was still overrun with a bad acid trip that took a wrong turn at Albuquerque.

At first, a high-pitched ringing drowned out everything else. The ringing intensified, and it sounded like my head was submerged in a raging river. As I stared at the colors, the constant shift of the colors was impossible to concentrate on. I wanted to close my eyes, but I didn't have eyelids to close. But not having a stomach meant I didn't want to vomit.

After who knows how long, I felt a sensation of falling, and my speed quickly increased. *Does this mean this is over soon? Thank you, because I don't want to be on this ride anymore.*

I'm starting to feel sick looking at all these colors. Are they going away? Why is everything turning red? Now it's going white. Ow, my head, why is there more pain? Wait, pain in my head? Does this mean I have a body again? Yeah, let's do this. Overwhelming pain immediately stymied my excitement. *Please make it stop. Why does death have to involve so much pain? Don't answer that question.*

2

BURNING FIRST IMPRESSIONS

Wetness was the first sensation I felt. I tried to open my eyes and move around. *What? My body isn't moving. Oh no, this isn't a good start. Why do I hear a ringing sound? It sounds like it's raining. That would explain the wetness.* Also, The Voice said that it would easily be understandable why I don't know anything and have a changed personality. Head pain, loss of memory, and potential personality changes make it sound like I have a concussion. Thanks a lot, but why is my body not responding to me? *What am I hearing now? Wait, is that light? Are my eyes finally opening? Does that mean I can move my body? Finally!*

I could hear people screaming in the distance. Water blurred my vision, and the only thing I could see, I guess, was mud. *Mud usually doesn't have this red of a tint to it.* More screams assaulted my ears. *This is terrible. It sounds like people are dying.*

The screams slowly disappeared and were replaced by the sounds of metal plates banging against each other, followed by loud footsteps coming my way. *Now I know I need to get up and see more than this red mud. Um, is that blood? That explains the red.* I tried to move my head. It shifted, albeit slightly and with even more pain, but it was better than nothing. I tried to take in my surroundings.

The Voice could have said many things, but it still wouldn't have done anything to prepare me for the horror that lay before me. My first view of the new world I had been sent to was full of blood-soaked mud, burning houses, bodies of animals and headless corpses. *Yeah, I don't think this is a good place to be. I'm in a new world with a new life, and the first thing I wake up to is a village being slaughtered? I think it's safe to guess that this village is being raided.* The only thing I could hear clearly was the sound of burning wood.

I looked around and, amongst all the death and destruction, there seemed to be some living people.

Maybe "people" wasn't the correct word.

They were huge, and their skin was a pale green. Most of them looked like they were wearing armor of some sort, ranging from just simple fur hides to chain mail. Two of the strange beings walked towards me. *Did they see me move my head? This will be the shortest reincarnation ever. Worst second-life experience ever, of all time. I demand a do-over. Why is my body not responding? I need to get running or I'm going to die. Come on, I need to do this.* I tried to move my arms and legs. *Nothing. Well, this is where I die. Again.*

Four mud-soaked boots stopped inches away from my face, interrupting my attempt to get my body moving. *I wish I got to know you, world.* A large hand grabbed me by the back of my neck. *Is he using three fingers? How small am I? I know I'm a child now, but come on. How young am I?* I was hoisted up to see a horrifying face, one that not even a mother could love—scarred, pale green and so full of teeth that it would be right at home in a shark.

"Looks like we've got a live one here, boys." The face was frightening, but the voice was far worse. It sounded like someone had taken a voice synthesizer and lowered the voice to an unreasonable level. It was deep, horrifyingly deep. *Please don't eat me.* "Tie her up and put her in a cage," the creature said as he held me to his partner, who had a rope in his hands.

"Her?" I'm a girl now? If I ever meet that entity who put me here again, I will have some words with it.

They tightly tied the rope around me, almost to the point of restricting blood flow to my extremities. *So I'm a prisoner now. At least I'm not dead. This life keeps getting better and better.*

As the creature finished tying me, he held me up by the rope and carried me away from the others of his kind. He took me to a bunch of cages, all of which were empty. *I'm the only prisoner they're taking? Lucky me. Or not, I still don't know where this is going.*

My head still felt like it was being split open, but it wasn't as bad as when I first woke up. The jarring movements sent a sharp pain through me every time my captor took a step. *The rope was unnecessary. I still have almost no control over my body. But I guess they don't know that.* The cages had a wooden square base with metal bars for the walls and ceiling. The door to the cage was at the top, and it looked to be a simple hook-and-latch system. I admired my new accommodations as he dropped me into them like a sack of potatoes.

I didn't control my fall, causing more pain to shoot through my legs and side when I landed. As I collided with the wood, I noticed that I had more than enough room to fall and not hit the sides of the cage. *Either this cage is large or I'm just that small.* As I lay on the floor of the cage, I looked at the carnage that had befallen the village my body was born in. I didn't see a single human being. All I saw were the pale, green-skinned raiders grabbing sacks, crates and chests as they approached the cage I lay in. *I can understand them. Although I'm not sure I'm glad about that. But it looks like The Voice made sure communication wasn't going to be a problem.*

I counted seventeen of the green-skinned raiders. There could have been more, but it was still frightening to know that they sacked this entire village with so few numbers. *They might be extraordinarily strong.*

All the other bodies on the ground were butchered nearly beyond recognition, but I couldn't find anyone who looked like a raider among the dead. *So the villagers didn't even kill one that I could see. This is a hopeless situation that I've been dropped into. Can this get any worse?*

Looking down gave me yet another sight I would never have been ready for. *I just had to say something, didn't I? I think I'm getting a little desensitized to these sights.* I had on a simple shirt that was long enough to be a dress on me. I knew I was a girl now, so that was within expectations. What was not, however, was the fact that both my arms and legs were completely covered in short hair. It might have been better described as fur. I also had a foot-and-a-half-long tail attached just above my butt. *Now I'm not even human anymore.* I suddenly felt an emptiness in my heart. *I think I'm in shock now. Yay. Why am I still conscious? Can this all be a dream and I wake up soon? Is this an elaborate joke? I can't do this, nope. I give up.*

My cage moved violently as it was picked up by one of the raiders and placed on a sled. They put an empty cage on top of mine and loaded the rest on the sled, stacked two high. Other sleds had several chests and or crates on them, while others had many brown and dirty sacks on them, stacked haphazardly. Then the raiders pulled their sleds by a cord and left the razed village with only one occupant in any of the cages: me. They walked into the night, and, at some point, I finally passed out. Whether from exhaustion or blood loss, it didn't matter. I wanted to wake up from this nightmare.

3

MIRRORED DREAM

I woke up and found myself on an island in the middle of an enormous lake or a serene ocean. *Is it over? How did I get here? Where is here? Is this a dream? Lucid dreaming... this is a new experience.*

I looked around to take stock of my surroundings. The first thing I noticed was that I was still in the body of a little girl with furry arms and legs and a tail. I was still caked in mud and blood. *I don't even know what color my fur actually is. And why do I even have have fur? This is a new kinda weird. How is the mud covering every inch of me?*

The island I was standing on was small, though calling it an island would have been generous. It was a twenty-five-foot radius, near-perfect circle of sand raised out of a still body of water. Strangely, a single palm tree rose from the center of the land with a piece of paper attached to it.

Can I move? I took a few cautious steps and found that I could walk. I started heading over to the tree.

Walking was a bizarre feeling. My new furry feet were bare, and, with each step, I could feel that they were not the same as human feet. *My feet are small, and my heels don't touch the ground.* It seemed my heels had to hover above the ground, and trying to make them go lower felt impossible. *It's almost like I'm perpetually walking on my toes and the balls of my feet. I guess I should look at the rest of my strange new body. My feet are probably only the beginning.*

I looked down at my hands. *Yeah, they're weird.* They were a cross between a paw and a hand, leaving my fingers looking short. My hands were completely covered in fur and were smaller than I would have anticipated. There were also callous-like spots on my fingertips and palm. *I know what these are. I have pads or "toe beans."* With a flex of my finger, I noticed I didn't have fingernails anymore. The things on my fingertips were too sharp and too long to be nothing less than claws. I could relax my fingers and retract my claws slightly, but they were omnipresent. *I guess I need to be careful not to scratch myself, anybody else, or anything in general.*

Oh, that's right, I have a tail that's dangling from just above my butt. I looked down at the matted and tangled fur of my tail. *It looks terrible.* My tail stuck out from a small hole in my dress-like shirt, which was brown and covered in blood and mud just like the rest of me. *I can't seem to move my tail outside of just grabbing it. I guess it isn't usable.*

A thought bubbled into my brain after looking over my body. *I wonder if I can see my reflection in the water.*

I changed course from walking to the tree to the water. *know I might not be long for this world, but if by some strange chance I do make it out, I'll need to know about this new body.* I peered over the water and gaped at my reflection. Only one word could truly do the description of my face any justice.

That word was, without a doubt, cute. *Of course I'm cute. Why would I be anything else? What are my other options? Ugly? Beautiful? Handsome? Plain? Nobody wants to be ugly. 'Beautiful' and 'handsome' are more for mature people. I guess if I was plain it wouldn't be that bad. So, cute it is.* But that wasn't the worst part.

I look like an animal! A cute animal, but still an animal. Large, round blue eyes stared back at me. A tiny triangle-shaped button nose, also covered in fur, sat in the center of my face. Again, more blood and mud coated my hair. And that included the fur on my face and neck. I had a pair of thin lips that covered my normal, human-looking teeth.

Next, I focused on the two protrusions from the top of my head. *My ears are on the top of my head?* I tentatively touched one with a clawed fingertip and shuddered. *They're hypersensitive. So this is why pets always enjoy scratches behind the ears. I can also see some grayish hair, or is that fur? What's the difference anyway? Is there anything human about me anymore?* Seeing the hair on top of my head soaked in the bloody mud, matted and tangled, annoyed me. It wasn't long, and it fell just past my chin.

It's very convenient there's a lake right here. I could clean this mud off and see what color my hair is. I stuck my hand in, but it didn't feel wet or like I was even touching anything despite being submerged in the water. I marveled at that. *I guess I'm not allowed to clean myself up in my dream.*

Deflated, I walked towards the tree in the center of the island. *That paper on it is likely important.* Arriving at the tree, I could see someone had placed a note at my head height. It wasn't long, but the handwriting was immaculate. I couldn't find anything holding the paper to the tree, so I grabbed the note, and it released itself with no effort.

First, do you remember how I said even I have rules? I'm able to communicate with you once.

Second, I'm sorry.

The body you now inhabit is not the one I intended for you to have. I know that it likely won't mean much, but you have my most sincere apologies for the predicament you find yourself in now. I failed to aim your soul correctly, and now you find yourself in the body of a beastkin.

To show you how sorry I am, you are free to live your life in any way you see fit. I will send someone else. Also, you

don't need to worry about the orcs that have you imprisoned. You will wake up after you finish this letter and be freed from your confinement.

   Just so you know, we wish you good luck and a happy life.
The Voice

   I stared at the letter. *I don't even know how to process this information. My second life will be as a female animal-human hybrid. I don't know how to feel about that. In my first life, there was a fifty-fifty chance of me being a male, so why couldn't I be born as a female this time around? Being a girl doesn't make me a freak, but looking like an animal might. Although the creatures that captured me make me suspect I might be more normal in this new world than I think. I don't know anything about this world.*

   As I stared at the letter after finishing it, lost in thought, everything brightened until my vision turned white.

4

THREE LITTLE WORDS

I found myself bound and in a cage again, lying down uncomfortably. The creatures that captured me, the ones referred to as orcs by The Voice, looked to be taking me out of a forest and into some plains full of rolling hills. I could hear the sleds scraping on the ground and heavy footsteps, but also something new in the distance. It was quiet at first but quickly grew in intensity. *It's getting closer, and it sounds like horses running.*

The sound was getting louder with each passing moment. The orcs didn't seem to hear them like I could. *Is my hearing better than theirs? With these satellites on top of my head, that wouldn't be surprising.*

I remembered what The Voice told me in its letter. *After I woke up, I would be free. It looks like I'm still tied up in a cage. So, The Voice has rules about how much it can affect this world. That's why it sent me in the first place. But how are horses going to help me? What's going to happen to get me out of this cage and not immediately killed by the orcs?*

When the orcs finally reacted to the sound that I was hearing, I saw what I believed to be knights galloping towards me. I stared at them in awe, not because I hoped they were going to save me, but because their armor was completely white. *That seems like an odd and slightly impractical choice.* Twenty of these mounted knights charged fearlessly towards my captors.

The orcs had almost no time to prepare as the battle began, but the orcs met the knights' charge with whatever weapons they had on hand. Unfortunately for them, all the knights had long spears. All but three of the orcs received a wound somewhere on their bodies, and four of the orcs didn't get back up from the blows they received.

The knights lost most of their spears in the charge, but that didn't stop them. They drew their swords as they wheeled their horses around to attack the war band again.

The orcs that survived the initial charge met the knights, this time more prepared for a fight.

I could see how seventeen of them had sacked a whole town so easily. The remaining thirteen each killed a horse as they were being charged, but three more orcs were killed in the exchange. I watched as the seven remaining mounted knights dismounted and formed a wall of swords and shields. The group that were forcibly dismounted kept their composure, and many rolled to their feet.

The knights wasted no time in gathering together with each other and fighting defensively. The orcs attacked the knights brutally, with little regard for their own safety. The knights, brilliantly, did not face the attacks directly. They instead dodged them or deflected them so that they would miss.

One orc broke a knight's weapon as he tried to deflect an attack. The orc's ax swing collided with the knight's sword; the sword shattered, and the ax sank into the shoulder of the knight. Destroying the sword was testament enough to its strength, but after it buried the ax a solid foot into the metal armor and chest of the knight, I worried about the knights' survival.

The orc struggled to dislodge its weapon from the knight's corpse, leaving himself completely defenseless. The seven knights who had dismounted arrived in time to cut the orc down as they joined the fray. It took several deep attacks to bring it down. *Great, so they're hard to kill too.* Now that the knights were a full team again, they killed off the orcs systematically, one by one. *It looks like the orcs individually are much stronger than the knights. But the knights' tactics and teamwork more than compensate for the deficit.*

After all the orcs were dispatched, the knights took a moment to catch their breath. They surveyed the battlefield, and a few of them looked in my direction.

"Captain, it looks like there's a captive." A single knight pointed in my direction as he looked at another knight with a helmet that had a long plume.

"It's surprising that they took a captive, but by the looks of the number of cages, they were looking for more for breeding stock," the captain replied.

My heart dropped. *I was almost reduced to becoming a baby-making puppet for orcs. The Voice better be sorry about that. Although, if I understood the letter correctly, it did get me out of this mess. But it was still to blame for this from the beginning.*

"She looks a little too small to be breeding," a third voice chimed in.

"She's a beastkin too. What do you want to do, Captain?" the first knight who spoke asked.

Alright, I need to get out of this situation and see if these knights in shiny armor really are just that. "I can hear you from over here." My voice sounded more like a wheeze. *I guess I didn't realize how dehydrated I was.*

The captain didn't waste any time directing his squad. "First off, secure the horses, burn the corpses and collect Dave and Girart. Their families should be able to have a body to lay to rest. You and Jenkins can start by going through the war band's supplies and plunder. Don't release the beastkin yet; we don't know if it's feral or not." *At least he knows how to keep his head in the game and not get distracted. What was that about being feral?*

Now I have to prove to them that I'm sane and not going to bite them. Fantastic.

While I waited for them to decide what they were going to do with me, ideas ran through my head about what I should do. *I guess my first goal should be to sit up straight to at least look civil. It looks like the knights are going to take some time to sort through everything.* I tried to worm my way to the sidewall of my cage and use that as leverage to sit up against it. My arms and legs weren't doing a lot for me since they were bound to my sides and together. *I imagine I look like a fish out of water. I really am in deep trouble here.* After many careful and numerous small movements, I made it to the side. *Now for the hard part: sitting up. I tired myself out just getting here. How much blood did I lose from my head wound?* I brought my back all the way to the wall with my legs out in front of me, and I attempted to roll sideways and stop halfway through. If the knights were watching me, I must have entertained them since it took me several tries to get off the ground and even more to get into a true sitting position.

Exhausted and successful, I celebrated with a heavy sigh and laid my head against the metal bars of my cage, enjoying the cool feeling on the back of my head.

While I enjoyed my reverie, I heard footsteps coming closer to me, but I noticed them too late. A voice startled me before I opened my eyes to see who was walking towards me. "That's a good sign. Moving around to sit up." It sounded like the guy the others were referencing as "Captain."

I opened my eyes after jumping just a little, but managed to remain sitting. I looked at the source of the voice and saw a human male. His face looked like he rarely smiled and his green eyes were staring down without hiding his scrutiny. "You don't look good. Are you injured anywhere?" His eyes narrowed on me as he looked to be scanning my whole body. The closer he got, the larger he looked.

"Water," I got out, but it sounded feeble and strained. The man brought his ear closer to me, and I tried again. "Water, please." I put everything I had into saying those two words.

He looked at me as if he was considering something. He put a gauntleted hand to his chin, showing how tanned his skin was compared to the white material of his armor. It looked like he was almost through with his idea when he ran his hand through the dark-brown, short hair on his head. Suddenly, his eyes lit up. "Dex, canteen!" he shouted, and held out his arm.

Finally, I can get something to drink.

Shortly, another knight who had also taken his helmet off came up. His complexion and hair color were similar to the captain's, but his hair was slightly longer and he looked boyish. He handed him a teardrop-shaped leather skin with a nozzle on it.

"Thank you. As you were, soldier." He then turned from the one who'd brought the water skin to me. "I take it you can understand me." I nodded. "You aren't going to cause any trouble?" I shook my head. "I'm going to place this next to you and cut your bindings. You are not to leave that cage. You will not touch anyone. Finally, you will not speak to anyone unless they speak to you first. If you try anything I don't like, I will kill you. You'll behave, won't you?"

I nodded my head enthusiastically but immediately regretted it as I got dizzy from the rapid motion. *I understand that my life's at your discretion.* The captain placed the water skin leaning on my leg and pulled a dagger from his belt. He walked behind me, and I heard a small snap, and suddenly my arms were no longer constricted to my torso.

I lifted my arms to unravel the rope and, as soon as I could bend my elbows, I reached up and grabbed the rope and began tearing it off of me. With my arms free, I snatched the waterskin and inspected the nozzle to see how it was sealed. It looked like a piece of leather, but it was perfectly sized. I gave it a tentative pull. It budged, so I took the claws from my thumb and pointer finger and pierced the leather to get a better grip. *These claws are surprisingly sharp.* I pulled this time with more effort and was rewarded with a satisfying pop.

My goal was right in front of me and finally accessible.

I put the water skin to my lips and drank a little too quickly. Immediately I started coughing as some of the water entered my windpipe. I got my breathing back under control and went back to drinking.

Before I could finish half of it, the captain grabbed the canteen away from me. I must have looked shocked, because he held out an open hand to me and he started talking. "Don't drink it all now. This should last us two days as we head back to the city now that our mission to kill these orcs is complete. Please hand me the stopper." He gave a slight nod to the leather thing still stuck to my pointer-finger claw. I pulled it off and gave it a closer inspection. It was indeed leather, but it was leather wrapped around some type of wood. *My claws just pierced wood like it was nothing?* I handed him the stopper and then looked at my claws, fascinated at how dangerous they were. Still curious, I took a single claw to the rope binding my legs and hooked it in. I pulled gently, and I severed the rope with almost no effort. *That is kinda cool.*

"Now, will you answer my question? Are you hurt anywhere?" Straightening his posture, the captain stood at his full height.

"My head, I think. It hurts a lot," I replied in a still-raspy voice.

He didn't ask another question, but walked around to my back. Before I could turn to look at him, he grabbed my shoulder to hold me still. His one hand not only covered my shoulder, but part of my bicep as well. Then I felt something touch the back of my head and pain shot through me. I flinched at the touch as I yelled.

"Do you remember getting hit in the back of the head?"

Didn't he see the blood in my hair as he cut my ropes? I wondered, but said, "No."

The pain was manageable until he poked it again, making the agony resurge with a vengeance. My head throbbed with the pain pulsing from the wound.

"How old are you?" The captain walked into my view again.

"I don't know." My voice was still weak, but it was getting easier for me to talk.

The confusion showed on his otherwise stoic face. "What village are you from?"

"I don't know." *Great, I think I can tell where this is going.*

"Do you have a name?" He was almost pleading now.

"I don't know." *Yeah, I was right. What's next, is he going to see if I know anything? Has he figured out that I have no memory?*

With a heavy sigh, the captain opened the cage and reached in to lift me out.

The feeling of being carried was disconcerting. The knight placed one hand under each of my arms and picked me up without hesitation. He then set me down on the ground, and my legs, still too weak to hold me, gave out. I slumped to the ground on my hands and knees. He took a knee and put his hand on my shoulder. It surprised me that I didn't fall completely to the ground with how weak my body felt.

"My name is Allen, by the way. How long did the orcs keep you in that cage?" he asked with concern in his voice.

"I don't know." *My new catchphrase.* "A day, I think."

He stood up, and the next thing I heard was the loud screeching of a woman. "You let it out of the cage? How do you know it isn't feral? We should kill it before it becomes dangerous." A knight slightly smaller than the rest came running up to us, drawing her sword. Her voice was high, and it sounded like she was running towards an emergency.

Her hair was short, but her face was obviously quite beautiful. Her ears were visible through her hair. They were longer than any human ears I had ever seen.

Her captain stood between her and me, halting her charge. "She's not feral; in fact, she has no memories. She's also extremely weak from her imprisonment. You're going to give her food and take care of her. I'll take her to Nora at the orphanage when we return to the capital."

"It's a beastkin. It will be nothing more than a wild animal once it grows up." *She has something against me, or, more precisely, my kind. It's good to know that there's racism in this world and that I'll be the target of some of it.* "That thing will never contribute to the kingdom. It will only cause problems. We should just dispose of it and save everyone the trouble of dealing with it once it can defend itself. Nobody will miss it." Her voice grated on me.

"Avollea, enough!" the captain shouted at the racist woman. "I don't care what happened to you in the past involving beastkin, but you will not kill this innocent child."

"What makes you think any beastkin is innocent?" The woman referred to as Avollea continued the shouting match.

"That's the type of thinking that leads to wars where nobody wins, wars full of senseless bloodshed. You will treat this child as if it were one of your own." *I think the captain might be a little angry.* He never gave the woman a chance for a rebuttal. "Your insubordination has tested my limits before, but you will not cross this line. You will care for this child because your life depends on it. If she dies, I will charge you with treason and you will be executed. Have I made myself clear?"

"You can't do that." Her screams hit a new high. Her voice started to break. I couldn't tell if it was from anger or sadness. "You're abusing your power."

"I can and I will." The captain balled his fists, squeezing the waterskin in one hand. "You took an oath to join my company. Defend this kingdom and all its inhabitants. We found this child within the kingdom's borders. We are a full day away from the capital. She is a citizen, whether she remembers it or not. You will not murder any of this kingdom's citizens. That's why it is treason to kill her." *I think this man has a hero complex to go through this much to save my hide. Not that I'm not grateful. I'm not interested in dying again.*

"I'll remember this." She sounded livid.

"You better." With those two words, I think the captain finally won the argument.

I knew my hearing was better than normal, but these ears, the size of satellites on my head, did their job too well. Before all the shouting began, my head was already pounding from a certain person poking a wound on the back of my head. The first shouts weren't too bad, but when they kept going and increasing in volume, all I could do was cover my ears with my hands and curl up in the fetal position. My head felt like knives were stabbing it repeatedly. I was feeling nauseous from the pain. Once the yelling was over, the pain slowly subsided.

"Get up." It sounded like Avollea. "Get up. I may have to keep you alive, but that doesn't mean I have to like you." Her foot nudged me out of the painful state I was in. I looked at her face and saw that everything was blurry. It seemed like tears had fallen down my face from all the pain. "Stop crying and do something useful. Help us set up camp."

"I can't stand up." My voice had recovered mostly at this point. *Wow, not only do I sound just like you expect a little girl to sound, but I also sound pitiful.* "I'm too hungry and weak."

"Ugh, here. Once you finish that, start building a fire with the wood from these cages." A piece of jerky the size of my fist fell from her hands and onto the ground in front of me. *She really doesn't like me.*

I quickly grabbed the dried meat and brushed off the dirt with my filthy hands. *Yeah, that was a wasted effort.* Still, I took a bite out of the provided food like it was my last meal. Wordlessly, I chewed the dried meat and savored the flavor. *I don't think I've ever had any jerky taste this good before in my previous life. If I'm completely honest, I don't think anything has ever tasted this good.* The piece of meat she gave me was gone in seconds.

There was an unfortunate side effect of eating the jerky; it awakened my hunger. *I might have been starving before they released me.* I felt livelier once I had food in my belly.

"More?" I looked at her with pleading eyes. "Can I have another one?"

"Absolutely not." The look she gave me made it sound like I was asking for her firstborn child. "You need to work for your food. Get to making a fire over there." She sounded angry, but wasn't screaming her words this time. She then pointed to the pile of orc corpses.

There's one problem that's preventing me from doing that. "I don't know how to make a fire," I told her honestly.

Her jaw dropped. "Can you cook?" I shook my head. "Do you know how to take care of a horse?" Again, I shook my head. "Can you clean a sword?" *I don't think I could do it properly.* Once more, I shook my head. "What can you do?" Desperation was evident on her face.

I thought of all the things I could do. Nothing was relevant to the situation in this medieval world I found myself in. "I don't know." *I said it again. Even I'm getting tired of saying those three words.*

"I knew you were going to be useless. Just take those cages and drag them to Drue and do whatever he asks you to." She pointed to a knight stacking the orc corpses.

I attempted to stand up, succeeded, and found that my body was much more responsive than earlier. *Although that bar was set quite low.* I still felt weak, but I walked over to the cages and saw they were still on the sleigh. I grabbed the cord that I assumed was used to pull the sleigh and prepared myself to pull a huge amount of weight, given the six large cages of wood and metal. I pushed with everything I had. Suddenly my arms were outstretched, and the ground was moving towards me. My arms didn't catch me as I hurled to the dirt. The impact was jarring and reminded me of how much pain I was still in.

I slowly recovered from my face-plant and felt there was a lot of slack on the cord that I was using to pull the sleigh, which was right behind my feet. *Did I just move this sleigh like it was nearly weightless? I'm in the body of a young child, and I can move something much larger than me. How is that possible? How strong would I be if I was at a hundred percent?*

"What are you waiting for? Those cages aren't going to move themselves," Avollea shouted.

Why is she yelling again? Snapping out of my confusion and picking myself off the ground, I stood up once again.

This time I prepared not to use my arms but only to use my legs. Leaning forward and bracing myself for the inevitable resistance, I pushed off with one foot. There was resistance, but not even close to the amount I was expecting. I almost stumbled again, but I was able to catch myself by bringing my trailing leg up in front of me. *These new feet are going to take some getting used to.* There was little surface area contacting the ground when I stepped. I shortened my stride, leaned forward less, put one foot in front of the other and pulled the devices of my imprisonment to my destination. *My guess is that they plan on using the wood from these cages to start a fire to burn the corpses, as Captain Allen ordered. Also, this is much easier than I would have ever guessed.* Eventually, I made it to the knight referred to as Drue, who was looking at me with admiration.

5

NEW MUSCLES

Drue was larger than Allen in all dimensions, and his face had several scars. One of the scars looks like it was caused by a large cat's paw that cut from his ear, part of which was missing, down to his chin. His bald head looked like he had regularly shaved it, although the stubble was growing and showed that it was time to shave again soon. "Did the princess tell you to do that?" His words sounded like a father questioning a lost child. I welcomed his deeper, calmer voice after listening to the women scream and yell.

"She's a princess?" I looked back at her in a panic. I saw that she was inspecting one of the chests and pointing toward another group of knights. I looked back at Drue, worried for my safety.

"Relax, kid, it's just a nickname we use for her." He put his hand on my shoulder to stop me from walking any further. He dropped to one knee and leaned forward a bit, but still looked down at me. "She's direct, rude, demanding and feels entitled to many things. Her combat abilities, on the other hand, are among the best. Her strategies are also ones that minimize the loss of life for all of her comrades. With the lives lost today, she's just in a bad mood.

Although I didn't know she was a beastkin-hater." Drue looked toward Avollea for just a moment, then back at me. "She cares about those who fight beside her, but only them, and doesn't give anyone else much thought."

"So she's just in a bad mood and thinks I'm useless?" I rubbed the back of my head to ease the pain just a bit, even if it was just momentarily. "I don't remember anything before waking up in the mud and everyone around me was dead. Then the orcs tied me up and put me in one of those cages." I turned to point at the cages behind me. "And my head really hurts."

Drue looked at me sympathetically. "Took a nasty blow to the head, did you?" I think he was asking a rhetorical question, but I still nodded. "That explains why the captain was quick to let you out. That, and he has a soft spot for kids. He has four of his own, you know? Three boys and a girl."

"He has a family?" I asked rhetorically. "I can believe that. But why did he order her to take care of me until we get to where we're going? And where are we going?" *This guy seems a lot more rational than the crazy elf lady. Hopefully he can answer my questions.*

He narrowed his eyes as he gave me a scrutinizing stare. *Did I say something weird?* "We're going back to the capital. Captain Allen has Avollea looking after you because she won't fail. Call it professional pride, if you will. He didn't need to add the treason clause on the order, but I think he was just angry with her at that moment." He removed the cord from the sleigh from my hands and stood up. "The captain said he'll take you to Nora and that she'll look after you. She runs the orphanage in Aquittemia. You'll like her. She takes her job seriously and understands that you're all children who have already lost more than you should. Her heart is much too large for her own good sometimes. There are those who have taken advantage of her kindness, but they always return to give back far more than they took. Nobody knows why." He moved the sleigh towards the pile of corpses. "So what did the princess tell you to do, anyway?"

"She said to help you by doing whatever you tell me to do." I gave him what I thought was my bravest face. "I don't know how to do much, but I can learn."

There's that sympathetic look again. Do I really look that pathetic? I guess the muddy hair and fur don't really help in that department. Also, I'm a tiny kid. "Go over to Jenkins and ask if the orcs had any oil and bring it over here. I'm going to show you how to start a campfire."

"Who's Jenkins?" I asked.

"Pretty boy over there." He pointed to one of the men who was sorting through the chests. Avollea was also there with Jenkins, but I still walked over there because I was on a mission. *A simple mission, but I'm a kid again, so I'll take my small victories. After all, walking is still something I need to get good at, and this is good practice.*

Each step I took was slow, and it felt like I was constantly on the edge of tipping over. *Having digitigrade feet really is going to be the hardest thing to get accustomed to.* Even though during my dream I walked around just fine, I stared at my feet and watched how they moved. *It's like I'm walking on my toes the entire time while at the same time spreading my toes as far apart as possible.* After taking several practice steps, I noticed that the walking motion wasn't all that different from my last life, but constantly feeling everything my feet were stepping on was a painful reminder of how inhuman I was. Balancing myself was the real problem, since my center of gravity was nowhere near where I thought it would be. Once I got about a third of the way towards Jenkins, my foot slipped off a small rock. I threw my hands out to catch myself as I leaned towards the ground. My hands easily caught my fall.

"You alright, kid?" I heard Drue call out as he jogged towards me.

I carefully put my feet underneath me and stood up again. "Yeah, I just tripped." I brushed my hands together and accomplished nothing.

"Maybe you should just take it easy. Your injury might be worse than you realized." Drue slowed down for the last few strides as he came to a stop and kneeled next to me. "Actually, how about you go take a seat over there? I'll get the oil."

I followed Drue's finger and saw that it pointed to a saddle resting on the ground. Another human female knight was leading a horse away from it and towards the other horses. "I'm sorry I couldn't help you. It's just everything is all weird for me right now." I lowered my head.

Drue chuckled. "Kid, I'm surprised you're walking at all. You look like you've had a really bad day. Head injuries can have complications. Since you moved those cages, consider yourself relieved of duty." A wide smile spread across his scarred face. "If the princess gives you any trouble for not working, I'll take all the responsibility. Do you need a hand to hold to help you?" The man stood up and offered his hand.

I guess should take it easy. I reached up and grabbed the large man's hand, making sure none of my claws would cut him, even though he had on leather gloves. "Thanks. This means a lot to me. Really, it does." I still couldn't look him in the eye.

"The Brilliant Crusade never leaves anyone behind."

Drue walked beside me, never moving forward until I took my step first. Patiently, he helped me walk to the saddle he had mentioned. While we walked, I tripped on a rock again, but this time he caught me. I noticed something while I was leaned over. I turned my head and saw that my tail stuck straight out. *That's right, animals use tails for balance. But why can't I use mine?*

Eventually, Drue and I made it to the saddle, and I sat down on it sideways. It wasn't comfortable, but it wasn't as hard as the ground.

Satisfied that I was now safe, Drue walked towards Jenkins to continue his duties.

Drue and Avollea couldn't be more different. Avollea saw me as nothing more than a wild animal that needed to be put down, but Drue saw an injured kid that needed a helping hand. So when

Avollea was shouting and screaming, why didn't he come to my defense then? Was it because Allen was already defending me, or is it because he's scared of Avollea? If he was scared of her, then why would he use such a derogatory nickname behind her back? What if she overhears him?

I could feel a headache coming on, so I decided that thinking such complicated thoughts needed to be put on hold. The mystery of my unusable tail, however, needed to be solved. I carefully grabbed the base of it. As I felt my hand holding my tail, I could feel my tail being held by my hand. *Having another limb and feeling it feels natural and alien at the same time. But tails are controlled by muscles and muscles can be trained. I remember hearing about how some people can learn to move their ears up and down.*

As that thought ran through my head, I placed a hand at the base of an ear and felt some muscle. I pressed the pad at the end of my finger into the muscle and I could feel my ear pull back. *Can I move my ears too?* After I removed my finger, I tried to move my ear just by focusing on the muscles that I felt. Both ears moved back and swiveled. *I moved them! That's so cool! Weird, but cool.* A thud sounded behind me as I felt my tail collide with something hard. I turned around and saw that I was wagging my tail.

I continued to watch, enraptured by my tail wagging faster and faster the more I got excited. *Alright, now that I know it moves, I should try to control it.* There were muscles just above my butt that flexed and relaxed as my tail whipped from side to side. I tried to stop them, but my tail just kept wagging. *Come on. Stop moving.* I reached and grabbed for my tail, only for it to slip out. I growled as I turned further to reach for it again. This time I grabbed it. *Did I just growl? How animalistic am I?*

While I contemplated my ability to growl, I failed to notice my shift in balance and that I was no longer seated on the saddle. With my hands holding my tail, I fell to the ground.

Laughter erupted from several of the knights. I released my tail, and my heart plummeted as they continued to laugh. I turned my head to look at the saddle and, without thinking, I scrambled behind it. Curling up to make myself as small as possible, I could feel my heart pounding in my chest. I noticed my tail had also curled up with me. *Oh, so now you stop moving. I guess my tail's movements are based on my emotions. No poker face for me until I get it under control. If I get it under control.*

Someone's footstep grew louder as the laughter died down. "You alright?" Drue's voice started once the footsteps stopped. "Why are you trying to hide?"

I poked my head up from behind the saddle and saw Drue holding a glass flask with a black fluid inside it. "I just—just couldn't handle everyone laughing at me." My response surprised me. It was like my words just flew out of my mouth without so much as a second thought.

"A real shy one, are you?" Drue turned towards the pile of bodies and cages I had moved. "Even I have to admit that watching you play with your tail was one of the cutest things I've ever seen."

My cheeks warmed as I felt my ears flatten. *Is it because I'm a cute little animal or a cute little girl?* I ducked behind the saddle again.

"I'm sorry. I didn't mean it in a bad way." Drue took a few more steps towards me. I looked up and felt minuscule as the man towered over me. "You really are shy."

I need to calm down. Is there anything left in my memories that I can use to calm down? As I dug through my memories, many of them were disjointed and didn't make sense. Nothing helped until an image of a grand waterfall appeared. The waterfall flowed from the top of a sheer cliff into the river below. A fine mist circulated at the base of the waterfall. In stark contrast to the roiling water at the base of the waterfall, the river looked calm. I could see that the water was flowing quickly, but there was hardly a ripple. A rainbow arced from the river into the mist and disappeared into the falling water.

Everything felt calmer while I looked at the waterfall.

Drue kneeled down next to the saddle and placed the bottle on the ground next to him. He extended his hand towards me. "Come out from behind there. There's nothing to fear. If you want, I can teach you how to make a campfire."

I don't know what persuaded me. Was it his gentle-sounding voice, or his fatherly smile? Either way, I cautiously took his hand and crawled out from behind the saddle.

6

A MAGIC TRICK

Drue showed me how to make a campfire, and everyone slept for the night. I kept my distance from the fire. It felt like something was telling me to avoid it at all costs.

The next morning, after packing everything of value up, we marched towards the capital city for an entire day. I spent most of it riding Avollea's horse because I had short legs and couldn't keep up otherwise.

We traveled through hilly plains most of the time until we finally found a road made of heavily packed dirt with small round stones with a slightly raised center. I learned that the stones tell everyone that these roads connected to large towns.

Everyone's tired faces livened up when stone walls crested into our vision.

With their destination in sight, the knights suddenly changed their attitudes. Instead of the stiff marching on the way here without so much as a word spoken to each other, small talk erupted from everyone, and they seemed to speed up. The most common topic of conversation was who they were going to sleep with. Some had wives, others committed relationships, and someone named

Marvin said he was finally going to ask out some elven seamstress by the name of Catherine. Others were talking about how they were going to spend their stipend. Avollea forgot about my existence entirely and even joined in the camaraderie. She had her eyes on a new home, and the money from this mission would give her enough to buy it.

I felt like a fly on the wall with all the different conversations I could hear. With my large ears, I could hear all of them all at once, but I could only focus on one at a time. Every once in a while I would feel dizzy and curl up on the saddle. There were a lot of noises, and I tried to ignore them as much as I could. I focused on the stone walls of our destination to block out as much of the conversations going on around me as possible.

The sun was about two or three times its diameter from setting when we reached the walls and a gate. As we were getting closer to the city, there was a merchant caravan-looking collection of wagons that moved out of our way. Everyone in the caravan was dressed in heavy, dark-colored cloaks. Many of the people lifted a hand and pointed at me then whispered amongst each other. Their stares felt even more unnerving. Regardless of their opinion of me, they let us pass like we were some conquering heroes who'd come home from a long war. *I guess this knight company was a bit more famous than I thought. But how do the people know? They were only wearing their padding, not the silver plates that they're likely known for.*

Drue walked close to me, talking with one of the other knights. I didn't know his name, but his reddish hair and light complexion stood out from the rest of the group. The two guys were talking about a waitress's bust size at a certain tavern. *It seems like guys will be guys no matter what world they're from. I guess that years from now, I'll almost certainly be the subject of that conversation between two guys. I don't know how I feel about that.*

"Hey, Drue."

Drue practically jumped at the sound of me calling his name as I

THE BIG BAD WOLF

interrupted his conversation. "Oh, yes, kid. What do you want?" Drue turned toward me. The redhead also looked in my direction.

"Why is everyone making way for us?" I asked, waving my arm around towards everyone else's strange behavior.

"We're a knight company from this city. The merchants recognized that. They have to go through inspections, but we don't." *He said that with far too much enthusiasm.*

"So, if you were a part of any company, would you receive the same treatment?"

This time, the other guy piped up. "Yes, but we're the Brilliant Crusade. Captain Allen only accepts the best, so we're treated with more respect than others."

"Oh, okay. Thanks, you can go back to talking about breast sizes." I waved them goodbye.

"Wait, you could hear us?" The redhead sounded surprised.

"Not such an innocent child, are you?" Drue added afterward. "Are you getting some memories back?"

I pointed to the fuzzy organs on the top of my head. "I can hear everyone's conversations with these. No, I'm not getting my memories back. I know what breasts are, just like I know that I'm riding a horse right now. Although I don't know what type of horse it is."

"I'm sure you're going to grow into a lovely woman." Drue grinned from ear to ear with that comment. "I believe you'll be so beautiful that you'll have every man swooning over you."

I looked at him, not hiding my confusion. *He knows he's talking to a child, right? Not that I'm one on the inside, but he doesn't know that.*

Drue simply laughed.

"The *breed* of horse you are riding right now is Rophmna's signature warhorse, the Grimerakke. Our horses are stronger, larger and hardier than every other horse." The other guy's chest ballooned out with each word. His chest was so puffed out that I felt an urge to poke him with a claw just to watch him deflate.

13 PITCH BLACK CATS

Our little talk about the horse I was riding ended as we formed orderly lines and entered through the gate, which looked like a metal portcullis that was split down the middle and opened like a cathedral door.

Three soldiers at the gate raised their left arms straight out, with their hands level with their eyes. Each held their hand as a fist, just as one would hoist a drink or weapon. Allen put his right hand on his left shoulder and bowed slightly as he walked by. After his bow, the guards dropped their salute.

As we entered the city, I saw crowds of people in the streets, but they didn't make way for us like the caravans did. The entire knight company gathered around Captain Allen as he stopped shortly after we entered the city. He gave orders to a few knights to sell the salvaged goods to the respective stores. He then told everyone that they would meet at their headquarters so they could receive their pay for the mission. Everyone went in all different directions, except for a certain elf.

Avollea approached Allen with heavy steps. "I did as you commanded. I brought the beast to the city alive." Her words were a little calmer. *Is being called a beast an upgrade from being called "it?"* "You can take it to the orphanage like you want." *And now we are back to being an "it" again.*

"I release you from your duty of watching over her. I will take her from here." Allen placed a hand on her shoulder as he walked by her to reach me. He reached up and lifted me off the horse and set me carefully down on the ground.

As soon as Allen removed me from her horse, Avollea grabbed the reins and walked off with the creature.

"Okay, kid, this is where you get your shot at life." He looked a little sad as he said that. "I know this isn't going to be the life you should have had with a mother and father, but this is the best I can give you."

"I understand. I probably should thank you for rescuing me, shouldn't I?" I realized I hadn't yet. "Thank you."

"You can thank me by being a good kid for Nora." His voice was serious. I gave him a thumbs-up, carefully not stabbing myself with my sharp claws. I smiled, and hopefully he accepted that I would try. "Good enough." His face eased a little, and he grabbed my hand and strolled down the street.

Now I know how short people feel when walking next to a tall person. I have to take three steps just to keep up with his one step. The streets weren't highly populated, but some people were moving around. *I think they might be getting any last-minute tasks done so they can stay home for the night.* The people that were out and about only half-paid attention to the human being walking with a beastkin kid down the stone road. Those that paid any attention stared at us like we were an oddity. Allen paid them no heed. *I guess a child walking like this isn't a normal sight. Alternatively, is it because beastkin aren't what most people call civilized? Now I'm getting self-conscious. Is the reaction that Avollea had more normal than what I was expecting? Everyone else in the company didn't have any problem with me being a beastkin.*

The buildings in the town were mostly wooden structures, except for when there was a larger building. Those seemed made mostly of stone. Everyone that I saw was a human or an elf, and the clothing that people wore was simple and monochromatic. Shirts and pants were the norm for men, although some women wore them too. Other women wore simple dresses. Everyone had heavy-looking boots, regardless of what else they were wearing.

After walking and looking at people and the city, it wasn't long until we arrived at a larger stone building that looked like a church to me.

The building looked like it received regular maintenance. It was larger than all the others nearby. A single wooden door was positioned on the left side of the building wall we faced. I found it odd that the entrance wasn't in the center, but on one side instead. The face of the building continued to our right. There were several windows along the rest of the wall. None of the windows had glass, but they were all covered with wooden shutters instead. The gray stones were uniformly cut, almost like bricks, and mortar filled the gaps to make the walls. *So this is to be my new home. Not bad, so long as this Nora lady is as nice as people say she is.*

Captain Allen released my hand once we were about five steps—five of his steps—away from the door. I walked beside him as best I could with my much shorter stride. Once he reached the door, he struck it with his fist so hard I thought he was breaking it down.

When the door opened, what greeted me was almost expected at this point—a tall elven woman with her green hair tied in a bun. I wasn't calling her tall because everyone I'd seen was tall to me; no, she was taller than Drue. She wore a plain brown dress and had a white apron over top.

She looked Allen in the eyes and recognized him instantly. Her face turned worried as she looked to Allen's right and then to his left, to me. Her beautiful brown eyes expanded as they almost popped out of their sockets.

After she examined me from head to toe, her youthful face snapped with rage. She poked a finger into his chest as she yelled at him. "Allen, you had best have a good explanation for this child's appearance!" She kept poking him in the sternum. "Not only is this the first beastkin you've brought me, but you keep trying to find children in a worse condition than the last!" Her volume rose with each word. Her screaming wasn't high-pitched like Avollea's. It was more like what you would expect a mother to scold a child with.

Allen threw his arms in the air in surrender to the elven woman. "It wasn't my fault, Nora. The orcs had raided a town before we dealt with them. She was their only captive. This is how we found her." He tried to defend himself from the finger-stabbing woman. Because of my sensitive ears, I had already cowered and covered my ears from her yelling. "We took care of her with what we had. Avollea fed her and made sure she had water to drink."

"You had Avollea take care of the child?" Her rage reached a boiling point. "No wonder she looks like she's done nothing but roll around in the mud for an entire day." She then looked at me, covering my ears. When her attention fell on me, breathing became much more difficult. *I have this urge, I'm guessing from my animalistic instincts, to run as far away from this lady as possible.* "Oh, my dear, I'm so sorry. Are you okay?" Her personality flipped so hard that I got whiplash.

"Your shouting is loud and it hurts," I said. "But I've been covered in mud for the last two days, I think."

"Two days?" she nearly shrieked again. And again, I flinched and covered my ears. "I'm sorry. We'll get you straight to the bath, then. Come on, let's go." She held out her hand as she stooped down closer to my level.

I slowly extended my hand and grabbed her long, slender fingers. As soon as I grabbed her hand, she pulled me gently and scooped me up into her arms. Without saying a word to Allen, she carried me into the building and shut the door in his face.

As the slammed shut, I couldn't help but feel a sense of loss and loneliness. *I think there's a little more history between these two than him just delivering orphans to her.*

She picked me up and set me on her hips. The dress she wore hid the fact that she had extensive hips. Also, now that I was at face-level with her bosom, I realized her breasts were the size of my head. *She's not thin or frail; she's well-fed and decently fit too. I hope the kids are taken care of as well as this lady is. Why do I still have this nagging feeling to run from her, though?*

Nora pulled me into what I speculated to be a coatroom, with rows of shoes of different sizes along the wall near the door and longer cloth objects were hanging on the wall on the opposite side of the room. We walked through it into a much larger room. There was a hallway on the right, a set of double doors straight ahead, a door on the right and on the left was another door.

We went to the door on the right, and the room we entered had four toilets in stalls whose walls only went up a few feet. Across the room was another door, and, as we passed through it, I could see where she was taking me: straight to the bathtubs, just like she said. The bathroom was a communal with four full-size tubs. They were all made of copper and looked like giant metal buckets.

She set me down by the first one by the door. "Okay, we need to get you out of those ruined clothes." Nora spoke quietly as she closed the door to the bathing room.

I was mindful of the fact that my tail went through a hole in my shirt dress. Carefully, I fed my tail back through the hole before removing my clothes. Once all my mud-laden clothes were on the floor, I looked at my naked body and almost flinched. *I really need to get used to the fact that I'm a little girl now, a little girl who is covered from head to toe in fur. I'm filthy. This is going to take a while.* There was mud everywhere on me and even some blood. *Although I think some of that blood might be mine.*

"Are you hurt anywhere?" Nora dropped to her knees and scoured my body for injuries.

"Yes, I was hit in the back of the head, apparently," I answered cautiously. *I don't know why, but this feeling of running away from her just got much worse once we were alone in this room together.* My gaze kept wandering towards the door we'd entered through.

"What?" Nora screamed, and I covered my ears and flinched away. The horror on her face showed the sincerity of her apology afterward. "I am so sorry. I keep forgetting about your ears. I'm not used to them yet." *Neither am I, but do you hear me yelling, lady?* "Let me see your head." She then inspected my scalp.

"Please be gentle. It still hurts from time to time." I braced for pain.

To my relief, the pain never came. "We'll need to see Phannidoritthin about that." She turned to the bathtub next to us, which still didn't have any water in it. I didn't see any faucets or anything where water could be pulled from.

"Do you have to go and get pails of water for baths?" *I think this whole bath thing might be a bigger ordeal than I originally thought.*

"No, silly." Nora giggled a little. She waved her hand, and water suddenly formed like a small waterfall over the tub. "I can use magic."

Something in the back of my mind pulled at me, causing me to flinch backwards a couple of steps away from the tub. But as I saw the water materialize over the tub and cascade down, filling it quickly, everything seemed to slow down. My jaw hit the floor so hard it bounced. *Is this what magic looks like?* "You can do magic?"

Nora waved her hand again, and the water stopped forming. She turned to me and, with a single finger, closed my mouth with a grin on her face. "That never gets old," she said as she giggled. Then her face turned serious and she waggled her finger in my face. "That doesn't mean I'll teach you magic, though. It isn't a toy you can play with and learn any time you want. It takes hard work to learn it."

I don't know why magic got me so worked up, but my tail was wagging. *Magic is so cool! It looks like some kinda miracle. How does it work? It would be amazing to learn magic. Didn't The Voice say I could learn magic?*

"Alright, get in." I nearly jumped as Nora interrupted my admiration of magic and pointed her thumb at the tub. *I guess it's bath time first.* As I walked over to the side of the tub, I noticed its sides went to about my shoulders. As I grasped the side of the tub, a thought popped into my head. *I might be able to jump in.* So I did just that. To my surprise, I jumped over the side of the tub with no difficulty. Of course, when I did that, I made quite a playful splash and sent water everywhere. I then slowly turned to look at Nora. *Oops.*

"Are you having fun?" Her voice dropped low and sounded menacing. *That little voice saying I need to run is screaming now.*

7

BATH TIME

"We need to scrub all that mud off you before we go and get you checked out." Nora's deadpan expression showed that this wasn't the first time someone had jumped into the bath and splashed water on her.

Where did that sponge come from? Why is the water getting colder? "Sorry. I'm sorry. Please don't be mad." My tail hugged my legs as I shrank down into the water.

Nora responded with a quick glare that turned into a soft smile. She retrieved a small jar from a cupboard, then dropped six drops of an unknown white milky liquid into the tub. Whatever it was, if using only six drops in this amount of water was enough, it had to be potent.

Using a sponge, Nora washed my face and hair first. She scrubbed me vigorously, and I began squirming from her rough treatment, especially when she worked around my ears. But she was extra gentle around the back of my head. With all of my movements, I noticed the water had turned dark brown.

Both Nora and I saw how dark the water got, and I looked at her sheepishly. "Sorry, I didn't realize I was this dirty."

"How did you even get this dirty, anyway?" Nora continued to scrub my back. "I know I said it looked like you had been rolling in the mud for an entire day, but can you tell me the specifics? Also, there's a lot of blood too. It isn't yours, is it?"

"I woke up in the mud after the orcs probably hit me in the head." *I can only assume they were the ones to knock me out.* "Some of the blood is mine, but most of it is from corpses that were nearby, I think."

"'Probably?' Why did you say it like that?" She stopped scrubbing.

I guess I should have phrased it differently. Too late now. Here we go with the bombardment of questions. Yay, I get to use my catchphrase again. Actually, I think I'll take a lesson from The Voice and answer as many as I can to speed this up.

"I don't remember anything before waking up in the mud. And before you ask..." I took a deep breath. "No, I don't remember my name. I don't know anything about my family or anything about myself." I took another breath. It was more difficult this time. It felt like something was catching in my throat. "I don't know what village I was from. I didn't know those were even orcs until the knights said that they were. And I don't know anything about beastkin, either." *Am I crying? Why are my emotions running away?* "And I don't even know why I'm crying!"

I heard a splash. Suddenly, I was pulled to the sidewall of the tub. I felt something grab me as my face was pressed into something soft. When I opened my eyes, I didn't even realize I had closed them, and was greeted with darkness. *I think Nora's hugging me. It feels like it.* I shifted my head to look up and I could see light, although it was blurry through the tears. I could make out Nora's face. She started holding me tighter and put her head on top of mine in between my ears.

"It's okay. You're safe now," she whispered. *Thank you for whispering when you're that close to my ears.* "Everything's catching up with you. It's alright to have a good cry. Get it all out. We'll work through this together, and we'll get you as many answers as possible."

I tapped her on the elbow. *As pleasurable as her bust is, it would be much better if I wasn't talking to her from this position.* She relaxed her grip on me but didn't let go.

Something about her response caught my attention. "What do you mean, 'find the answers?' Everyone who lived in the village is dead. I was the only one they captured."

"We'll use the oracle stone." She held me out at arm's reach and smiled. Her eyes shimmered but didn't shed a tear. "We'll have to pay for it. Hopefully, Phannidoritthin is familiar enough with beastkin to tell me anything I need to know about you physically."

"Oracle stone?" I tilted my head and felt my ears turn towards Nora. *Wait, money?* "If it's too much, maybe we shouldn't worry about it."

"Sweetie, don't worry about the money. Although that is very grown-up of you to care about that." Her inquisitive look scared me. *I'm supposed to be a child. If I started saying that I was reincarnated, The Voice said that nobody would believe me. If that's true, then I'll sound crazy, and medieval mental health services are something I would very much like to stay away from.* "The oracle stones can tell us who a person is, and if they have done something or not. They're mostly used for determining guilt or innocence in court since you can't lie to them and they can't be tampered with, either. We can ask to use it for you, since you have amnesia."

Wait, there's a way we can learn my name? We aren't just going to come up with a name for me? This sounds way too convenient. Also, this court system sounds way too convenient as well. If it can prevent the wrongly accused from getting punished, why not? It probably works by magic; magic makes everything better and more efficient.

"But, before we go any further, young lady, you need to look presentable." *There's the scolding mother look again.* "We're going to get all this mud off of you no matter what it takes." I felt the blood draining from my face.

She retrieved the sponge and began washing my furry arms. She felt like she was attempting to scrub my fur off. *That's a weird sentence I never thought I would say. I have fur. Let's just staple that to the list of things I need to accept as my new normal.*

She accomplished her goal of getting the mud off of me. The bathwater was so full of dirt, blood and whatever else was on me that it had thickened. Nora pulled me out of the bath and drained the tub. There was a small tube at the bottom that ran into the floor. She pulled a handle connected to that small pipe, and the water slowly drained.

I looked at myself now that I was a lot less covered in mud and blood. *Gray fur. I'm a little girl, and I have gray fur. I guess since I likely have some canine traits, gray is a normal color for wolves.* Unfortunately, after looking at myself, I could see that we weren't done with my bath. I stood still, examining myself while soaking wet and creating a puddle at my feet. *Nora cleaned most of my fur, but my tail and legs still need work. I wonder what color the hair on my head is. Is it the same as my fur?* I pulled some in front of my eyes to see that it was the same color as my fur.

As the first tub was still draining, Nora picked me up and placed me in a tub near the first one. *There were four tubs, and I guess we have to get this done in less than four tries.* A sudden downpour of water pulled me from my internal joke.

It was like standing outside in the middle of the heaviest rainstorm you could imagine. While I stood in the deluge, I could feel a slight tingling sensation all over my skin. I sat back down in the tub as the water filled the tub. The downpour didn't last long. Nora didn't fill the bath as much as last time, only halfway.

I guess that was the first rinse cycle.

Wordlessly, she grabbed a new sponge and began washing my tail. I watched her, and I had to tell her to slow down because she was pulling too hard. *That thing is attached to me. I think it's best if it stays that way.*

I took the sponge when we got to my feet. I knew there were

sharp claws on my toes. Also, after her rough treatment of my tail, I didn't trust her with my feet. It was also a good excuse to study them more closely.

I have some weird feet. No one could ever prepare me to own a pair of digitigrade feet. They looked just like those of a canine, only much larger, pads included. My "heels" had limited motion and it looked like they couldn't touch the ground while I walk. The rest of my leg felt just like a human leg, so long as I didn't go below the knee. The same gray fur covered my legs. *Are my legs on the short side or are my arms longer? I don't need to bend forward much to touch my toes.*

Nora had taken the time it took me to clean my legs to get three towels and two combs. I was given another rinse cycle, thought it was much lighter than the first one.

Finally completely cleaned, I took the towel Nora gave me. Getting out of the tub, I could feel a difference in my weight. *My fur can hold some water, it seems. I need to make a personal note not to get too dirty, because getting clean and dry will be a much larger ordeal.* We spent a long time getting me dry, and once the towels were completely soaked through, I felt much lighter without all the mud or water in my fur. I looked down and saw that the floor had as much water as the towels did.

Then came the task of combing through my hair and fur. With a brush in her hand, Nora gave me an apologetic look. *Why is she giving me that look?*

Most of my fur wasn't bad at all since the it was short and didn't get tangled much. My head and tail weren't so lucky. Getting every single knot out left me in tears from how painful it was. Nora mentioned something about that if I didn't want to experience this again, I would be a good girl and brush everything once or twice each day. My pain tolerance was way down because, in the end, I was crying like a baby. *I guess if the shoe fits...*

After I finished crying for the second time that day, Nora put a simple gray cotton dress on me that went down just past my knees.

She also gave me some underwear to put on. She went and grabbed scissors and cut a hole in the back of the dress for my tail. The hole in the dress was perfectly cut so that my tail, when it perked up or was wagging, wouldn't flash my underwear to everyone behind me.

Nora also got a change of dress. She was no longer in her brown dress with an apron. Her dress was green, darker than her hair, but this one had no sleeves like the brown one. The dress also covered her up to the base of her neck.

As I watched her enter the room, I noticed there wasn't a nagging need to run away from her. *That's weird. Why am I not scared of her? Why was I even scared of her in the first place? Do my instincts just not trust strangers? But why didn't I freak out while I was with the knights? There has to be something about Nora that was making my instincts want to fear her, or at least be cautious of her.*

"We're going to head to the courthouse first. We'll learn your name so that I don't have to call you 'little one' anymore." She was back to using her sweet and caring voice again.

"You don't have to do that." *I really don't care about what this body was called. With a new start, I should have a new name.* "You really could just give me a name and I would be happy with that." *For some reason, I can't come up with a name for myself.*

"No, no, that isn't right. You never know when you'll run into someone who knows you." She tapped the tip of my nose with her finger. "You never know. You might have a connection with someone out there. If you don't know your real name, you could miss out on that connection. Also, when you use the oracle stone, it will use the name you were given first. So even if I do rename you, the stones will never recognize it."

"I don't understand." I tilted my head in confusion. *This sounds like a good time to raise my concerns.* "How do these oracle stones know my name, and why can't it be changed?"

"Honestly, I have no idea how they work. Nobody does. They just work, and we accept that they do. Mostly because nobody has proved them wrong yet. Some believe that some deity answers the questions presented to them. Others say that they are intelligent items that share consciousness with each other. Then the stones are capable of powerful divination to get all their answers." She stood up and put her hands on her hips.

"Who makes them and how?" *That should be the question that leads to the source of their inner workings.*

"Who? That's easy. The monks at the crown of the world do it. How? They keep that secret closely guarded."

That's another convenient answer.

Nora grabbed my hand and led me back to the front door. "There have been infiltration attempts to learn the secret. Those have all ended in failure since the stones were used to discover the infiltrators before they could get any answers. Those that make the orbs take an oath before they learn to make them. The oath forces them to take the secret of how to make them to their graves, unless they're teaching someone who has taken the same oath. If they attempt to break that oath, they turn to dust. Also, the monks never leave the little haven they made for themselves."

That seems a bit extreme and, again, convenient.

As we left the orphanage, Nora smiled at me. "But enough of that depressing talk. Let's go learn your name and get you registered."

8

A ROSE BY ANY OTHER NAME

It was a straight shot from the orphanage to the courthouse. It was all the way across town, but a straight shot nonetheless. Nora walked with slow, measured steps. I had to take two steps for every one she took. But at least I didn't feel like I was almost running the entire time. I didn't try to hold a conversation because I was too busy trying to keep up. Also, I tried to get a look at the town I was going to be living in now. There were many storefronts with an equal number of homes on the road we traveled. I didn't get a close look at what the businesses were since we walked so fast. There were even fewer people out than when I first entered the city. *They must be getting settled in for the night.* The sun hadn't set completely yet, though the buildings' shadows completely covered the road.

We arrived at our destination, a large brick building with no windows on the ground level but several on the second and third floors. We walked up a few stone steps to the heavy wooden front door. Nora released my hand and opened the door without stopping to knock.

As we entered the building, I saw three directions to go. There were doorways on my right and left and a staircase up to the second level straight ahead. The doorway on the right had iron bars and no handle, but it did have a keyhole. Through the bars, I could see a room that had more of the same iron bar doors. *I think that's the jail, or a holding area for minor offenses.* The doorway on the left was a normal wooden door that was wide open. Through that doorway, I saw tables and benches, but nobody was in the room.

I think it's a little weird that nobody's here to greet us or question why a woman and child just stormed into the courthouse. Regardless of my pondering, Nora kept up her march and proceeded up the stairway. *Stairs. I hope I can get up them without trouble.* Using the wooden handrails attached to the wall, I carefully made my way up the stairs at a much slower pace. Once Nora reached the top of the stairs, she turned around to watch me slowly walk up the stairs. *It isn't my fault that these stairs are taking me longer to get up. I've had to relearn how to walk, and I'm short.*

Once I finally reached the top without falling down or tripping, I looked at Nora and she had a proud smile on her face. I couldn't tell why, though.

At the top of the stairs, there was a straight hallway with doors in each direction and two staircases, one at each end. As we walked down to the right, I noticed the doors were labeled. I looked at the labels and saw unique runes that I have never seen before. *I've been speaking the language just fine, but what's the story behind the runes?*

"Hey, Nora, what are the strange symbols on the doors?" I pointed to the top of the door we stopped at.

"That's writing." She looked down at me. "It tells us this is the office of a person who will let us use the oracle stone."

"I can't read?" *Oops, I shouldn't have said that.*

"Don't worry, honey, I'll read everything you need to know." *Whew, dodged that bullet.* She opened the door and walked through it. She grabbed my hand when I just stood there. "We'll teach you how to read. I'm surprised you don't know how to read given how well you talk."

As we entered the office, I could tell that this was going to be a bureaucratic nightmare. The walls were lined with bookshelves from wall to wall and floor to ceiling, and books filled each shelf with no visible organization to them. *If they need to look something up, how are they going to find it quickly?*

There were four chairs in the center of the room on a nondescript rug that covered the wood flooring. The chairs all pointed to a large desk where a man sat, and he couldn't have been plainer. Nothing about him was memorable, from his short brown hair, expressionless face, a complete lack of personal effects on his desk and the monotone voice that he greeted us with.

"Good evening, Nora. What can I do for you?" His voice sounded way too rehearsed. He did at least look up from whatever he was working on. "Although I think I can guess the reason, since you have a little one I haven't seen yet."

"Yes, Dairein, but this one is a bit more of a special case than the rest I've had." She talked to Dairein with familiarity. "I know you like to be efficient and everything, but there are going to be some extra steps before registering her."

The man lifted one eyebrow. *Am I seeing emotion coming out of this bureaucrat?* "Coming from you, that's quite a statement. What else needs to be done?"

"She has no memory of who she is." *Well, that was blunt enough to give me another concussion.* "We need the oracle stone to tell us her name and other information," Nora continued.

Dairein looked down at me, his skepticism obvious. "Well now, that's new." He moved from looking at me to blatant staring. "Also, a beastkin child is new to this entire town. Do I even want to know?" His stare left me feeling uncomfortable, so I stepped behind Nora to break up his vision.

A sharp whistle pierced the air, causing me to flinch. I realized it came from Nora, and I looked at Dairein and saw his attention had returned to Nora. "Allen brought her to me. He said that he and his knights saved her from some orcs. I didn't ask him why they only had one prisoner, and such a young one at that. Also, since I know Allen so well, I know he didn't stop to ask the orcs either." *Was that a joke from her? Also, does she use her mom voice on everyone? Who is she to this town to be able to do that?*

"I agree that's odd, so I guess that's what you want to do first?" Dairein went through a few drawers at his desk until he pulled out a couple pieces of paper. "You know I have to ask this. Is this going to be an open tab for her?" He sat there with a fountain pen in hand, ready to write something.

"Unfortunately, yes." The sadness in Nora's voice frightened me. *I'm going to be placed in an orphanage and learn my name, so am I going to owe the government money?*

"Wait, you don't have to do this. You can just give me a name," I blurted out a plea to Nora again. *I don't want to be in debt as a child. Who knows what I'll have to pay back in interest alone?*

"Sorry, kid, that's against regulation. For her to take care of you, you'll need food, clothes, housing and an education." Dairein's voice was emotionless again. *I think he's going to give me a speech that he's given too many times before.* "To do that, she needs money. That money has to come from somewhere. Nora is an employee of the kingdom because her orphanage is owned by the kingdom. All expenses must be accounted for, and each child in her care increases her stipend." *Money, it's always about money.*

"But what does that mean for me?" I asked meekly. *I'm not going to like the answer, am I?*

"The kingdom has no problem giving money to care for orphans, but the kingdom sees it as an investment. You're required to serve in the military for a time based on your tab. I'm guessing someone at your age will need to serve for five years once you come of age." He was looking at me this time, but not staring, thankfully. "However, extra expenses like the use of the oracle stone and extensive medical bills can extend this service. That is, unless you can find someone to adopt you and pay for the expenses you've accrued. Although, because you're a beastkin, don't count on it."

THE BIG BAD WOLF

Could you be a bit more blunt next time? I still have some memories you can knock out.

"So I've been drafted?" I muttered in disbelief. That was a lot to take in. I looked away and stared at the ground to think about everything.

I can see the point of the government wanting something in return for taking care of orphans. It saves them from having to find as many willing soldiers. There's a part of me that sees the logic and reasoning. It sounds a lot like a program from my world, but instead of paying for me to go to college, they're paying for me to live with the basics. But I can't bring myself to like the prospect of being raised just to go to war if needed.

I moved to sit in a chair and hoisted myself up into it. I was oblivious to the conversation that Nora and Dairein were no doubt having. *Maybe it isn't so bad. In my previous life, I was never in the army. I could be part of the equivalent of the national guard for this kingdom and never go to war. They're only asking for five years, minimum. What sort of country am I in that openly and readily drafts orphans into their military?*

What Dairein said about being adopted was extremely rude. But Avollea's reaction to me when Allen released me from the cage tells me there may be more people who have that type of reaction to me. The casual racism I receive probably won't bother me. I just need to avoid the hyper-competitive levels of racism. Or is it species-ism? Probably racism, I still feel like a person. It doesn't matter since people always fear what they don't understand or what's different from them. I haven't forgotten about being a girl now, either. There are so many social stigmas attached to that alone. It's obvious I'm a girl, and they're still going to draft me into the military. That's right, Allen has a few women in Brilliant Crusade. This shouldn't have been surprising. Maybe that might get me a job doing something off the front lines. You never know. If I have to, I'll use stereotypes to my advantage. I'm not eager to die again; it wasn't a pleasant experience the first time.

"Let's go." Nora's voice pulled me from my internal revelations.

"Huh, what?" I shook my head back and forth in surprise.

"We're going to the oracle stone now, sweetie." Nora was holding her hand out for me to grab. "Are you okay? Do you feel sick? Are you tired?"

I guess I could use that as a lifeline. I doubt she would understand that I was lost in thoughts about joining the military and coming to terms with the fact that I would be subjected to racism and sexism. "Yeah, I'm getting kinda tired." I grabbed her hand and removed myself from the chair. Or tried to, at least. I might have forgotten that I had an extra appendage attached just above my butt. When I slid out of the chair, my tail didn't clear the seat as I dropped. I leaned forward to alleviate the pain as I yelped. *Two lessons learned. One, I need to think about how I get out of chairs now. And two, my tail does not fold straight up. It will go a maximum of ninety degrees from my butt.*

"Careful, are you okay?" She put her hand on my back as I rubbed the base of my tail, attempting to ease my pain. "Does it hurt? Can you walk?"

"It does, but I'll be fine, I think. I guess I'm a little more awake now." *This new body is going to be hard to learn.* I walked to the door to move on from the embarrassment.

Dairein stood, waiting for us at the door without saying a word. Nora caught up with me quickly, and we followed him down the hall to a door just before the stairway. He pulled out a key from his pocket and unlocked the door. It opened to a completely dark room.

Before we entered the room, Dairein stopped us. "Nora, if you would, please." He waved his hand as if inviting us to go first.

"Maybe you should grab a wand next time." Nora sounded disappointed in the man. She then snapped her fingers four times in rapid succession. The black room suddenly had orange lights brightening it from the corners.

"Ladies first." Dairein bowed slightly.

Complying with his wishes, Nora and I walked into the small room, now lit by four sconces.

"Is that it?" I said, disappointed. In front of us, on the far wall, was an altar made of stone with a perfectly square tablet with no writing on it. "How is this thing going to tell me my name?" *Honestly, I was expecting a crystal ball on a table that we sit around and hold hands while talking to it.*

Dairein looked at me and then back to the altar as he walked past us. "I think you're going to have to hold her up." He continued to size me up. "She's shorter than I realized. I should have brought a box or something."

"That won't disrupt the functions?" Nora looked around the room for something.

"No, you have to be in direct contact with the stone for it to work." He looked at me while putting a finger on his beardless chin. "She actually could be small enough to sit right next to it while we ask the questions."

"Alright, sweetie, all you need to do is just put your hand on the oracle stone and we'll do the rest." Nora picked me up by lifting me by my armpits and set me next to the extraordinarily plain-looking stone tablet.

"Like this?" I placed my furry-clawed hand on the top of the tablet.

"Correct. Now no matter what, don't move or let go until we say so. Understand?" Dairein looked at me with a stern face. I only nodded my head, readying myself for something to happen. "Alright, we'll start with the basics." Dairein extended one arm and a small light grew in the palm of his hand. The light extended from his hand to the stone. More strange-looking runes made of light formed on the tablet. I guessed they were words because they were groupings of symbols like the ones I couldn't recognize from earlier. "Go ahead and read it for me, Nora."

"First, it says her name is Lucia. What an adorable name for such a little cutie." Nora beamed a smile at me. "Beastkin, wolf subtype. That isn't much of a surprise, considering the shape of your tail."

"Lucia, Lucia, Lucia, Lucia." I tried to get used to my new name. *It feels weird to say, I don't know if I like it. I know your parents pick your name like they did in my other life, and in that life I just accepted my name. Although I've been stripped of that name and am not even allowed to remember it.* "So, this is who I am?"

"It's just a name. But it's your name." Nora brought her face close to mine. "It's your job to give people a reason to remember it. You have your whole life to define who Lucia is. All you have to do is decide what to do with the time that is given to you."

I looked at her in surprise. *That's an interesting pep talk.* I lowered my head to consider what she had just said.

"Age: four. Sex: female." Nora raised an eyebrow and turned her head slightly towards me. "You're a little tall to be four years old." Nora returned her attention to the stone and resumed reading. "It also says 'physical' and 'recovery.' Those are her aptitudes, right?"

"Two?" Dairein sounded completely surprised. *I guess Nora said something important.* "Sorry, kid. Lucia, was it? It looks like the kingdom won't leave you alone. You're correct, those are her aptitudes. The fact that she has two of them and that they are broad areas means she'll have a lot of room to grow."

"But what do they mean?" I asked. *How about some details for the one who knows nothing about what's going on here?*

"First, physical aptitude is one of the rarest. As you grow up, you'll be faster and stronger than almost everyone with little effort. If you train and focus, with enough time you'll be faster, stronger, more flexible and have more endurance than everyone else." He was staring me down again. *He still creeps me out when he stares at me. Is it because I can't figure out what he's thinking?* "Second, recovery is a little more common. However, because you have a second aptitude, that puts you on the same level as some legends."

I really don't want to be in the limelight right now. I'm surprised that I've taken everything in stride, if I say so myself. "So does recovery mean I'll heal faster?" I tried to get this guy back on topic.

"I apologize. That's part of it." Dairein rolled his shoulders and straightened his back. "A secondary effect of it is that you recover from exhaustion and training faster too. I imagine once you're older, a single night's rest will heal superficial wounds and return you to top form, even from complete exhaustion."

He's said that twice now. "Why do you keep saying once I get older?"

"Because, like every muscle in your body, as you get older, they get stronger. Your aptitudes will also become more pronounced, especially if you nurture them." *The strange look in Dairein's eye is unnerving me.* "Don't worry, if I know Nora, she'll make sure they're nurtured to their absolute most. But, on to the second part of the oracle stone's use."

"He's right. We'll make sure you'll be the best you can be." Nora attempted to put her hand on my head between my ears, but I ducked my head away. "It also looks like you'll make the others jealous."

Dairein, not waiting for us to finish our little side conversation, brought both hands up this time and a blue light grew from both palms. "Oracle, assessment."

The light didn't extend to the stone this time. Instead, it shrank from his hands and grew on the stone, and it gradually dissipated from his hand until it fully manifested on the tablet. The light then flattened into the stone, where it revealed a single image of two crossed swords, but they were made of a red light. "That's unfortunate."

"Nora, what does it mean?" I asked, looking at her nervously.

"It can mean many things, but the most common is that you will spend a lot of time fighting in your life." Nora looked at me with sadness. "It can also mean there will be a massacre and you'll be at the heart of it." She took both my hands in hers. "This is the oracle stone's assessment of your most definitive prophecy. Or it could have been the moment your village was attacked by the orcs."

"But you don't know what it means exactly, right?" *I hope I don't end up in another massacre.*

"Listen, kid, reading the oracle stone is more guesswork than anything when it comes to the assessment," Dairein said. "We've kept a record and know what the basic symbols mean, and the light's color changes the meaning slightly. But the exact meaning is difficult to tell because it can be a single moment or a lifelong achievement. That's why Nora gave you three possible answers."

"Are there other things that it could mean?" *I don't know how much this stone can really see into the future, but I want to be ready for anything.*

"There are, but the people who study the runes and what they mean have gone home for the day. Besides, I doubt you want to spend the next several years listening to what could happen to you or what you could do." Dairein went to the door and opened it.

"There's no sense in worrying about anything. Just forget about it and live your life as you want." Nora picked me up and rested me on her hip.

"If you'll follow me, I'll have the paperwork ready for you in short order." Dairein held the door for us to walk through. "She might have a high recovery rate, but she still needs to get her sleep."

It sounds like he cares for my well-being. I'm shocked. Is he just awkward around people?

We returned to his room, and we watched him take a piece of paper and I assume write some form of contract, because at the bottom of the paper he drew four horizontal lines and wrote something in on one of them. He handed the paper to Nora after blowing on it for a few moments. "Arsane should be in the room across the hall. She'll be able to finish everything."

"Thank you and good night, Dairein. Please tell Minilla I said hi." Nora smiled politely.

"I was simply doing my job." Dairein gave a slight bow. "I'll tell

THE BIG BAD WOLF

her that at dinner tonight. It's going to be rabbit stew." He had a wide smile on his face. *Is that drool coming from the corner of his mouth?* We left the man to his dream of rabbit stew.

Nora carried me to the room directly across the hall and knocked on the door. We waited a few moments before there was a reply. "Come in," a woman called.

Nora opened the door and set me down as we entered. Everything in the office was the same as one we were just in, with only one massive difference. Instead of a plain man sitting behind the desk, it was a petite elven woman with an angular and emotionless face. Her auburn hair flowed into her light-red top. *It looks like all bureaucratic jobs are soul-sucking no matter what world or universe you go to.*

"What do you need?" Arsane's voice was as monotone and dead as her facial expressions.

"I'm here to finish the registration for Lucia," Nora said in her normal uplifting voice, handing over the paper Dairein just gave us.

The elf read through the paper silently. "Ah, registration of guardianship for one Lucia. So is this Lucia?" She turned to look at me, then she turned to look down at the document. "So that is what a beastkin looks like." *You didn't even know what a beastkin looks like?* She glared at me intensely for a few seconds before returning to her document. "She is a wolf beastkin with silver hair and fur, not gray. I will make that correction. You are Lucia, correct?"

"Yes." *This lady feels like talking to an angry librarian that you returned a book to two days late.* I straightened myself up and looked at my fur. *Is it really silver?* "But my fur looks gray to me."

"No, it is silver. It's too light to be gray." Arsane shook her head. *She said it like it was supposed to be a good thing.* "The paperwork now says silver regardless of your color sense." The cranky lady made her correction on the paper by crossing out a spot and wrote something next to it. "Do you, Nora Stormleaf, hereby take full guardianship and responsibility for Lucia? If so, please sign here."

"I do," Nora said without hesitation as she walked to the desk and took the pen from the lady and signed.

She continued down her list. "Do you, Lucia, agree to obey all laws and decrees from the Rophmna royal court?"

"I don't know what they are."

"Irrelevant," the bureaucrat shot back.

"Don't worry, we'll teach you," Nora whispered.

"Fine, I will."

"Do you, Lucia, understand and accept that you will be given care and education at Nora's discretion? In return, you will serve in the town guard of Aquittemia or as a knight, should you be accepted into a company, for the number of years determined by the kingdom of Rophmna when you reach the age of seventeen." She never looked at me as she read from the sheet that Nora had just signed.

"I do," I said with no confidence behind my voice. *What other choice do I have? Live on the street like a beggar or a thief? I'll pass on that.*

"Then sign here." She held out a pen and paper while pointing at a line at the bottom of the paper. "If you don't know how to write, then sign in blood."

"I don't know how to write. How do you sign in blood?" I looked up at Nora.

"Just place a drop of blood on the paper on the line where you were supposed to sign," Arsane said nonchalantly.

I looked at the lady and saw that instead of a pen, she had a needle in her hand.

"Is it alright if I assist her?" Nora asked with concern in her voice. She placed her arm on my shoulders.

"Please do. I don't want any mistakes." Arsane's emotionless voice annoyed me.

Nora lifted me onto a chair to stand on next to the desk. She laid the paper down and grabbed my left hand, holding the needle with her other hand. "This is going to hurt for just a second, sweetie."

Of course it's going to hurt. You're going to stab me! I kept my small tirade to myself as I looked away from my hand and extended my thumb. A sharp pain in my pad informed me that she had just stabbed me. Then I felt her turn my hand over and give it a slight squeeze. "All done. See, that wasn't so bad."

I looked at my thumb and saw a red pool of blood, then stuck it in my mouth to clean and seal the prick. There was a single drop of blood on the line that I was told to sign. I then noticed something tasted sweet in my mouth. *The only thing I should taste is my thumb. I didn't think my claw had a taste. Wait, does my blood taste that good? Am I part vampire or something?*

"Thank you. Is that all you required?" Arsane's voice was still devoid of all emotion.

"That's all. Thank you, and have a nice day." Nora placed me back on the ground and began to lead us out of the office.

"Good night." Those were the last words we heard from the elf behind the desk.

Once we left the room and closed the door behind us, I had to ask. "So what was her problem? Why does she feel so soulless?"

"Arsane is outstanding at her job, but she doesn't do much else." Nora frowned. "She used to be such a bright child, too. I think she needs to find love. That should cheer her up." Nora then put a finger to her chin in contemplation.

"Why did she call you Nora Stormleaf?" I interrupted her thoughts with my question. *She can play matchmaker some other time.*

"It's my title from when I was in a knight company." Nora's face soured with sadness. "It was a long time ago, and I'd rather not talk about it." She looked at me directly as she forced a smile. "Let's go. We need to get you checked out at Phannidoritthin's." Nora lifted me again and adjusted it so I sat on her hip. Without me walking beside her, she walked much faster, her pace quick and decisive.

By the time we left the building the sun had set, but there was still a bit of light originating from over the horizon. I knew that once we were done with this Phil guy, it would be night.

Before I knew where we were, she stopped in front of a storefront. It had a sign above the door, but I couldn't read it. This time, Nora knocked on the door, and we waited a few moments before it opened.

9

MEAT IS BACK ON THE MENU

"For the last time, leave me alone." A scaled humanoid with a single horn growing from his forehead stood in the doorway. His scales were a dark blue and his eyes were red with vertical pupils. He was just standing there dressed in robes that almost glistened in bright blue. His blue scales were slightly duller in contrast to his robes. I looked at his hand and saw that he also had claws on his fingertips. Even though I was smaller than him, my claws appeared longer and sharper. He was shorter than Nora, but not by much, just like everyone else I'd seen with her. *How tall is this lady?*

"Oh, sorry. I thought you were someone else for a moment." He relaxed as he recognized Nora. "Care to explain yourself, Nora? What are you doing out so late?"

"I can—" Nora began.

Something welled up from inside me and took over. "Why does everyone ask her? Why doesn't anyone want to hear my side of the story?" *I don't know why, but I'm getting annoyed with everyone ignoring me. I know I'm a child, but that doesn't mean I like being treated like one. Am I so tired that I'm irritable? I guess I am feeling tired. It's been a long day.*

I looked at the scaled individual in the doorway and saw his look of astonishment. I then turned to Nora and saw her giving me the same look. She recovered and simply said, "Go on then."

Uh oh, these emotions are getting out of hand. What's wrong with me? As I was contemplating why my emotions were running amok, the rage from earlier returned. "My village was being killed by orcs when I woke up buried in mud. I don't have any memories from before I woke up. I was taken captive and then rescued by knights. Then I was dropped off at an orphanage, where I was scrubbed mercilessly. I was then placed on an altar and told by a stone who I am and what would happen to me. Now I'm here to see if there's anything wrong with me!" *Now that I've done it, I need to calm down.* I tried to slow down my breathing.

"That about sums it up." Nora looked at the lizard-like being. "Well, except for the 'merciless' scrubbing." She turned her head to me and gave me a look. It was the *we are going to talk about this later* look. On the bright side, I felt like something lifted from my shoulders. "But we're here for you to make sure the wound on her head is alright. Also, I don't know much about beastkin. Could you teach me a bit about them? Also, possibly add it to the curriculum for the kids in the future?"

"What? Who? Why? When? What?" I watched the lizard guy, Panni-something, stumble with his words. *I think he's in shock.*

We stood staring at each other in silence. *This has gone from weird to uncomfortable. A horned lizard man is standing in the doorway of this store. I'm guessing he's the Pand-something person we are looking for. I heard his name, and I'm having trouble remembering what it was.* I could see into his home, or business, and saw bookshelves filled with books, although the place was dimly lit.

Shaking his head, the lizard man looked even more confused. "Just come in. I'm sure you'll explain why you're here once the child has settled down." Standing next to the door, he motioned for Nora to enter.

It wasn't well lit here, but there were a few candle sconces attempting to remedy that. It looked like we walked into a library, not a hospital. *Why did she take me here to get my head checked?* I guessed Nora had been here many times before, because she walked towards a door near the back of the library. The lizard guy followed us, and, with a wave of his hand, the door opened before we got there. *So he can do magic too. Am I going to get to learn magic? That would be awesome.*

The back room was small, with a chair and a table at its center. "You can set her down on the table." The lizard man pointed to the one table in the room as he headed for the chair. Each wall of the room that didn't have a door was lined with cabinets and pantries. Everything was made of wood, and it looked like it had been treated with some kind of stain or finish. It looked more like a nurse's office than I was expecting.

"So, why are you here?" The question interrupted my investigation of the room.

"Well, little Lucia here is now one of my charges." Nora sat me down on the table and placed a hand on my shoulder while she turned to look at the other person. "I'm not very familiar with beastkin. I was hoping, since you're in charge of the kids' education, you could educate me too."

"It's because I run a bookstore, isn't it?" His eyes narrowed.

"I want you to check on her head as well." Nora moved her hand from my shoulder and placed it gently on the back of my head. "She received a head wound. Like I said, just about everything she said was correct."

"You're going to have to remind me what she said." He looked tired. "She said it so fast. And I wasn't expecting a child to snap at you like that, either."

"Don't worry about that. We're going to have a little chat about that later." I could feel her eyes burning a hole through me. I didn't want to see that look, so I just attempted to make myself smaller by tucking my arms and legs in and hunching down. "Both her and the knight who brought her to me said that she has memory loss because of her head injury. She was saved from orcs and given to me to raise because, according to them, there were no other prisoners and they didn't know of any other survivors."

"Okay, first off, I'm sorry, kid, that you had to go through that." He moved closer to me in his chair. "I do want to ask, how extensive is your memory loss?"

"I don't even know how to answer that." *That's the dumbest question to ask an amnesiac. I guess I have to commit to that role now. I'm young enough that I'll have to explain that a lot for the next few years, but hopefully it'll become something that doesn't matter.* "I only recently learned my name from the oracle stone. I also know I'm a wolf beastkin. I know that Nora is an elf, but I don't know what you are. I also know that I can't read. I have no knowledge of my family or anyone from my village. I also don't know what village I'm from. That about covers everything, I think." At some point, I started to look at the floor. My instincts were screaming at me again to run away.

"I'm glad you aren't throwing a tantrum again, but you can relax. Nora is strict, but fair. You're just a kid, so at worst you're going to get a warning."

I couldn't bring myself to look at him. *It's taking everything I can to keep from jumping off this table and running with no plan in mind. I need to get these impulses under control.*

"Alright, let's start with that head wound. Please hold still for me." I saw his legs move, and then I felt him grab my head as Nora placed her hand on my upper back. "How many days ago did you get hit?"

"Two days, I think," I said hesitantly.

"Two days? If you told me two weeks, I might believe you." The shock in his voice was unsettling. *Am I healing that fast? Maybe that might be a good thing.*

"Just so you know, Phannidoritthin, while we were at the oracle stone, we learned she has the recovery aptitude." Nora stepped in and used this guy's name. *So that's how you pronounce it. Wow, I've been way off.*

"Lucky girl, that would explain it. Although if it's this effective at this age, I'm curious to see what it'll be like once she grows up." He let go of my head and walked around in front of me with a hand on his chin.

"She also has the physical aptitude," Nora slipped in quietly.

"I take that back. You're not a lucky girl. You must be blessed by an angel." He sounded shocked. "This might be completely unnecessary, but I'm going to use some magic to see if anything else is wrong."

"What do you need me to do?" I asked, still staring at the floor.

"Don't move and relax." Those four words were the only warning I received before I felt something strange.

In my previous life, I had torn a ligament in my knee. My doctor had done an MRI test to see the extent of the damage. The feeling of being in a small, enclosed space was uncomfortable. The noise that the machine made was a little frightening. It was by far the most awkward test I ever received. Still, that paled in comparison to what I felt when Phannidoritthin cast his spell on me. I felt every pore in my body invaded, and also like something was crawling under my skin. Every muscle in my body seized up, and I couldn't move even if I wanted to until the feeling of something crawling under my skin stopped.

I curled up in the fetal position and lay down on the table. Holding my legs to my chest, my tail curled up in between my legs with my head touching my kneecaps. I felt violated. Everything about me felt disgusting, but I had no good reason for feeling that way.

"You handled that better than some kids." Phannidoritthin was talking to me and sitting in the chair, watching me. *I hope you learned something, because I'll never allow you to do that again.* "First off, it looks like she's in good health. Her sinuses are blocked by something, but I have something that will clear that up in a few moments. Also, you said you needed advice about how to take care of her. Is that correct?" He stood and turned to Nora.

"That's correct. I've never dealt with any beastkin children, or beastkin in general," Nora responded. After she said that, he walked off to one of the cabinets, and Nora turned her attention to me. Her voice was sweet again as she combed a few fingers through my hair. "About half of children react like you the first time scanning magic is cast on them."

"What does the other half do?" I asked, worried that I had made a fool of myself.

"Run around like they were on fire, screaming and rolling around." She said it in a matter-of-fact tone. *Great options.* She sat me up and pried me open like a clam. I just sat there, unable to decide to curl back into a ball or relax.

When Phannidoritthin returned, he carried a stone bowl with some yellow seeds in it. He used a stone stamp-like thing to crush them. *I think I remember something like this being called a mortar and pestle.*

"Alright, kid, this is going to make your nose run. Nora, could you go to that cabinet and grab a towel?" He pointed to a cabinet behind me, and Nora walked off in that direction. "If you don't close your eyes, you'll be sorry. I need you to take a deep breath through your nose when I say. Got it?" He was looking at me as sternly as he could. I nodded and closed my eyes. "Now." I breathed in as deeply as I could through my nose. It was difficult. It felt like my sinuses were clogged with a severe cold.

I heard him blow out his breath, probably to aerosolize the seeds he'd crushed.

I screamed as my face burned from the inside out. I threw myself off the table and hit the ground hard. My face still felt like it was burning, and now my right side throbbed with pain from the fall. I rolled around, still screaming.

Someone grabbed me by my shoulders and held me down, preventing me from rolling. I heard some shouting, but I couldn't pay attention. I had more pressing concerns, like my burning face. I kept screaming in pain from something I couldn't do anything about, until what felt like a bucket of water was dumped on my face. It may have been exactly that, because I stopped screaming in favor of expelling the liquid that had entered my lungs.

Someone turned me over and I opened my eyes. Everything was blurry, but I could see a towel below me.

Still coughing out some water, I noticed that there was some brown liquid pouring from my face as my vision slowly cleared.

"Explain what you just did." Nora held her volume back, but none of her rage.

Hearing Nora interrogate Phannidoritthin made me feel a bit better after what he had just done to me. *My head is dripping wet again. How many towels it going to take to get dry this time?* She placed a towel she had grabbed on my head to dry my hair.

"I've used mustard seeds for this many times, but nobody has had such a bad reaction to them like that." *He sounds defensive. I wonder why?*

"It looks like it's working, but why did she sound like someone was killing her?" After finishing drying my hair, Nora held me in her arms as some of the brown liquid started pouring from my mouth as well as my nose. It tasted terrible, like dirt, with the consistency of snot. A towel was held under my face to collect it.

"Of course it's working. I guess she has a very sharp sense of smell. I haven't done this to a beastkin before," Phannidoritthin admitted. *Why is he talking like he isn't a beastkin? What is he?* "Although there might also be another reason too. I'll be back. There's an easy way to check for this."

"You okay?" Nora spoke sweetly in my ear. "How are you feeling?"

"I feel as if life has it out for me," I said. *Wait, no, I shouldn't have said that. She's already suspicious of me not being normal, and now I'm throwing more clues. I'm trying to blend in, not stick out.* "My face still hurts, but not as badly." I coughed up some phlegm in between words.

"Sorry about the water, but I had to try something." Nora continued to hold the towel to my face. "It looks like it's almost done." The brown-colored mucus had stopped, only for it to turn yellow and lighten up some. But the flow hadn't slowed down at all.

"It isn't stopping." My voice shook. *Hopefully, the worst part is that I just get really dehydrated.*

Nora put a new towel on my face as I soaked the other towel with my mucus mixed with something unidentifiable. "Blow it all out as best you can." Nora held the towel to my face.

I blew my nose. It was still full of mucus, and I felt the towel would be insufficient for the task. I took a deep breath and blew again until it stopped. After the fifth round, I was worried that we were getting nowhere. I grabbed the towel and pulled it off my face.

"Is that blood?" I asked, noticing the red on the towel. "Is this going to stop?"

"Calm down, it's okay. Phannidoritthin will fix this," she said as Phannidoritthin came back. Still being a mother figure, she then shot one word in a tone that sent chills down my spine. "Right?"

"Yes, yes, of course," Phannidoritthin responded before he closed the door. "It looks like I was right; your nose is much more sensitive than ours." He pinched the bridge of my nose as he kneeled next to us. An itching and tingling feeling invaded my nose as he let go. "There, that should settle things down."

"Ah, it itches now." I sat back, released the towel and fervently rubbed my nose with my wrist. I had sufficient presence of mind not to involve my claws.

"That's good." *Is that all he's going to say?* I recovered from my little itch attack and looked back at the lizard man. He was holding a carrot. "Feel better?" Noticing my nose wasn't running at a million miles an hour, I nodded. "Now for the most important test for a beastkin. Eat this." He held out a carrot for me to grab.

I looked at him in utter confusion. "Why?"

"Beastkin can have varying diets based on their subtype. Since you said you were a wolf beastkin and wolves are natural carnivores, we need to see if you can eat plant-based food." *He's lecturing me right now. I can feel it.* "So eat the carrot."

I looked at Nora, worried that something else could go wrong. She shrugged, then simply motioned to the carrot, inviting me to eat it. Tentatively, I grabbed the vegetable and noticed that my hands were not well suited to holding anything. I bit into it, like I had done so many times in a life that was growing further away with each new experience.

"Auk!" I spat the piece of carrot out after chewing it for just a few seconds. It tasted like sour dirt. "That is the worst thing ever, of all time."

Nora sighed as Phannidoritthin looked apologetically at Nora. "I'm sorry. She's a carnivore. She can only eat meat."

I snapped my head around to look at Nora and saw the sadness in her eyes. "Don't worry, we'll make it work. This doesn't change the fact that I'll still take the best care of you I can." She looked like she was forcing her smile.

With obvious confusion on my face, I looked back and forth between Nora and Phannidoritthin. *I'm lacking some critical details to make sense of these reactions.*

Phannidoritthin spoke up first. "Meat is much more expensive than vegetables. I'm aware of how much they give you kids for a stipend, and the cost for you alone could be used for about three kids." My jaw dropped. "So to keep you fed, your service to the military could triple."

Fifteen years in the military! I can see why they had the reactions they did. It looks like I'm going to be an expensive child.

"I'll need to do some more research on beastkin so I can help you with her. I only have a very basic knowledge of them. But I believe I have a few books lying around somewhere. It's been decades since I read them," Phannidoritthin said.

"First thing's first. We have to teach her how to read and write." *Nora sounds like an advocate for public education.* "But let's give her a few days to acclimate and get acquainted with the other kids. She's had an exciting past few days."

"I'll be by next week. Or as soon as I find those books. I'm sure the other kids will need to get used to her," Phannidoritthin said mirthfully. "Good night, and don't forget to take care of yourself too."

"Good night, Phannidoritthin." Nora turned to me. "Alright, let's get you to bed."

"Okay." I stood up and looked up at Phannidoritthin. "Good night, Fanidrat, Phonador, Pandriot..."

"Okay, stop before you hurt yourself." Phannidoritthin put his hands up. "Listen, I know Nora likes to use a person's full name, but I understand my name is a mouthful to most people. You're going to see much more of me and it's alright if you call me Phan." His face shifted to what I think was a smile, but it was hard to tell.

"Okay Phan, good night." I tried to sound as chipper as I could. "By the way, what are you?"

Phan laughed. "I'm a dragoon. Don't worry, kid. You'll learn what that means later. That and many more things. Go home and get some sleep."

Oh good, more schooling. Great. I rolled my eyes as I turned away from him.

Our walk back to the orphanage was quick and quiet. I was carried in and taken to the right hallway. Nora made almost no sound, and we stopped at a room three doors down on the left. She carried me into a small room with a bed, a dresser on the back wall and, at the foot of the bed, was a small, empty bookcase. A window sat above the dresser to allow natural light in. There were no curtains or glass; instead, only wooden shutters sat closed as my barrier from the outdoors. *I guess I'll get up when the sun rises.* There were sheets on the bed, along with a pillow.

    Nora placed me on the bed, whispered "good night" and left me to sleep. I took off the dress, grabbed a single blanket and a pillow and curled up on the sheets. It wasn't soft or hard, but I fell asleep nonetheless, more from exhaustion than comfort.

10

CONTROL ISSUES

I slept through the night without dreaming, or at least I didn't remember any dreams. The sunlight brightened up my room. I sat up in bed and stared at my new furry female body. *I died and was given another chance at life. In exchange, I had to help defend this world from some coming evil. The one who sent my soul to this world messed up and put me in the wrong body. I'm now a female wolf beastkin named Lucia, and I live in an orphanage. Orcs attacked the village I "woke up" in and killed everyone but me. I was rescued by some knights in this kingdom called Rophmna. I live in the city of Aquittemia, the capital of Rophmna. Nora, an elven woman who runs the orphanage, will take care of me with funds supplied by the government in exchange for years of military service. That's a problem because I can only eat meat now. I was told that keeping me fed would triple my expenses, and thus triple my required service. Even still, the government is going to follow my every move because of the "aptitudes" that I have. According to the clerk at the courthouse, I'm going to be faster and stronger than most everyone and recover from everything quickly.*

There was an odd odor in the air. The smell reminded me of

stale air. I looked at the window and noticed a simple hook and latch keeping the shutters closed. I climbed on the dresser and opened the window. The bright light of the sun blinded me. But I was rewarded with fresh air as I returned to my bed.

If anyone told me this is what would happen when you die, I would never have believed them. But this isn't a dream, and this is as real to me as anything before. Now I'm sitting in a bed that was given to me, and have to live my new life. My last life was all about going to school to get a good job, finding a wife, having a family and not causing trouble. What do I do now? Do I just live a normal life? Get a job and have a family? Well, except this time around, I'm going to be the wife. What do I do if the demon king shows up?

There was a rumble from my stomach. *Regardless, everybody needs to eat sometimes, and my empty stomach is getting my attention.* I could smell something sweet as the air. *Oh, that's right, two or three of my senses are sharper than they were compared to when I was a human. Most notably, my hearing and smell. My eyes might be better, although I don't have a good reference. I need to test that.*

I hopped off the bed, making sure my tail cleared the edge of the bed. As I landed, I looked at my feet. *Right, I'm not human anymore. Even though I'm not human, I am still a person, right? I think, therefore I am? Am I a human with the appearance of a wolf? Or am I more wolf than human? This is too complicated to figure out. It doesn't help that The Voice took away most of my memories. I know I was human and a guy, but I can't remember what that's even supposed to mean. The weirdest part is there doesn't feel like there's something missing. What body did it plan on putting me in if this wasn't it? My previous life is drifting further and further away. How soon will it be before this life is all I know? Is that a good thing? Maybe. I did agree to start over. So I guess I'll start over.*

This time I have to live my life as Lucia.

I put on the dress I was given yesterday since I had no other clothes. *I'll likely be going clothes shopping today.*

Once dressed, I left my room in search of the source of the

scent. I turned left from my room and took another left turn and walked through a pair of double doors. *Here it is, the kitchen. The smell is strongest here.* I looked at the kitchen, and there were counters, cupboards, a stove, a large sink and someone standing at an island countertop in the center staring at me.

The person was new, a human woman with bright-red hair tied into a bun, wearing a white short-sleeved top with a gray apron over top.

She screamed. "Monster!"

I covered my ears reflexively when she started shouting. A knife flew through the air towards me, but kitchen knives aren't balanced for throwing, so I easily dodged the projectile.

"Help!" She screamed even more.

"Stop screaming!" I yelled, trying to get her attention. *I need to convince this lady that I'm not here to hurt anyone. At the very least, I have to convince her that I'm not a monster.* "I'm not a monster, and I don't want to hurt anyone. I just smelled something... " I stopped to duck an airborne cutting board.

"Stay away!" *She's hysterical. I think it's just better to get away from her and get Nora.* I made a quick getaway through the doors I had entered from.

After exiting the kitchen, I saw two individuals, a male and a female teenager, brandishing weapons in the hallway. The girl held a dagger in each hand and the boy had a thin sword with a large guard to protect his hand. They were looking at me with obvious bewilderment. I looked at them with a matching expression. We stared at each other for what felt like forever, until Nora came running in behind them, holding a ball of fire.

Every alarm went off in my head, telling me to run away from the fire, and I bolted back into the kitchen. Or I tried to. I slammed into the doors. I ran my claws down the wood, trying to force my way through, but they didn't budge. My hands tingled whenever they touched the doors.

"It's okay, calm down," Nora blurted out. "You're up early."

THE BIG BAD WOLF

Her tone changed to a much sweeter one. "Stand down, you two. This is our new addition."

"Huh? What?" Both teenagers responded simultaneously. I turned to look at them and saw them staring in disbelief with their weapons lowered. I noticed Nora got rid of the ball of fire too, but the other two were still holding their weapons, keeping me on edge.

"We'll do introductions soon. Put those away. Can't you see that you're scaring her?" Nora was now pointing at their weapons. *You scared me more than they did.* The two walked away while watching me. Their expressions never changed.

"I'm sorry," I said, attempting to defend myself before anyone could accuse me of a crime. "I smelled something good, and I wanted to know what it was. I walked into the kitchen, where a lady started screaming and throwing things at me. I didn't mean to scare her. Could you please tell her that I'm not a monster?"

"It seems you've met Melody." Nora walked up to me and moved me to the side. "Stay here. I'll calm her down and we'll get you introduced to everyone at breakfast."

When Nora put her hand on the door she looked disappointed. She waved her hand and it sounded like there was a shriek from the woman in the kitchen. I watched Nora enter the door that wouldn't budge for me, unimpeded.

I did exactly what Nora told me to do: stood right where I was. Nora entered the door that wouldn't budge for me, unimpeded. I stood still, unable to hear anything being said on the other side of the doors. *Why can't I hear anything now? The doors aren't that thick. What did she do?*

Instead, I heard footsteps coming from down the hall. I saw the boy who was wielding the sword earlier walking in my direction. He was dressed in a simple gray shirt and shorts with bare feet. He was much taller than me, almost double my height. His skin was dark brown, just like his hair. His long ears pointed out of his short hair, and he stared me down with bright-green eyes that I could tell were taking in every detail. His lean build showed how toned his muscles were. He may not have been strong, but it looked like he could handle himself in a fight.

He stopped to inspect me and, after a few nerve-racking moments, he resumed his march. Once he reached the door, I called out to him to stop him from interfering with what Nora was doing. "I wouldn't do that if I were you." I tried to sound as non-threatening as possible.

It didn't work. I sounded like a brat.

"You can speak?" He sounded surprised.

"Yes, I can speak. What made you think that I can't?" *Either he's foolish, ignorant, or both.*

"Given how much of an animal you look like, I almost expected you to bark at me." He chuckled.

I knew it was a possible joke, but it was a poor joke if it was. *If it wasn't a joke, that would be by far the rudest thing anyone has said to me yet. Even Avollea said nothing that rude.* The more I saw him laughing, the more enraged I became. I growled. "I'm a person just like you."

"If it looks like an animal, sounds like an animal and moves like an animal, then it must be an animal." His smug look never left his face.

I will not be everyone's doormat. Nobody will tell me I don't deserve to live or that I'm some stupid animal! I will wipe that stupid smile off your face! I leaned forward to charge him. My vision shifted as everything held a red tint to it.

He stopped laughing and straightened up when I released a louder growl. I charged at him and we tumbled through the door. I reached for his face with my claws, but he grabbed my wrists to keep me from inflicting any damage. He landed on his back but used that momentum to throw me over his head and further into the kitchen.

Unable to contort my body to land properly, I fell on my back. I didn't feel any pain. I just got angrier. I rolled over and got up on my hands and feet in a four-point stance and charged at the elven boy again. *He hasn't completely stood up yet, so this is my best chance at getting him.* He saw me charging again, and instead of continuing to get up, he swung his legs around to kick me. I recognized what was happening, but I couldn't stop myself in time to avoid his kick.

This is going to hurt.

I was right. His foot collided with my cheek, and the kick redirected me towards the center island in the kitchen. This time, I managed a controlled roll and got back to my feet even faster. My face was numb on the right side where his foot connected, but I didn't care. I was furious.

"Lucia, stop right now!" The volume nearly shattered my eardrums. I dropped to the ground, holding my ears to my head in pain. I was terrified. My anger simmered down in favor of self-preservation. "Evandol, explain yourself. Now!"

"She attacked me first!" he shouted, attempting to sound justified and proud.

My anger returned after hearing his defense. This time I tried to rein it in. "He started it by treating me like an animal!" I was still holding one ear down with one hand and keeping the other flat with new muscles I hadn't registered before. My other hand was outstretched to point at the boy.

"So you attacked him?" Nora turned to face me. The other woman who'd thrown kitchen hardware at me was cowering behind her. "What possessed you to charge at him when you've just met? What did he say?"

"He said he was surprised that I could talk and that he expected me to bark like a dog." I stared at the elven boy. "Then he started laughing at me, and I got angry."

"If you act like a wild animal, what else are people going to think?" The boy and his smart mouth were at it again.

Something in me snapped again. I charged at him again, but this time I was aiming for his legs. But, after only two steps, my feet were not underneath me. Instead, they were behind me, and the rest of my upper body was quickly becoming parallel with the ground yet again.

I caught myself before completing the face-plant. I looked back and saw my feet were together. It felt like something was forcing them together, but I couldn't see anything. Instead there was that annoying tingling sensation I have felt several times now.

"I said enough, Lucia!" Nora snapped at me. Her attention quickly changed to the other kid. "Evandol, I know I raised you better than this. Did you not remember what happened last time with Anna? I will punish you the same way. Do you really like the taste of soap?" *Who's Anna, and what does she have to do with this?* "Go to your room. Now!"

Evandol looked shocked. He turned to me with the same look. My face turned into a grin. Knowing he was going to suffer for his treatment of me left me feeling justified.

His face turned angry as he saw me grinning. He stomped out of the kitchen and down the hall. As he exited through the double doors, five more kids walked in, three girls and two boys. I could feel whatever was holding my feet together release them, and I quickly stood up and brushed myself off.

Nora was in my face as I looked up from my dress. Her eyes felt like they stared into my soul.

"I know it's been a trying time for you lately, but you will behave." She drilled every word into my heart. "Is that understood?"

Terrified, I barely moved my head into a tiny nod. "Yes, ma'am," I said as my voice shook as much as my body.

"Five strikes should serve as a warning," Nora said as she grabbed my shoulder. "All of you sit at the table and nobody eats until we get back." She turned to the older lady and gave her instructions. "Feed these five like normal, but make a plate of just eggs, with a little extra, for Lucia."

The other five kids scrambled past us without getting close to me, and Nora forcefully led me out of the kitchen. She took me down the hall to my room. While we traveled through the hall, I heard some muttering from one of the rooms. I could pinpoint the location—inside the room closest to the main entrance—but not what was said. *I think Evandol is pacing back and forth and probably cursing me quietly so as not to warrant more attention from Nora. I have really good hearing, but what stopped me from hearing on the other side of the kitchen door? Also, people need to stop shouting around me.*

11

I AM LUCIA

As we arrived in my bedroom, Nora closed the door quickly and then put her hand on her hips. "There are rules, and if you break the rules, you will be punished. Do you understand?"

"Yes, but he called me an animal." I pointed in the direction that I had heard Evandol pacing.

"And he will be punished accordingly." Nora stepped towards me. "You will not attack anyone unless your life is in danger. Here, I will be more forgiving than if the guards saw you attacking someone in the streets. The two worst crimes you can commit in this kingdom are treason and murder. Even though Evandol said something he shouldn't have, you still can't just attack him like that."

"I wasn't going to kill him. I just wanted him not to call me an animal. He made me so angry. I'll try not to do it again." I held out my hands pleadingly.

"This will help you remember to control yourself." Nora's eyes looked like she was looking elsewhere. *She said five strikes. What strikes?*

THE BIG BAD WOLF

The moment I had finished my thought, a stinging slap struck my butt. I yelped in surprise and pain. I turned to see who spanked me. There was no one behind me, just an empty room. A second slap hit my butt again. More pain flooded from my backside. I turned around again to see Nora staring at me. Panic slowly started to set in.

A third spanking clipped my tail and hurt the most so far.

"Stop, I get it. Don't hurt anyone." I held back my tears.

"I said five, there are two left." Nora sounded as distant as her eyes looked. It was like her emotions disappeared along with any sense of self.

A fourth slap struck my posterior, causing my knees to give out as I slumped to the ground clutching my butt. The stinging was just beginning to abate as my arms were pulled away just long enough for the final spanking to hit me. Tears fell down my face as I rubbed my backside to try and make it feel better.

"Please don't attack the others. I know you're lost, confused and probably lonely, but that means you just need to get along with everyone all the more."

You don't know the half of it, lady. "I'm sorry." My voice cracked as I cried.

"Stay here until you're ready to sit with the others to eat breakfast. I'll deal with Evandol now," Nora said before she left me alone in my room. Her eyes were still unfocused.

I moved to sit on the bed as I waited for the pain to stop. It didn't take long for the stinging sensation to dissipate. *I guess I recover from everything faster. But I need to control myself and not let anger get the better of me. Why does that keep happening? This is my first full day and I've already earned a spanking. I need to get it together. After all, I promised Allen that I would be a good kid for Nora. But I tell them I'm not an animal, then I go and act just like one. Why are these impulses so hard to control? Is it because I haven't gotten used to them yet?*

I opened the door to head back to the kitchen and saw Nora walking towards me. She wasted no time getting me back to the table. The closer we got to the kitchen, the more I smelled cooked eggs. As we entered, there was nobody present, but I could smell the scent of cooked eggs emanating from here. *I hope nobody tries to turn me into a bloodhound. This nose is strong, but I'm afraid of what people will make me smell.*

Nora led me through the kitchen, past an archway. *I guess I missed that when someone was throwing stuff at me. And when I lost my temper.* We entered the dining room which had a large rectangular wooden table with ten chairs set around it. Four windows allowed the rising sun to illuminate the room. There was a door on the left wall, where one window sat, showing outside. *Is this building the shape of a U? If that's the case, there must be a small backyard that this door leads to.* My curiosity would have to wait, because at the table sat five kids who looked at us with varying levels of confusion. The lady who'd decided that kitchen implements were a sound choice of weapon also stood there.

Nora stopped near the center of the table, with me following in behind her. *I don't know why, but all of these eyes staring at me are making me extremely uncomfortable.* Nora noticed I was trying to use her as a human shield, and she grabbed my shoulders and presented me in front of the others.

"This is our newest addition to our makeshift family." Nora used her sweet and caring voice. *She has way too many distinct tones. I guess she might have split personalities or something.* "Go on, introduce yourself to your new siblings."

So she wants us to act like a family? "Hi, I'm Lucia and I have amnesia." *Well, that was smooth, if I was at an Amnesiacs Anonymous meeting.*

The reactions that followed were mixed.

"What are you talking about?" The oldest-looking girl, a human, spoke first.

"She's so cute!" The youngest girl, also a human, squealed and jumped out of her chair to rush me.

"Where did a beastkin come from?" the third girl said, whose hair was in a long braid that revealed her pointed ears. But her ears weren't as long as any other elf's ears.

The two boys had less vocal reactions, but their facial expressions told different stories. The youngest of the two boys, at least the shorter of the two as they looked of similar age, looked at me with his mouth agape and head tilted. The other boy, who was larger and taller than the one who sat beside him, looked at me with disgust. *Great, another racist. At least he had the sense not to vocalize it in front of Nora. Especially after Evandol's display earlier.* The lady—I thought Nora said her name was Melody—just stood there, expressionless.

Nora looked down at me disapprovingly. "What happened to you? A few moments ago, you got into a fight with Evandol. Now you're so shy, it's cute."

Was she expecting something different from me? I gave my name and a fact about myself. Isn't that what it always is?

The little girl who'd left her chair tackled me in my confusion, reaching for my ears. "They're so cute. Are they real?"

The little girl, who, albeit taller than me by a few inches, was acting crazy. Looking at her skin and eyes, I would believe it if I'd been told she was of Asian descent. Her black hair and light brown skin tone were different from everyone else around her. Her thin build held a surprising amount of strength.

Oh no, I'm not going to let that happen. Not after what it felt like when that knight touched them. Grabbing her wrists, I pushed them as far away from my head as I could. "Don't touch them!" There was a little growl in my voice. *Maybe I should try not to panic so much.*

The girl squealed as she attempted to flee from me, and I quickly released her wrists. She only went a few steps but did give me some distance to stand up. She was holding her wrists in her hands like she had been released from imprisonment. "I'm sorry."

She almost started crying. Her eyes expanded as she looked at me with sadness. *She's giving me the puppy-dog-eyes treatment.*

"Oh no, I'm not falling for that." She was only a bit little taller than me. *I have actual puppy dog eyes, so you have no power here, little girl.* I gave her a stern look. "Don't touch them!" I crossed my arms in an attempt to look tough. I don't think I succeeded, because the look the girl gave me told me she wanted to squeeze the life out of me with a hug.

"Okay, everyone, please introduce yourselves from youngest to oldest." Nora attempted to break up the situation. "Let's not take too long; the food will taste better hot." *Oh right, breakfast is supposed to be served after introductions.*

"I'm Molly. I'm ten years old and cute things are my specialty," the girl who tried to touch my ears moments ago said as proudly as possible. *Yeah, this kid is Crazy with a capital* C.

"Anna, thirteen years of age, and I'm curious why a beastkin is here." The girl with the almost-elf ears spoke next.

The largest boy said: "My name is Martin. Leave me alone and I'll leave you alone." *I was wrong about this kid twice. He isn't a racist; he just doesn't like dealing with people at all. I can deal with that. And also, he's going to be huge once he grows up.*

"Oscar's the name, and magic's my game." The one I thought was the younger of the two was actually older. "My birthday's next week, so you're gonna look up to me even more." *I think this kid has a few screws loose, but not the same ones or as many as Molly has.*

The final girl spoke up. "I'm Eleanah, and I will watch you closely." She was the one who had two blades brandished towards me earlier. "What do you mean, you have amnesia?"

"I don't remember anything from beyond... is it three days now?" I said to Eleanah. "It wasn't until last night I learned my name."

Eleanah's brow furrowed, but she said nothing else.

"Now all of you will get along and treat little Lucia here kindly." Nora was as motherly as ever. *She's going to make us all get along whether we want to or not, isn't she?* "Alright, who's ready for breakfast?" Nora beamed as she clapped her hands together. She nudged me towards the table. "Go ahead and take a seat."

Molly returned to her seat between the other two girls. I looked for a seat with nobody seated next to me. I noticed that they'd split the table, with the boys on one side and the girls on the other. I saw that sitting on the sides with the other kids would put me next to one, so I headed to one chair at the end. But as soon as I got to the chair and grabbed it to pull it back, I heard Anna clear her throat, and I looked at her, confused.

She shook her head slightly. *Is she trying to warn me that I shouldn't sit here? She seems like the most sane person here. I think I'll sit next to her. It should be safe, I hope.* The chair didn't have much room for my tail, so I moved it so that it was sticking out to the side, away from Anna.

Once I was seated, I watched Melody place plates in front of the boys first, since they were closer to where she was standing. There was a small pile of scrambled eggs, a piece of bread and strawberries. *Eggs and uncooked toast with sugar-free unprocessed strawberry jam, not a bad breakfast.* Each child was presented with the same plate, except for me. There was only one thing on my plate, the scrambled eggs, and there was about twice as much compared to everyone else. When all the other kids saw my plate, they all protested immediately.

"Calm down, everyone." Nora's voice carried over the spontaneous shouting match. She held her hands out and waved them up and down. "I can explain…"

"Why does she get special treatment? Why does she get all the eggs and doesn't have to eat this bread?" Martin pointed at me as he interrupted Nora.

All the shouting forced me to cover my ears once again. *Why is everyone always shouting? And what's wrong with the bread? It looks fine to me.*

Nora looked at Martin with a glare as she leaned forward. Even though he was the largest kid here, he backed down. *I guess Nora can be scary to everyone else too.* Even though Martin relented, he still held the resentment on his face.

With everyone silent, I decided that I should explain it. "I can't eat bread or strawberries," I said as I lifted my head out from under my hands. Even with my ears released, I still decided to lay them down flat. *Am I nervous? Why? They're a bunch of kids. Yes, I'm the smallest one here, but I'm simply stating facts.* "When we saw Phan, he said I was a carnivore and could only eat meat."

"Can you even eat eggs?" Anna looked at me skeptically.

"Honestly? I have no idea." I shrugged. "Probably." *Eggs are embryos and therefore meat at the earliest possible stage... That's a dark thought when I put it that way.*

"Prove it, then." Martin threw a strawberry at me. It landed next to my plate.

"Martin, behave. Lucia, you don't need to eat that." Nora was trying to get control of the situation, but I didn't think she would succeed. *I'm curious to see what will happen if I eat something plant-based.*

Picking up the strawberry, I looked at Nora. "If this will shut him up, then I'll do it. Just so you know, I'll probably vomit this back up." *That's nothing more than a guess. I know that dogs eat grass and vomit it up shortly after.*

I ate the strawberry whole, minus the green stem, of course.

I remembered what strawberries should taste like, and I remembered liking them. But strawberries never tasted like *this*. And nothing had ever tasted that bad. The strawberry's opening salvo bombarded me with a gag-inducing sourness. *I'm doing this to prove a point. I will swallow this fruit.*

After surviving the first attack, the strawberry moved in and swarmed my taste buds with an acidic flood. I nearly regurgitated at the taste of so much acid. It tasted like I was already vomiting. *I'm almost there. How much worse can this get? I won't lose to a berry, of all things.*

Eager to end this torment, I gathered what willpower I could muster and forced myself to swallow the little red offender. I panted as I looked around and noticed that I was sweating from the pads in my hands and feet. Everyone was staring at me like I was about to die.

"It was just a strawberry!" Oscar's shout broke the silence.

"I told you, I can only eat meat," I said haggardly. I turned to Martin with a stern look. "I hope you're satisfied." My stomach had already begun its revolt.

"You were just faking it. You can eat it just fine." Martin sat straight up and crossed his arms. He had a smirk on his face.

I narrowed my eyes at him. "I really hate you." The strawberry was making its return trip sooner than I'd thought. "Let's see if you think I can fake this." I felt the bile climb to the back of my throat. I turned my head to the side, away from Anna, and faced the ground.

The floodgates opened wide as I opened my mouth.

Vomit spewed from my mouth at an alarming rate. It also seems that my mouth wasn't large enough; my stomach contents found their way out through my nose too. Considering the only content in my stomach before was one little innocent, seed-covered red berry, most of what I threw up was acid, and it burned as it exited. Tears rolled down my face as I could do nothing more than watch as I threw up.

As quickly as it started, it ended. *That tasted just like strawberries.*

Gasping for air, I waited for the last drips of bile, snot and saliva to fall. I saw a pair of feet standing by the pool of vomit. An apron was lifted to my face and used to wipe away the consequences of my idiotic decision.

"Could you have held on long enough for us to get a bucket?" Nora's voice was soft.

"Nope." *I did warn you that this might happen, though.* "Can I have some water to drink?" *I need to wash this foul taste out of my mouth before I eat something that I can handle.*

13 PITCH BLACK CATS

Melody placed a copper cup in front of each child. After Nora finished wiping my face, I took the cup and inspected it. *It looks like water to me. It smells fine too.* I tentatively sipped some and found that it was clean water. I downed it quickly to wash out my mouth.

The awkward breakfast continued as everyone started eating. After my display, nobody talked as we ate. Martin and Eleanah gave me sidelong glances. Anna didn't give me much attention while Molly watched me with awe. *After I saw the orcs, I thought that my animal-hybrid body would be a little more accepted. I guess not. I'm still a freak.*

If I had to describe the taste of eggs in one word, it would be "nothing." There was no taste, but I didn't have the urge to either spit them out or throw them up. I was hungry, so I ate them without a fuss. I noticed that my earlier display of regurgitation didn't put anyone off their breakfast, either.

12

GETTING TO KNOW THE NEIGHBORHOOD

We all finished eating at roughly the same time, with Martin clearly finishing first. The other five children all got up as they finished their food. I sat with an empty plate in front of me until Eleanah finished last and started collecting all the plates, forks and cups. *I'm guessing the other kids all have different chores, and Eleanah's is doing the dishes.*

Eleanah was the tallest of all us girls, but that only put her at the same height as Oscar. Her blue eyes were slightly darker than mine. Her wavy brown hair threatened to cover up her right eye. She brushed it back behind her ear to reveal her maturing face. Her body also shows other signs that she'd hit puberty, although it looked like she is still growing.

A pair of voices caught my attention. I turned to see Nora and Melody talking to each other in the doorway to the kitchen.

"I need to take Lucia to get some clothes," Nora whispered.

"I take it you want me to watch the others while you're gone?" Melody asked in a pleasant voice. *Her voice sounds so calming if she isn't shouting and throwing things at me.* "Which chores do you want me to leave for her?"

Of course I'll have to help with the chores. They're going to treat me like the kid I appear to be. I turned an ear towards them and focused on their conversation.

"I think cleaning the bathroom will be enough for today," Nora said with a contemplative look on her face. "Last night, when Allen brought her in, she was filthy. She needed two baths just to get clean. Also, there is that little display she had earlier." *Is she tailoring her choice of chores to who gets them the dirtiest last? That's intriguing information.*

"Hopefully she can keep her mood swings in check while we're shopping." She turned her head and looked right at me.

Why is she accusing me of having mood swings? "Hey!" I blurted out. *I just exposed myself for eavesdropping.* I also noticed that Eleanah was staring at me. *Did she figure out that my hearing is better than a normal human's?*

Nora walked over to me. "How much did you hear?" She didn't sound threatening, but her tone still scared me a bit.

"I can hear what sounds like Molly skipping down the hallway," I said nonchalantly. *That should give them a clue how good my hearing is. Although I don't know if that really is Molly skipping, but she looks like the only one who would skip in this place.* "I started paying attention when you started talking about chores."

I watched Eleanah's jaw descend to the floor after hearing my boasting.

"Since yesterday, you've been overzealous one moment and flighty the next." Nora waved her hand out over the table.

"It isn't my fault; everything has either scared me or made me angry," I said while pouting. *Why does everything I say make me sound like a brat?* "I'm sorry for throwing up on the floor, though." I dropped my pout and slumped in the chair.

"Eleanah, go take care of those dishes." Nora gently nudged the girl into action. As the other girl scurried off to the kitchen, Nora looked at me with a smile and stood by the chair I was sitting in. "I know your unique physiology will give you an upper hand, but remember, you'll need to work hard. But we'll start with the necessities. You need something else to wear." She extended a hand to me.

I remembered my lesson from last night and pushed off the chair so my tail would clear the edge before I dropped down. As I landed, I grabbed Nora's hand, ready to follow her. She led me out of the dining room, through the kitchen and down the hall. I smelled that sweet smell again but couldn't pinpoint where it was originating from in the kitchen.

"As you've figured out, the dining room and kitchen are connected to one another. You can get to them by going down the hallway with all the bedrooms. Each room is labeled, and yours will be too." We stopped in front of my room as she pointed out a blank plaque on the door. "You can also get to the kitchen by going in from the courtyard to the dining room." We continued walking down the hallway. "My bedroom, should you need me, is the first one on the left if you're coming from the front door or the last one on the right if you're coming from your room." To punctuate her point, Nora stopped in front of her bedroom and waved her arm towards the door.

"I know the bathtubs and toilets are down that way, but what's through that door?" I asked, pointing to the one door straight ahead.

"That's the way to the classroom, and above that is the training room," Nora said cheerfully. She clapped her hands together and continued, "We'll spend plenty of time there in the future. We're going to head out once you use the toilet."

This brings back partial memories. I know I had parents in my previous life, but I can't remember a single detail about them. I do remember that, before going out of the house, they would make sure we didn't need to use the restroom. I only understood the importance of them doing that later in life, so, in this life, I'm going to put that lesson into action immediately. I simply nodded my head in agreement.

13 PITCH BLACK CATS

I didn't look closely at the toilets when we walked by them last night. They were glorified raised holes in the ground, and I couldn't bring myself to look down the hole. *Who makes toilets out of wood? Wait, let me think about that. Nope, that makes things even more gross. Wood retains moisture, and the moisture that comes into contact with a toilet—I won't continue that line of thought. When in Rome, do as the Romans. But that doesn't help me enjoy this at all.* Toilet paper, though, was large, absorbent leaves stacked in a wooden dispenser.

Nora followed me in and watched me go. I will admit that it was far more nerve-racking than when she gave me a bath. Her stare and critique of how I wiped myself made me uneasy. She knew better, so I followed her instructions, resolving to learn from them. After enduring that embarrassment, Nora went to her room to change her clothes, and I was told to wait for her in the hall.

While I waited, I saw Anna walk out of a room carrying a pile of clothes in a wooden box. She walked to the room where I heard Evandol pacing around and knocked on the door. "Evan, I need your laundry," she said through the closed door.

The door opened silently, and Anna held out her arms as Evandol placed a pile of clothes in them. She continued on her way, with all the clothes in the box, to stand in front of me. "Do you have any laundry?"

"I'm not sure what happened to the clothes I wore last night. Other than what I'm wearing, I have nothing else." I shrugged.

"I figured as much." Her tone was very nonchalant. Then, suddenly, she dropped the box of clothes and her face shifted like she had just remembered something. "Wait. That means you're going clothes shopping. I need to go clothes shopping too." She stomped her foot.

I stared at the girl in shock.

"Then you can come along with us." Nora surprised the two of us as we both jumped to attention. "You can do the chores later. I plan to be back with enough time for Lucia to clean the bathtubs."

"Yay!" This calm and collected girl from before had completely changed her personality. *Apparently this girl loves to shop. That can be dangerous.* "I'll get changed right away," she shouted as she sprinted down the hall and dove into a room.

I guess that's her room. Hey, isn't that right next to mine?

I turned to look at Nora and saw that she was in a similar dress to the one from last night. This one, instead of green, was blue with an embroidered trim of clouds. The dress went down to a couple of inches above her ankle.

It didn't take Anna long to change her clothes. She walked out in a faded yellow shirt that went down past her waist. It had short sleeves, and she had the front tied up with strings to the base of her neck. Below the shirt was a skirt that was a darker yellow than the shirt and went down to right past her knees. Her boots were short compared to all the others that I'd seen. They looked similar in every other way, except that they barely went past the ankle.

She walked towards us excitedly, taking a brush to her hair. "I'm ready to go once I put my hair up." As she spoke, the brush in her hand disappeared in a quick flash of light that folded in on itself. She took a small string and tied her wavy brown hair into a ponytail. She beamed at Nora as her blue eyes shimmered with happiness. "All set, let's go shopping!" She pointed to the door like she was leading a parade. She began marching to the door.

My mind was catching up with two major epiphanies. *There happens to be one of these kids that proved she could do magic, while the other claims he can do magic. Also, the one I thought to be the calmest and most normal of the kids here has become a woman on a mission, and that mission is to shop 'til she drops. Nora is acting like this is normal. What kind of world is this? Is everyone crazy? If I walk out this door and see a white rabbit with a timepiece saying, "I am late," I'll just quit. I don't know how, but I'm going to.*

Anna turned around to look at me and found her enthusiasm again as she ran up to me. "Is she okay? Why is she staring at me with her mouth wide open like that?"

"I think you using magic caught her off guard." Nora giggled. "I impressed her with my magic before her bath last night." I felt her finger lift my mouth closed, and she snapped her fingers behind me, causing me to jump a bit. "Wake up. If we take too long, we'll be late for lunch. I believe, of all people, you won't want to miss this lunch."

"Why?" I tilted my head to look at Nora.

"Because Melody is cooking braised boar." Nora grinned and folded her arms in front of her.

Does she think she can bribe me with food? Unfortunately for me, she's right. "Is that what smells so good in the kitchen?" *I have to know now.*

"Wait, you can smell it cooking already?" Anna shouted as she leaned toward me. "From here?"

"Volume," I said, flinching away from her. "And yes, to both questions." Anna stared at me, bewildered. *I think I should tell her about my enhanced senses.* I pointed to the ears on top of my head and wiggled them slightly for emphasis. "My ears are excellent. Which is nice for listening to those who are talking about me, but makes loud noises, like shouting, painful."

"We'll need to have a meeting with everyone later," Anna said as she straightened up. "But first, shopping!" Her hands clasped together as she stared straight ahead. I thought I saw some drool pooling in the corner of her mouth.

Again, Nora is acting like this is normal.

"This looks like the beginning of a beautiful friendship," Nora said jovially.

We exited the orphanage behind Anna and saw a horde of people walking in the streets. I followed Nora and Anna through the town and felt all the stares that followed me wherever I went. I ran up and grabbed both Nora and Anna's hands, trying to alleviate the anxiety. Anna jumped from surprise but didn't break her stride and carried on with her happy stroll.

As I tugged on Nora's arm, she turned to look at me. "What's wrong?" she asked.

"I have some questions," I said, doing my best to ignore the stares people were giving me.

"What sort of questions?" Her voice didn't hide her concern.

"Last night, when you were talking with that guy, you talked about me serving in the guard when I turn seventeen. What does that mean?" I asked. "I remember Phan mentioning something about a stipend. Am I really going to be required to serve for fifteen years?"

Nora raised an eyebrow. I could tell she was thinking something, but not what she was thinking. "How did you come up with that number?"

Ah, I did it again. I'm supposed to be a kid. A kid who doesn't know how to read. So how do I explain how I can do math? I need to fit in. I don't want to draw attention to myself. People treat me like a freak enough as it is. "I guessed." *Yeah, that won't convince her.*

Nora narrowed her eyes for a moment before turning back to see where she was going. "As Arsane said last night, in return for the money to feed, clothe and care for you, the kingdom requires you to serve in the guard or as a knight. I regulate how much money they provide for you and adjust it as needed. If you get hurt and need extra to cover the cost of care, I can ask for an emergency withdrawal. The kingdom keeps track of everything based on the accounting ledgers I provide, and, when you turn seventeen, they will tell you what is required."

Why the option? "What's the difference between serving as a guard or as a knight?"

"If you serve as a knight, you're required to spend fewer years in service. Knights are also responsible for dealing with crimes as they see them, but their major concern is fighting in wars and defending against invasions. The guards are the ones in charge of peacekeeping in the cities and villages." Nora's voice trailed off at the end. She shook her head a few times before her step resumed its usual liveliness. "If you're worried about getting some spending money to buy anything extra that you want, we can see about getting you a job around town, something simple and easy to handle."

"Then I'll be a knight," I whispered. *I want to spend as little time as possible indebted to the kingdom. But I still need to grow up. I'm still just a kid.*

Even though the stares never stopped, Anna walked on, ignoring everything. It was a short while before we arrived at a section of town with no buildings. Instead, tents and different styles of stalls were erected, with people shouting and talking all around. *My head is spinning from the walk here. And now there's this?* I felt like I wanted to run away again; the noise was unbearable.

The organization of the market was impossible to follow because every vendor had different sized and shaped storefronts. Some used large, round tents, some used rectangular wooden stalls and others used nothing more than a cart. Everything they did, they did to present their wares. Vendors showed off their goods, haggled with customers and completed their sales. *The world feels much larger when you're a child.*

Nora grabbed both mine and Anna's shoulders and dragged us to the side of the road. "Alright, Anna, you can go shopping with Lucia and help her get some clothes." Anna's eyes bulged and sparkled with excitement. Nora raised a finger. "A few rules first."

Anna waved her hand as she spoke. "Yes, I know. Don't spend too much, don't go with strangers and no free samples," she said with all the attitude a teenager would give their parent.

Nora stared Anna down, unamused. "Also, everywhere you go, Lucia goes with you. If anyone causes you trouble, just leave. If you see anything strange, let me know immediately. You are never to be separated from her, understand?" Anna's peppiness and sass evaporated as she nodded meekly. "Good, here's how much you can spend." She held out a pouch, and I could hear a jingle of metal in it. "Try to get five full outfits with underwear. I'll handle the other things she'll need. You can use this time to get what you need too."

"Mission accepted!" Anna slammed her fist against her chest and grabbed the coin purse. Her vim and vigor restored, she grabbed my hand and pulled me into the horde of people. My head spun and my heart raced when I saw that every direction I looked in was crowded.

13

DRESS FOR SUCCESS

How did I get here? I'm in my room. What am I carrying? I looked down at a bundle of cloth tied together with a string. *Oh, that's right, I went clothes shopping with Anna. What happened? The last thing I remember was Anna pulling me towards the market area. Did she traumatize me with her shopping habits? At least I made it back to the orphanage. Should I call this home now? I don't know.*

I placed the bundle on the bed and cut the string with my claws. *Why did I just do that? I understand my claws are sharp and can cut strings easily. The part I don't understand is why I acted on impulse and didn't think about it. I also noticed that I'm more aware of my tail's position too. Walking feels much more natural now; I barely have to concentrate on it anymore. Have I been adjusting to this body slowly and soon everything will feel completely natural? If I'm honest, that's relieving. But what if I start acting more like a wolf than a person? No, that's not what's happening, right? I'm just using the parts of my body as they are. Nothing to worry about.*

After I finished my self-reflection, I looked down at the clothes. There were four outfits: one solid black dress with no sleeves; a black short-sleeve shirt with a black skirt; a gray short-sleeve shirt with a gray skirt; and a brown tank top that had a slightly longer shirt tail with a long, slightly lighter brown skirt. The black and gray skirts both reached my knees, while the brown skirt fell just above my ankles. *I need to ask why there are so many skirts. Why didn't I get any pants? I know I'm a girl, but this still doesn't feel right. I need to find out what happened.*

As I moved to leave, I noticed there was another small leather sack next to my door. *It can wait.* "Anna!" I shouted as I left my room.

"What?" I heard two voices respond to my call. One came from the person I was looking for and the other was from Oscar. I turned to see them standing in the hallway. *Were they just talking? I guess I wasn't paying attention.*

"What is it?" Anna ran up to me, looking worried. "Why aren't you wearing any of those cute outfits we got for you?"

"What happened?" I dropped my volume back to a civilized level. "What's with those clothes?"

"Nora said to get five outfits. Unfortunately, because of the tailoring we needed done, we had to pay extra. We could only afford four with what we had on hand. Don't worry, we'll get you one more later. We needed something in case you needed an outfit for a formal event, then something for when it's colder and the other two are for regular use." She appeared perplexed. "Don't you remember going shopping with me?"

"You went shopping with Anna?" Oscar joined in on the conversation, walking over. He stood a head taller than Anna, and his light-brown hair contrasted with his tan skin. He wore a gray tee shirt with brown shorts. His right foot was bandaged up and covered with a slipper-like shoe. There was a matching slipper on his other foot, but there was no bandage. He didn't limp as he walked.

His face didn't match the concern in his voice; he had this perpetual look of paranoia. He looked around everywhere and focused on us at the same time. "I'm so sorry for you. Are you okay?

Did you need me to get you anything? How much money did you give her?"

What's with these questions? Why did he ask how much money? That doesn't seem relevant.

"Nora gave her the money. Why do you ask?" I watched him closely as I tilted my head.

"Curiosity mostly," he answered in a nonchalant tone. "I hear lunch is going to be a big deal because of you."

I took a sniff of the air. I smelled something similar to the sweet smell from this morning. *It's different, and there are more scents mixed with it.* "I can smell it, and it's making me hungry." I tried to walk towards the kitchen, towards the lovely scent, but a hand halted my progress. I looked down to see Anna had stopped me. "What?"

"Not dressed like that, you aren't." Anna waved her finger at me. "We went shopping and got you some cute outfits. You're going to show them off to everyone." She moved to stand guard in the hall.

I guess I can't go to lunch until I pass her inspection. That reminds me. "You didn't answer my question. Why do I only have a dress and skirts but no pants?"

"You don't remember our experience of shuffling through all the clothes? You tried on some pants, but you said that they felt weird against your fur." Her face changed so that it looked like she was thinking about something. "Your eyes were a bit glossed over, and you didn't talk unless I asked you something. Oh well, it doesn't matter. Go, pick out an outfit and put it on. There'll be no lunch for you until you do." She returned to her sentry stance.

"I'll see you at the table." Oscar waved as he headed down the hall.

Thanks for nothing, Oscar.

There's no reasoning with this girl over clothes. Might as well get it over with. I went back into my room and grabbed the leather sack by the door as I entered. After shutting the door, I placed the sack on my bed and opened it to find underwear, a brush and comb. *Anna said I needed to pick an outfit.* I picked the black shirt and skirt. *I guess if I said that I didn't like wearing pants, I might have to look into some type of replacement. Maybe I can try again some other time.*

Putting on the new clothes was a simple endeavor with one problem: my tail. Anna had ordered the clothes to be tailored to have a small horizontal cutout with a string tie that went above my tail. My claws kept impeding me from tying the knots behind me. I growled. *Why can't I do this? I know how to tie knots.* After several more failed attempts, I swallowed my pride and poked my head out the door and saw Anna standing vigilant.

"Um, Anna?" The hesitation in my voice was obvious.

"What?" Concern filled her face as she looked at me.

"Could you kinda come in here and give me a hand, please?" *Now I have to ask for help to put on clothes. Why does everything have to be so difficult?*

Her face shifted from concern to skepticism. "Okay." She drew out her response as she walked towards me and my room. Once she entered, she closed the door behind herself. "So, what do you need help with? It looks like you did just fine. I liked the black on you way more than the other colors. It really brings out your silver fur."

"Thanks, I think." It sounded like a compliment, but I wasn't looking for her opinion. I needed hands that could tie a knot. "Can you tie up my skirt, please? It's too hard for me to tie anything while trying not to cut it with my claws." I averted my gaze from Anna as I asked.

"How do you tie a knot?" She held the other skirt, that was still on the bed, out in front of her.

She wants a demonstration? Okay. I grabbed the strings and crossed them over with no problem. I took one string and made a little bunny ear pinched between my thumb and pointer finger pads. Then I took the other string and wrapped it around my two fingers, pinching the other string. Once it completed the loop, I attempted to force the second string past my thumb claw and struggled.

Seeing me struggle, Anna stepped in. "Stop! Even if you get it through, you're going to keep getting stuck on your claws. Who taught you how to tie a knot like this? It's completely impractical for you to tie this knot." She sounded disappointed in me.

"I don't remember." *My favorite three words return. It isn't like I can tell her that is how I tied my shoes every day in my last life.*

"Oh right, I forgot—amnesia." I watched her deflate. She straightened her shoulders and handed me the skirt. "Hold this." I took the skirt from her and she grabbed the strings. "Watch me closely. Your first part was right, but after that, this is much simpler. I believe you can do it, even with your hands." *That's one of the nicest things someone has said to me so far.*

She took one end in each hand and wrapped it around the pointer finger and thumb in each hand. "Look at how I wrapped them around in opposite directions." She spread her two fingers apart and interlocked them. "Make sure the strings cross one another." She pinched her right hand's thumb and pointer finger again. Then she hooked the pointer finger around the string that wrapped around the pointer finger of her right hand and pulled both hands into a simple knot.

I stared at her hands in complete disbelief. *This method is astoundingly simple.* "Do that again."

Anna shrugged as she pulled the two single strings originating from the knot to undo it. She then tied the knot the same way.

"Wow, that is so cool." *I never saw a knot like that in my previous life.* My tail wagged lazily back and forth. "One more time."

She obliged. Anna undid the knot before taking the skirt from me. "Your turn." Those two words were more intimidating when accompanied by the playful smile on her face.

I did the first step with no problem. I followed her instructions and, with a lot of effort and a couple of attempts, succeeded. Anna made me practice several more times until I could do it in one fluid motion.

"You learned that really quickly, almost too quickly." She was staring down at me, looking for something. I was just excited that I could tie a knot. My tail was wagging in full force, and that caught Anna's attention. "Well, I'm glad you're happy to learn something. So I'll leave you to tie yourself up now. It's cute to see your tail wag like that. Molly's going to latch on to you the first chance she gets when she sees that."

Success! I did it even with my hands behind my back. That was harder than I would have liked, but I did it. What was she saying about Molly?

Her kind act overwhelmed me with gratitude, so I thanked her with a hug. My head lay against her stomach as I wrapped my arms around her. "Thank you for teaching me your cool knot-tying skills."

"You're welcome." Anna sounded a little shocked and unprepared for the hug, but embraced it nonetheless.

"I can smell the food and I'm hungry. So how about now, can we go eat?" I asked as my tail continued wagging behind me vigorously.

"Let's go show you off and get some food." She put her hand on my head and patted it.

I melted in her embrace as my tail went from excited to ecstatic. I jumped out of the hug, my eyes wide and my jaw clamped shut.

Anna's eyes were open wide too, but soon her expression turned into a knowing grin. "You like your head patted, don't you?"

"Please don't tell anyone." I grabbed my tail to calm down and get my emotions under control. *I should use the waterfalls tactic again.* "It's embarrassing. Could you also not do it anymore?"

Anna walked over to me, put her arm around my shoulder and led me out of the room. "I won't tell anyone or pat your head in front of them. But once they find out on their own..."—her pause buried a seed of fear in me—"I won't be letting this cuteness stay hidden."

What is it with girls and cute things? I don't see the appeal.

The two of us walked towards the kitchen together. "I have a question, if you don't mind me asking," I said as I slowed our pace. "Why do you almost change into another person when you talk about clothes?"

"What are you talking about? I'm still the same person." She glanced at me with a bewildered look. "Are you asking why shopping gets me all excited?"

"Sure, that."

"Why wouldn't I get excited? The kingdom doesn't provide us much of a stipend. Most of us use our jobs to help pay for necessities like clothes. But for me, clothes shopping is about what I want. Every day the people I work for tell me what to do. My teacher tells me what to practice and learn. The kingdom tells me what I'll do once I turn seventeen." Her eyes seemed to glow as they looked straight ahead. "When I go shopping for clothes, none of them can tell me what to do. I can go to a store and pick out something I like. When I pay for it, the store owner won't judge me or tell me no. They'll take my money with a smile and thank me. When I pick out my clothes, it's the most control I have in my life."

I blinked several times. *She isn't crazy. She's just happy to have some semblance of control as a kid. Maybe I should take a few lessons from this girl and take control of what I can. Now I just need to find something for me. Thanks, Anna, you're something special.*

While my thoughts ran through my head we went through the kitchen into the dining room. Everyone else sat around the table and waited for us, sitting in the same seats they were in for breakfast. Nora and Melody sat at each end of the table, dividing the boys on one side and the girls on the other. Evandol joined us to eat lunch. Anger filled his eyes as he stared daggers in my direction. *At least by chance we'll sit as far away from one another as possible.* The table was set with all the food spread out for everyone to eat family-style.

Nora spoke up first. "Couldn't help yourself and forced her into her new clothes, did you, Anna?" She had her hands clasped together and her arms made a tent off the table. "You made us wait for a while."

"But she looks so cute now," Anna said. Her chest was nearly exploding with pride. "Besides, I taught her how to tie a knot." She waved her hand as she presented me. "Go on, show off."

I don't think so. Clothes are your thing, my thing is sitting on a plate. I was having trouble keeping my drool from escaping my mouth while I stared at the large leg of meat. Without stopping, I headed straight for the seat I used during breakfast. I noticed the evidence of my strawberry incident had been exterminated. I turned to see Anna's face in shock, as if I had betrayed her. A small amount of saliva escaped my mouth as I looked at the meat. I absent-mindedly wiped it without diverting my gaze. I heard Anna take her seat next to me with a dissatisfied huff.

"Well, everyone's here. And someone is going to soak her new clothes with drool if we wait too much longer." Nora stood up from her chair. "Begin eating. Please pass the dishes around." Nora pulled the large leg of meat closer to herself. Taking a large knife in one hand and the exposed bone in the other, she began cutting chunks of meat off and placed a large piece on my plate first. She started cutting smaller pieces off for everyone else to grab, including herself. There were what looked like baked potatoes, corn on the cob, bread slices and more strawberries in addition to the roast. Not wanting a repeat performance at breakfast, I grabbed the fork and knife and attempted to attack the meat on the plate before me.

14

A TASTE OF HEAVEN

First it was tying knots, and now it's using a fork and knife. Why does everything have to be more difficult with my hands? The knife wouldn't stay straight. Every time I pushed down, the knife tilted to one side and wouldn't cut anything. The fork was equally ineffective; every time I tried to stab the meat, it slipped through my fingers. I didn't have any problems with the eggs because I was simply scooping them up and not actually stabbing anything. *Like everything else I've been doing, I need to change how I do this.*

I adjusted my grip on the silverware. Instead of holding the fork between my fingertips, I used my entire hand to hold it in a reverse knife grip, so my thumb kept it from sliding out.

Using the fork that way was better for my bestial hands. The knife was a different story, though. I couldn't coordinate cutting it around the fork, and the sawing motion wasn't getting through the meat fast enough. I looked at the knife in my hands, and an idea leaped to the front of my mind. *I already have five knives; why don't I use one of those? It worked on the string.* After putting down the knife, I lined up the claw on my pointer finger and cut. There was no resistance as my claw sliced through. With my prize on the fork, I celebrated by eating the piece of meat.

"Oh yeah, mmm, that's good." I closed my eyes and savored the taste. I couldn't decide which tasted better: the jerky or this. Both tasted way better than anything else I'd had before, by a long shot. *If I can only eat meat and it tastes this good, I can live with that. I don't think I want anything else. Maybe this can be my one thing. There are all kinds of different meats out there. Maybe I can see if I can taste every different kinda meat there is in this world.*

I opened my eyes to see everyone else eating, but also watching me as they did. "What?"

"You really should use the knife, not your nails," Nora said flatly.

"I tried, and it didn't work. Besides, they're claws, not nails. And my claws are way better than any knife." I cut off another piece just to show off, then ate it. Enjoying it sent another shiver down my spine, and I noticed my tail was wagging and hitting the back of my chair with a thud.

"Could you stop that?" Martin curtly asked as he stopped eating.

I thought about it. *I'm in way too good of a mood, and if my tail shows it, oh well.* "Nope," I said as I went back to enjoying my heavenly meat. *I'm going to get addicted to this taste.*

Martin grunted his annoyance and returned to eating.

"Lucia is a beastkin. Being a beastkin, her body has some differences, and I expect you to respect them." Nora, being the peace keeper, defended my partially involuntary action. "But that doesn't mean you can do as you want. Be respectful of others." She turned on me and gave me a look.

I shrugged. "I'm sorry, but my tail's movements are mostly based on my emotions."

"I'm glad you're enjoying yourself." Melody spoke for the first time since we started eating. "I'm sorry about the knife I threw at you this morning. Please accept this meal as my apology."

Everyone turned their heads to look at Melody.

"But what about the cutting board?" I voiced my thoughts as I stared at her in confusion.

This caused everyone to turn their heads towards me. I could see some jaws dropping.

"Yes, sorry about that too." Melody looked down, ashamed.

Their heads snapped back to her again.

"This is the best food I've ever tasted. And I did kinda sneak up on you. Friends?" *It looks like she really is sorry, and, if I'm honest, if I had seen myself in my old life, I would have panicked just as much.*

It seemed the conversation had gone from shocking to wholesome, because everyone stopped trying to give themselves whiplash.

"Friends." She was smiling as she replied.

A genuine friend, this is a heartwarming moment. I hope nothing ruins it.

"I can't take it anymore!" Molly yelled, causing me to flinch from the volume. She jumped out of her chair and turned directly to me. "MUST. HUG. TAIL!" She sounded possessed.

That familiar feeling of needing to run wasn't there, but I ran anyway.

I jumped from my chair away from her. I wanted to keep as many obstacles between her and me as possible. It was odd to be chased by another little girl, who was acting crazy. The insane look in her brown eyes tracked me as I fled. The brown dress that fell to her shins hindered her running as it got tangled in her knees. *This girl is energetic.*

I ran around to the other side of the table faster than she registered. Upon reaching the other side, Oscar stood ready to catch me. I didn't stop myself and ran right into his arms. I noticed, as he wrapped his arms around me, I only came halfway up his chest.

"It would be better for everyone just to let her get it out of her system. Trust me, she won't hurt you." Oscar was both aiding her and trying to soothe me at the same time.

THE BIG BAD WOLF

I could see Molly catching up, and the fear compelled action from me. *I need to get out of his grip.*

I grabbed his wrists, but made sure I didn't use my claws. I pulled his arms away from me with every ounce of muscle I could muster. He was older and taller than me, but I was stronger. Slowly, I moved his arms, and eventually I succeeded at pulling him off me. I shocked both of us with how strong I was.

Molly continued her charge.

"Then you should do it," I said as I ducked under his arms and shoved him with all my strength towards Molly.

The collision that ensued was priceless.

Molly, running full tilt, collided with the off-balance Oscar, flipping him over her shoulder. She didn't clear out from under him before gravity took hold again, though, and he crashed down on top of her.

Laughter rang out from the two other boys and Anna. Nora, Melody and Eleanah were not amused by the display.

"Why are you so mean?" Molly slammed her fist on the floor as she flailed under Oscar, who was still trying to figure out which direction was which. "Why won't you let me pet you? You're so cute. First, you won't let me touch your cute ears. Is your adorable wagging tail now off limits too? It's not fair!"

I need to come up with something here. "This is a punishment for always yelling and hurting my ears."

It seemed Oscar had sorted out his directions, but was now trying to figure out how he'd gotten to where he was.

Molly turned on her puppy dog eyes. *I'm still not falling for that.* "I promise to be good," she begged.

"I don't trust you to let go or stop once you start." That was an honest assumption I had of her.

She just sat there and pouted.

Wait, she didn't deny it? I called it. Oh no. New mission: know Molly's location at all times.

"You all have way too much energy," Eleanah interrupted in a serious tone. "I know Lucia hasn't started her chore yet, and Molly needs to finish hers."

Oscar finally joined us again as he rolled off Molly and stood up. "Lucia's had a rough day. She went shopping with Anna earlier."

With that sentence, all the kids other than Anna gave me sad looks. The one that surprised me the most was that Evandol gave me the same look.

"Hey." Anna sounded annoyed at how everyone was looking at me.

I was still hungry, though, and the meat was still on my plate. "How about we all just sit back down and finish lunch first? Sound good?" I appealed to everyone's reason. I walked back to my seat, staying away from Molly.

"Yes, once lunch is done, then you can all play together." Nora put so much emphasis on that last word that I felt the word as much as I heard it. "But make sure your chores are all done before the sun sets. Oscar, you can show Lucia how to wash the tubs, as that will be her only chore for the day."

"No problem," Oscar said as he took his seat at the table.

I watched Molly head for her chair, trying to head me off. I slowed my steps down so that she would take her seat first. She passed my chair and went directly to hers and sat down. I walked past her, noticing that her hands were shaking as she held back from reaching for my tail as I passed. *It's almost like I'm looking at an addict searching for their next fix. Her fix is apparently either fluffy, fuzzy or anything she thinks is cute.*

I, however, headed for my new addiction: meat. I sat down, grabbed my fork, extended my claw once again and went to town on the boar in front of me. *Is boar meat considered pork as well? I don't care what it's called when it tastes this good.* I was so engrossed with my meal that I blocked out everyone else's conversations.

I finished the meat in front of me. It was a little more than I should have eaten, but I ate it all anyway. *It tasted way too good not to eat.* After I cleaned my plate, I cleaned the fork and then my claw that I had been using to cut the meat. I was careful with my claw because I knew how sharp it was. *I think I can feel a food coma manifesting.* With my hunger sated, I looked around the table to see what everyone else was up to. Martin and Evandol were still eating since it looked like they had refilled their plates. Eleanah still had some food on her plate, but everyone else had finished eating.

I looked at Oscar, my bathtub cleaning trainer, and waved him over. "Alright, show me the way, Oscar." *I really should thank Melody again now that I've finished eating.* I turned to Melody, who was beginning to stand and gave her a thumbs-up. "Thank you, Melody. That was the best thing I've ever eaten."

Eleanah looked at me with skepticism. "Aren't you supposed to have amnesia?"

I looked at her, confused. "I do."

"Then how much did you forget?"

She's giving me the inevitable amnesia questionnaire. I could feel my ears, shoulders and tail droop. "It's easier to say what I do remember. Even then, just assume that I don't know anything."

"So you remember the flavors of food but didn't know what was going to happen when you ate the strawberry?" *Eleanah is attentive.* I nodded at her. "How long ago did you lose your memory, and how?"

"It was about three days ago, I think." I relaxed a bit while sitting up straight. "I'm guessing the orcs that were ransacking my village hit me in the back of the head. Again, I'm guessing it was the village I lived in. Everyone else was dead when they took me captive. As for what I've eaten since, I've had four things before the boar." I held out my four fingers to help everyone follow along. I placed my pointer finger from my other hand on the other pointer finger and began counting, moving my finger down with each item I listed. "First was the jerky rations that Avollea gave me. It tasted pretty good, but not as good as this. The second was a carrot that Phan gave me to taste. I spat it out right away. Third was the strawberry, but you all know how that ended. Shortly after were the eggs, which didn't taste like anything. I mean it, there was zero flavor to be found."

Everyone just stared at me. The prospect of answering another barrage of questions again irked me. To distance myself from everyone else and calm down, I got up from my chair and headed out of the dining room. "If you're done questioning me, I'll be completing my chore." I walked through the kitchen without looking back.

Once I heard the door close, I ran to the bathroom. My heart was racing and I could feel my emotions unraveling. *Why am I so emotional?* I burst through the doors into the bathroom and then found myself in the room with the bathtubs. *Calm down.* I started pacing back and forth, concentrating on just walking. I also went to my waterfall thought bubble. Focusing on imagining the flowing water and the roar of the churning water at the base, I could finally feel my heart slow down. *This would be much harder if I didn't have a lifetime, cut short as it was, of memories.* I didn't know how long I had been pacing before I heard the bathroom door open and someone walk in.

15

JOKER'S WILD

There was a knock at the door as it opened. "Is it safe to come in?" I could hear more footsteps past the bathroom doors, but couldn't make out how many.

I turned towards the door and saw Oscar poking his head through the door. "Yes, it's safe. I'm not a dangerous animal, you know." *Why did he phrase it like that? I guess I need to learn why people don't like beastkin.*

Oscar slowly walked in with his hands up, as if he was surrendering.

"What are you doing?" I could feel my rage building. *This isn't good.*

"I'm trying not to get attacked by you. So I'm making myself as non-threatening as possible," Oscar said slowly.

"If you keep doing that and talking like that, you'll make me angry." I let out a small growl at the end. *I guess I need more time to calm down.* "Out!" I pointed to the door.

Oscar let out a less-than-masculine sound as he fled the room as if his life depended on it.

I grabbed my head as I repeatedly growled at nothing.

13 PITCH BLACK CATS

Waterfalls. Think about waterfalls, only waterfalls. Calm waterfalls. It isn't working. The sound of the door opening caught my attention. But before I could yell at Oscar to go away again, my vision blurred for a moment, and I noticed something moving.

A rabbit? What's it doing here?

Everything faded away, and the only thing I could think of was tearing this innocent, cute and possibly tasty morsel apart.

I leaped at the rabbit and reached out with my claws to snatch it up. My hand passed right through it, like it was never there in the first place. *I was angry before, but now I'm pissed off.* I caught myself in my dive and rolled onto my hands and feet. The bunny jumped over my claws to avoid me after I charged at it again. *You're going to die today, little bunny! I don't know how, but this rabbit is always a half-step ahead of me.* As the chase continued, my vision turned red. *I'm going to have hasenpfeffer tonight!*

The rabbit landed just outside my reach to my left. I stopped as quickly as I could and again found myself on my hands and feet for stability. I let out a loud growl before I chased after it. It started moving as soon as I did, but I could see I was catching up to it as we sprinted for the wall. I knew it was going to turn, but I had to wait for it to make the first move. I could feel my focus sharpening as I saw the rabbit's tail twitch to the left. *It's going to the right.* To prepare for the sharp turn, I placed my hand on the ground. *It made its turn on a dime, and now I need to do the same.* I extended my claws into the wood floor for traction and made the turn far sharper than I ever thought humanly possible. *I guess I left 'as far as humanly possible' behind when I first woke up in this life, didn't I?*

The chase continued and I was gaining ground on the rabbit. The longer we went on, the closer I got. It could gain some ground on each turn, but I was getting better at turning with each attempt, and soon it was inevitable. *I'm going to catch this rabbit and rip it to shreds for avoiding me for this long.*

The rabbit eventually turned to run towards a corner. *That's it, future fecal matter, corner yourself, you won't escape this time.*

The rabbit ran to the very corner and turned to look at me. No fear in its eyes, no emptying of its bladder or bowels. It just stood there, staring at me. I made one final aggressive leap towards the rabbit. But, just as my claws were about to skewer the furball, it disappeared.

What the...? I hit the wall hard. *That's going to leave a bruise in the morning.*

I heard laughter coming from the other side of the door, and I peeled my face off the wall and turned to look toward it.

Oscar walked back through the door. "Did you have fun?" he asked with a colossal grin.

After rolling to rest my back against the wall, I noticed I was panting. "You think that was funny? That hurt a lot." I rubbed my face where I collided with the wall. I also noticed that my thinking was clearer again. "Well, what do you know? That helped. I guess I needed that. But what happened exactly?" I tried to recall my antics of chasing an untouchable rabbit.

"I told you, magic is my game." Oscar continued smirking as he replied. "My aptitude is illusion magic."

There it is again: aptitude. "Everyone has one?" I asked, remembering something that was said when I was learning my name.

"Mostly. There are some people who have had more than one. They have all been important people, like heroes." Oscar made me feel he was more intelligent than he let on. "There have also been cases of those with no aptitude."

That's interesting. I think The Voice probably gave me mine.

I feel a little drained from my chase, but I still need to learn what I need to do with these bathtubs. "So, since you decided to tire me out, I'll sit here and you'll show me what I need to do here." I adjusted my sitting posture so that my tail was more comfortable.

"It's your chore. I just agreed to tell you how to do it." Oscar was giving me a smug look. "It isn't my fault that you didn't know it was an illusion and when to stop yourself."

I thought really hard about the whole encounter. I went over every detail to see if there was something that would tip me off. *The rabbit moved like it was real. Wait, it didn't sound or smell like anything. I just saw a rabbit. No other senses were involved. I'll never fall for that again.*

"Nora's words were to show me what to do," I said, grinning even brighter than he did. "But now I know how to distinguish your illusions. I think I can muster enough energy to make you sorry."

The color drained from his face. "You can?" He shuddered. His confidence and bravado were long forgotten. He had a slight twitch in his eye before he found his bravery again. "Okay then, prove it. How do you know what's an illusion?"

Nice try, kid. "Where would the fun in that be? Next time you use an illusion on me, I'll find you and pull your underwear over your head." *Yes, I just threatened a kid older than me with a wedgie. I already know I'm stronger than he is, so I think I can follow through on that promise.*

"I'll just pull it off my head." Oscar looked less frightened than I would have liked. *Maybe he doesn't quite understand what I'll do to him.* "Seems like a dumb threat."

Yeah, I'm going to need to spell it out for him. "You'll be wearing the underwear while I pull over your head." I gave him my best scary glare. *I should find a mirror and learn how my facial expressions work.*

He sat there thinking, and when he realized what I had said, his eyes widened. The look of fear tickled something deep inside me. He hopped up and ran to the cabinet on the far wall. "First, we need soap and water to clean the tubs." It sounded like the words were racing against each other to get out of his mouth. "We have this wand to summon a little water at a time. When we need a lot, like for baths, Mom does it for us."

Mom?! "Hold up, stop, just a second, one moment. Did you just call Nora 'Mom?'"

"Yeah, we all do." Oscar calmed down a bit. "She's more like our mom than our real ones. At least she didn't dump me off for someone else to take care of." I could feel the resentment in his voice. *So his parents, who likely were still alive, placed him here.*

"I think mine are dead. I don't know. There were a lot of dead bodies around," I said without thinking.

"That's right. You said that orcs attacked your village. Were they really orcs?" He sounded concerned now. *These kids change conversations faster than the wind changes direction.* "How do you know they were orcs? And how did you escape?" He walked towards me with a small bottle and a short stick in his hands.

"The Brilliant Crusade saved me, and Captain Allen brought me here because he knew Nora. I was their only captive." I recalled the first moments of this life. "They were the ones who told me that those were orcs." Oscar nodded along as I explained. "I woke up with my head injured and no memories."

"Didn't you say it was only a few days ago?" Oscar interjected.

"I did." *Where's he going with this? I guess I didn't stick around after I asked if there were no more questions.*

"You don't look like someone who was hit that hard on the head a few days ago." Oscar sat across from me.

"I learned that I have the recovery aptitude when I learned my name." I lowered my head, slightly embarrassed. *I don't know how readily I should share that information.* "Nora was adamant that I learn my name with the oracle stone."

"You got to use the oracle stone? That's so cool. How old are you?" His excitement was growing, and I felt more and more unnerved.

"It said I was four." I sounded wary, even to my own ears. "Why are you asking all of these questions?"

"You look too old to be four. Your birthday might be soon." Oscar changed his seating position so he could get to his feet sooner. "Don't be mad, but we're all trying to learn everything we can about you. We'd never seen a beastkin before, and both

13 PITCH BLACK CATS

Eleanah and Evandol ordered me to." He subtly flinched as he finished.

"I take it those two are the oldest here?" Oscar nodded sheepishly. I sighed before continuing. "What are the chances we can gather everyone together for a meeting? Anna said something about that earlier." Oscar looked like he was thinking. "I promise not to storm out as long as you don't make me mad."

"Mom was right; you do have mood swings." Oscar voiced his inner thoughts, only to stand up and flinch at realizing what he had said.

"I do not!" I slammed my hand on the ground. Shortly after, I relaxed a bit. "So what if I do?"

"Nothing, it's fine. Don't hurt me." Oscar was slowly backing away from me.

"Calm down. I won't hurt you." *Unless you give me a reason to. No! Stop that. Why is it getting harder to control myself? Maybe I need to distract myself.* I stood up, feeling somewhat recovered from my exercise. "How about you show me what I need to do now?" I tried to sound friendly.

"Cleaning the bathtubs is easy. You just take a few drops of the soap, which is in this bottle." He held up the bottle Nora used last night in his hand. "You pour it into the tub and use this wand to summon water to clean it." He held out the small stick to me. "There are washcloths in the cabinet over there." He pointed to the place where he had retrieved the wand and soap.

"Sounds easy enough." I grabbed the wand and the bottle of soap. I inspected the wand closely. It looked like a dowel rod with a slight taper and had a waxy finish. "How do I use this?" I held it up.

"Easy, just say the command word and it'll do the thing." Oscar had a glint in his eye as he answered my question. "First you need to hold it like this." He grabbed my hand holding the wand and adjusted the wand's position. I was now holding it with the narrow end closest to me. "This wand has three command words. Each word releases a different amount of water, but it always comes out of the same end. The words are sprinkle, spray and flush." He held up a finger to signal me to wait. "One use of flush is enough to clean a tub. So go ahead to the tub and fill it up." He then waved me to the first one.

I walked up to the tub, pointed the fat part of the wand at the bottom of the tub and said the command word: "Flush." Water poured from the end, pointing towards my face. Surprised, I released the wand, causing the water to spray my entire body. I was now completely soaked. *These were new clothes, too.*

I growled at a certain trickster who was going to face my wrath. He was already out the door, giggling his happy self down the hall. *So this is all a joke to you. Pick on the new kid. Well, this new kid has claws.* My vision shifted to red as I chased after him.

As soon as I left the bathroom, Oscar turned around to look at me. I growled even louder as I charged towards him. He nearly tripped when he turned to run from me.

A strange feeling manifested when I saw Oscar run. It was like I was looking at that rabbit running away from me in the bathroom again. My toe-claws scraped the ground as I sprinted towards the joker. I caught up to him before he could take more than a couple of steps.

I grabbed his shoulder and yanked him to the ground. My claws dug into his shoulder, tearing through his shirt effortlessly, and he hit the ground on his back. He cried out in pain and grabbed his shoulder where I scratched him. Fumbling, he turned himself over and tried to crawl away from me. I grabbed his leg and threw him into the wall, and I heard something crack.

Oscar rolled back and forth on the ground clutching his left arm, shouting in pain.

I slammed my foot on his lower back, and he screamed incoherent nonsense as he struggled to flee.

I leaned forward, the claws on my right hand extended as far as possible and stabbed him in the shoulder. I ignored his screams as I stared at the back of his neck. My mouth drifted open as I inched towards his vulnerable spine.

"Lucia!"

My vision returned to normal at my name. I looked to see who said it. I saw Anna, Eleanah, Martin and Nora staring at me with all their eyes wide and jaws on the floor. Everyone was speechless except for Oscar. He continued whimpering under my foot. I looked down at Oscar and saw that I was hunched down, ready to bite down on his neck. *I was about to kill him. Over a prank?* I turned back to Nora as I extracted my claws from Oscar's back. *I promised that I wouldn't fight the other kids again.*

Without a second thought, I ran to my room, still soaked, and slammed the door. I looked around. Because the door opened into the room, I used the bookcase to barricade myself in. I jumped onto my bed, kicking off the clothes that were bought for me. I grabbed my pillow and hugged it for dear life.

What have I done? Nora is going to kill me. If not, are the rest of the kids going to think I'm nothing more than a wild animal? Why did I do it? I'm acting on every impulse. I just attacked Oscar and enjoyed the sound of him in pain. Am I really a monster? Is this why I was released from the job The Voice gave me, because I'm going to get myself killed or be unable to control myself enough to do the job once the time comes?

Tears welled up in my eyes as my fears of every possible repercussion spiraled further out of my control. *I'm not myself. Every time something happens to me, I act like an unruly child. It's like I'm acting like I'm four years old. But I am four years old. I'm not even trying to act like a kid again to fit in. I'm becoming a kid again.* Unable to stymie the tears, I put my face into the pillow and cried.

I didn't know what scared me more: my slow, unavoidable regression to childhood, or my inevitable punishment.

16

NORA KNOWS

This is my first day. I got into a fight with Evandol, was traumatized by Anna's shopping habits and I assaulted Oscar. This is my first day, and my life might end just as Avollea desired. She's right: I'm going to become a menace to society.

Being this depressed after only being alive for three days is probably a record somewhere, not that it's a good thing. I don't know how long I cried, but eventually the tears stopped coming. I felt like I wanted to keep crying, but I couldn't. I lifted my head up from my now tear-and-mucus-soaked pillow. My clothes had dried somewhat but still had some wet spots, especially where they came into contact with the bed.

Nora was sitting on a chair on the opposite side of the room. She looked at me, calm and collected. I couldn't see any anger on her face and I didn't see any weapon in her hands, which were folded in her lap. *How long has she been sitting there?*

"Have you come to execute me?" I asked, through my sniffling.

Nora lost all composure. She stood up, her worry obvious. "What makes you think you deserve that? No, I would never do that to any of you."

"I'm a menace to everyone here. All I've done is cause trouble, and I'm unlikely to stop myself in the future." I clutched the pillow even tighter. *I've never felt this horrible, and that's not just because most of my memories were stripped from me. This feeling of depression is new to me. Compared to the other feelings I've felt so far, they've all been slightly familiar, even though I don't remember where I felt them before.*

Her face went from worried to the saddest I'd ever seen. "Who are you really?"

"What?" *I didn't see that coming. This might be bad.*

"You were never Lucia, were you? There's a level of self-awareness in you that no child your age should have." She was sitting in her chair again. "Who are you?"

"What do you mean? I've been Lucia ever since I woke up." *Is she on to me?*

"Who were you before you were Lucia?" Her head had lifted, and she gave me a steely glare. "This isn't your first life, is it? Don't bother with lying to me; I'll know."

The Voice never said that I was forbidden to say I was reincarnated. It just said that nobody would believe me. I think I've found the one person who will. "How did you know?" *That should be enough to confirm it for her, but not let her know that I don't remember who I was.*

Nora breathed a sigh of relief. Her shoulders slumped as she leaned back and her face lightened up. But I saw a sad smile had found its way onto her lips. "I thought so. You're here to defeat the demon king once he arrives, right?"

"Yes," I said wearily. *She's spot on.* "How?"

"I know because I made a promise to the last person who had your 'job,' as he put it." She closed her eyes. It looked like she was remembering a somber memory. "He asked me to assist him with defeating the demon king, but the demon still hasn't shown up. So I made a promise to him to assist the next person who inherited that responsibility, should I ever find them." A single tear fell from her eye.

"Why?" *I need to know.*

"Because he saved my life, and I loved him," she said without skipping a beat.

I could feel my eyes explode as my brain followed shortly. *That's a pretty good reason.*

"I hate to disappoint you, but I no longer have that responsibility." My voice trailed off. *I guess I should tell her the entire story.* "I was told that being in this body was a mistake, and, because of that, I could live my life however I wanted."

This time, I watched her mind explode as I told her my first secret. "So you weren't a beastkin in your last life?"

I guess I should spill all the beans, shouldn't I? "No, I was human—and a man, too. There were no such things as beastkin in my old life." I hung my head. I couldn't see her face, but I could hear the realization click in Nora's brain.

"Oh, that would explain a few things." *That's all she can say? I guess her knowing might make things easier if I make it through this alive.* She got out of her chair and walked towards me. "I guess we both have a lot of learning to do." Her voice was sweet and tender as she sat on my bed.

"That means you aren't going to kick me out or kill me?" I looked up at her with hope in my eyes.

Her face flashed with anger. She grabbed my chin and forced me to look her in the eye. "Do I have your attention now?" I gave a slight nod, as much as I could with my jaw held captive. "Good, now get this through your head. I will make sure you live." After the last word, she released my jaw. "I promised I would take care of you before I knew who you really are, and I will keep my promise. You're stuck with me until you're seventeen."

"Yes, ma'am," I hastily responded. *That could have been worse.*

"Now, I'm curious. Who were you before? You still haven't answered that question." She stared at me, waiting.

"When I said that I had lost my memories, I wasn't completely lying." I took a deep breath before I shoveled out more secrets. *At this rate, this woman is going to know me better than I know myself.* "I don't remember much other than basic information from my world. I don't remember my name or what I looked like. It will be easier to treat me like I don't know unless I say otherwise."

"Interesting." She looked like she was thinking about something for a moment before her eyes turned hard as they focused on me. "So, about what you did to Oscar." *Yeah, I knew this was going to come up.* "You know what you did was wrong, right?" I nodded my head. "So why did you do it?"

I slumped my shoulders as I prepared for my trial. "I was agitated at the lunch table with all the questions they were asking me. So I ran to the bathroom to try to calm myself down. I did, to some degree, until Oscar showed up. He treated me like I was a wild animal, and I got upset at that. I yelled at him to get out so I could calm down again. He left, but he played a trick on me with his magic. He made me see a rabbit in the bathroom, and once I saw it, I couldn't control myself. I was consumed with the need to kill it. I believed the illusion and chased it around the bathroom for I don't know how long. Eventually, Oscar tired me out and made me run face-first into a wall, then started laughing at me. I was angry at that, but I controlled myself. We started talking, and, when he eventually showed me what I needed to do, he played another prank on me. He showed me the wrong way to hold the wand and told me to use the strongest word. That's how I got soaked. He ran out of the bathroom. I have never been so angry, ever. I was about to kill him, but when you said my name, I snapped out of it." After giving my testimony, I braced myself for judgment.

"Well, that settles it. Tomorrow we'll start your education. But first, we need to figure out what to do with you." Her voice trailed off as she started thinking. "If this happened out in the street, you'd be tried for assault and attempted murder."

"I need to be stopped," I said as I set the pillow by my side.

"Something or someone needs to stop me every time I get angry. I don't know why it's so hard for me to control my temper. It's like I need to fight everyone over everything."

"I might be able to come up with something." Nora's voice was barely more than a whisper. She stood up and walked to the door. "Stay here until I get back." With a wave of her hand, my bookcase moved to its original spot.

I watched Nora leave. *What is she going to do?*

I did as I was told. It felt like an eternity as I waited for the door to open again. When my anxiety nearly overwhelmed me, Nora walked through the door again. She carried a small blue stone on a string in one hand and a small candle on a platter in the other.

"Sit up so I can put this on you," she said as she placed the candle on the bookcase. Her eyes were barely opened as she turned to me. Her voice was devoid of emotion, causing my tail to wrap around my waist.

I complied and waited patiently. Nora wrapped the necklace around my throat but didn't tie it. I felt a small amount of heat and a tingling sensation on my neck where her hands were. After she let go, she pulled her hands back to her lap.

I grabbed the stone to inspect it further. It was about the size of my pad on my palm and a foggy blue color, like raw sapphire. I thought I could see strange symbols swirling inside of it. The string looked to have melded into the stone seamlessly. *That's odd.* "What is it and what does it do?"

Nora took a deep breath before opening her eyes completely. "It's better if I show you. Also, we need to see if it works." My heart sank, and I tried to remove the necklace. No matter what I did, it wouldn't rise above my chin, and I couldn't find where she tied it off. I tried to cut it with my claws, then pawed at it frantically, but each time my claws just slid off the string harmlessly. *My claws cut the wood floor in the bathroom with ease. How is this string this indestructible?* I looked up to see Nora grimacing. "That works. Now I need you to get angry," she said with a wince.

You want me to get angry? Am I some sort of rage machine that can get angry on command? I know I have a short fuse now, and, once that fuse is lit, I can't control myself. But can't you see that I'm too busy panicking to get angry? I tilted my head slightly as I looked at her. "I can't."

She sighed. "The hard way it is."

What's the hard way?

She reached behind me and grabbed my tail, then pulled on it. Reflexively, I swiped my claws at the offending hand. Four straight, bleeding lines appeared on her hand.

I gasped when I saw what I had done. "I'm sorry." *I lashed out on impulse again.* "I didn't mean it!"

"This?" Nora held her hand up. "This is just a scratch." She reached for my tail again.

I jumped away from her grasp. "What are you doing?"

"I told you, we need to test it, and to do that, I need you to get angry. I know grabbing your tail will make you angry." Nora stood up and took a step forward. "This is the hard way, and I don't need you to worry about my safety." She reached for my tail again.

I backed up into the dresser. "Please stop. I don't want to hurt you again."

"Then make me!" she shouted, causing me to flinch. "I'm not worried about my safety. I'm worried about yours and theirs," she said as she pointed to the door. Nora grabbed my shoulder and turned me around. To my surprise, she had plenty of time to grab and yank my tail, hard.

I yelled in pain. *That's attached!* "Let go. That hurts. I don't want to hurt anyone." I grabbed the base of my tail in defense.

"It didn't look like that when you were with Evandol and Oscar!" she kept shouting. *Is everyone going to hear this?* She pulled harder, nearly lifting me off my feet by my tail. "The sooner you prove this thing works, the sooner we can end this!"

Adrenaline coursed through me. I turned and grabbed the hand that held my tail with both hands and raked with every claw. It had the desired effect. She released my tail, and I turned on her. "Fine! You want me angry? Congratulations, you succeeded." I stomped my foot down. "Why did you need me this angry for? What's supposed to happen?" I braced my ears as I yelled.

"Still not enough." Her voice was calm and calculating. "This should do it." I felt yet another pull on my tail. *How? She's still in front of me.* I turned my head and felt a slight tingling sensation wrapped around the base of my tail.

"I said—" My vision shifted and turned red. However, this time I didn't fly into a rage; instead I seized up and screamed in pain as it felt like electricity ran through all my muscles. Unable to control my body anymore, I fell to the ground and flailed. Everything ended as quickly as it came. I felt weak and my body refused to cooperate with my commands.

I'm now wearing, in effect, a shock collar.

"It works," I said, through a pained breath.

I felt awful, but a hand rested on my shoulder. "I'm sorry it has come to this." *This is my first day! I guess I have been rather extreme.* "The two worst crimes you can commit in this kingdom are treason and murder. Both end with you getting executed. Any attempt at murder will get you imprisoned in most cases. Other times, you'll be beheaded. This way the worst you get is a fine for assault. Let's sit you back up. Are you okay?" Her gentle voice put me at ease.

"Kinda. I guess I asked for this, didn't I?" My voice was slightly raspy. With Nora's help, I rested my back against my bed. "Can we try something a little less extreme first?"

Nora's eyes grew wide. "What do you mean?"

"How about if you notice me getting emotional or angry, we use a code word? So that I can get away and calm down before this thing becomes necessary." My fingers slowly curled around the stone amulet, reminding me of its existence. "Something you wouldn't use in normal conversation but is still easy to remember. I could use it too if I needed to get away. It might make things easier, and a lot less painful."

"You have the physical aptitude. You're going to be strong. Possibly too strong for anyone to stop you alone. Your violent outbursts are getting more and more extreme. This is the only thing I can create with a short notice that I know will stop you. I don't even know how long that will stop you for. But we can try your suggestion too. It would be preferable if you never activate that necklace again."

Why did she jump straight into electroshock therapy? She didn't think about something like this? I was right—medieval mental healthcare is something I want no part of.

"So, did you have a word in mind?" Nora asked politely.

"How about 'waterfalls?'" *I know I think about them when I need to calm down.*

"That's an odd choice for a word." She sounded surprised. "I'm guessing there is a reason for it."

"Yes," I said meekly. *Please don't ask me to explain. It's kinda embarrassing.*

"Fair enough." She stood up and looked around my room. "How about you get this room cleaned up and go to bed? It's been a long day."

I could smell something like iron in the air. I looked at Nora and saw the culprit. Her hand was dripping blood from my attacks earlier, but she didn't even consider it.

"Your hand!" I pointed at her wounds. "I'm sorry."

"Oh, this? I told you it's just a scratch." She looked down at her hand. "I guess it is making a mess of your room. I'll take care of that." With a wave of her hand, all the blood that had been falling on the floor evaporated into nothingness, and the wounds quit dripping. She headed for the door. "Good night, Lucia."

I looked at the door and remembered that it was still barricaded when she'd left for the first time. "How did you get in?" *I need to stop thinking aloud.*

She turned and looked at me with a smile on her face. "Magic." She turned to walk out the door and closed it behind her. *Of course it was magic. One of these days, I'll learn how to do magic.* I heard her walk down the hall and giggle loud enough for me to hear.

"I heard that!" I shouted loud enough for her to hear me. *Let's see who gets the last laugh now.* I giggled as I heard her stumble for a step.

I looked around my room. I'd scattered all of my clothes around the floor when I'd entered. The contents of the bag also found their way to the floor. *I guess I should put this stuff away.* Starting with the contents of the bag, I picked them up and placed them on the dresser. I looked at my furry arms and legs and took the comb to them, but it didn't get much done with each swipe. Instead, I switched to the brush and felt the difference. As I brushed myself, I could see small amounts of shedding building on the brush as my fur looked lighter. *I shed? I guess since I have all this fur, I should have expected it. Hopefully I don't have allergies. That would be awkward to be allergic to myself.* Brushing my tail and head felt soothing, even addictive. *I can't let anyone find out about that.*

17

A WOLF IN SHEEP'S CLOTHING

Unable to sleep after cleaning my room, I rested my head on the windowsill and stared at the moons. *Why is it so hard to accept that I'm not human and not on Earth anymore? Why does everything in this life have to be so difficult? Starting over isn't as easy as I thought it would be.*

Three moons of different sizes and colors illuminated the night sky. The smallest glowed with a dim yellow light and was almost the width of my claw. It was the only full moon in the sky. The largest was the red moon, at five or six times larger than the yellow moon. It was in its first quarter stage. The green moon was at about the waning crescent stage and half the size of the red moon. I continued to gaze at the stars, remembering every cheesy line about everyone sharing the same stars at night. *I really wonder if that's true.*

After I changed into my pajamas and blew out the candle, I used the mostly dry clothes to clean the crusted blood from my claws, then placed them next to the dresser so I could hand them off to get washed. I looked at my pillow as it sat alone on my bed. *My pillow should also get washed.* I flipped it over and didn't find any tears or snot marring its appearance. *I'll get it washed tomorrow, but for now it will do.*

I drifted off to sleep, only to be hounded by terrifying nightmares. During one, I hurt the other kids, and the collar didn't work. The whole town marched towards the orphanage and barricaded me inside, torching the place to the ground and burning me alive.

I had another nightmare where I sat by a waterfall. Everything was peaceful until the water turned red. I could smell iron and realized the water had become blood. There was a voice in my head. "This is all the blood you'll spill. You're a danger to all."

After having those two nightmares, I woke up before the sun was up and didn't go back to sleep. I curled up in the fetal position, clutching my pillow, afraid of where my mind was going. My thoughts continued to haunt me until the sun poured its light through the window.

I heard movement outside my door. The other kids were waking up and going to breakfast. *Can I even eat with them without worrying about being provoked? I understand if they want to hurt or ostracize me.* I couldn't bring myself to leave my mattress. So I huddled in the corner of my bed, holding my pillow.

After some time, someone walked to my door and knocked on it. A sweet voice followed the knocking. "Are you awake in there, Lucia?" *Nora? What's she doing knocking?* "Come on out and have breakfast."

"I don't think that's a good idea." I poked my head out from behind the pillow. "Can I eat after they're all gone or in my room?"

"You are going to eat with everyone else, young lady." Her voice dropped drastically. "You can't avoid everyone forever. Also, you're going to learn how to read and write today."

"You aren't going to take no for an answer, are you?" *I know the answer. I don't know why I'm asking.*

"Get changed and get out here. The food's going to get cold."

Her mom voice is scary. "I'm going to stand and count to thirty. If you aren't out by then, I'll bring you out myself. One."

Panic drove my actions before I gave them any thought. Leaping out of bed, I headed to the dresser and pulled out another shirt-and-skirt outfit. I tried to change my clothes as quickly as I could, but I struggled with the laces on my skirt again. My heart dropped when Nora reached thirty.

I turned in time to see her standing just inside my room with a scowl on her face. Her face relaxed as soon as she saw me struggling with my laces. Without a word, she reached for them and tied them for me. I couldn't look at her as I headed for the door.

"Aren't you forgetting something?" Nora asked from behind me.

I turned and saw the brush in her hand. "I thought you wanted me to get out as quickly as possible."

"That was to get you motivated to move. But you need to remember to take care of the unruly hair on your head. It's almost as bad as you." Nora waved the brush around with a slight smile on her face. *Not funny.* "Little girls need to take care of their hair so it will grow long and beautiful." I swiped the brush from her outstretched hand and turned to look away from her as I started brushing my hair. "You're strong for your size and age." *Is she trying to make small talk? She knows that I have the physical aptitude.* "Molly can't move her bookcase."

I looked down at my arms for any sign that I had more muscle than I thought, but all I saw was fur. *What was I expecting? But how much stronger will my physical aptitude make me?* I continued to brush my fur, then ran it through my hair, finding a few knots. *How rough was I sleeping last night to mess up my hair this much?*

After an approving nod from Nora, I placed the brush back on the bookcase. *I'll take care of it later.* I opened the door and motioned for Nora to lead the way, forcing myself to follow to the dining room.

I could feel my anxiety building with each step I took. When I entered the kitchen, I sheepishly looked around and saw Melody scooping out eggs onto plates. Her face was impossible to read. It looked like she'd forced a smile that couldn't cover her sadness. I kept the exchange wordless as I tried to put on a brave smile for her. Nora walked into the dining room, but I stopped short of entering. I made sure I was out of sight of the table. *This is going to be bad. Something is telling me to be ready to run if anyone stands up or moves in my direction.* I took a deep breath, grasped what little courage I could find and walked into the room.

Nora had turned to make sure I was still following her. All the kids were staring at the doorway, waiting for me to come out. I received a gamut of reactions. Eleanah and Evandol were full of hate, and they didn't hide it. Molly and Oscar's faces flinched at the sight of me. Anna was holding back her tears. *Why is she crying? I did nothing to her.* Martin stared at me with calculated indifference. *He has got to be scheming something. Eleanah and Evandol's reactions are the most expected, and I anticipate more reactions like theirs. I understand why Oscar and Molly might be scared of me.*

"Don't you have anything to say, Lucia?" Nora asked.

"Sorry, Oscar." I tried to sound as sincere as possible. I lowered my head and ears for a moment. "Please don't make me angry. I can't control myself. I don't want to hurt anyone."

Oscar rubbed his elbow which was a bright purple color. I also caught a glimps of the bandages peaking out from under his shirt on his shoulder. I turned to look at Nora's hand. Guilt flooded my senses as I saw the bandages wrapped around her hand.

"Then what are you doing here?" Eleanah stood up and shouted. Her blue eyes were bloodshot.

Time to get away from them. As I turned to leave, I ran into an invisible wall. I bounced off nothing and landed on my tail, eliciting a yelp of pain.

"You aren't going anywhere." Nora said sternly. "The rest of you will behave too. Give her the chance to redeem herself."

Eleanah sat back down with a huff, her arms crossed. I stood back up and Nora pulled the chair I sat in yesterday out for me. On the way back to my seat, I gave Eleanah the widest berth I could. I sat down next to Anna again, who still looked sad.

Breakfast was the same as yesterday, a pile of scrambled eggs for me. They even had the same flavor as yesterday—nothing. *I wonder why eggs have no flavor while every meat I've tasted has been nothing but fantastic.* Still, I ate my eggs in awkward silence. Everyone else ate in silence too, driving up my anxiety even further. I looked up occasionally and saw that everyone was staring at me while they ate. Their stares felt judgmental, and I cowered away from them. I deserved them. As soon as my food was done, I got up to leave the table to go back to my room.

"Where are you going?" Nora's stern voice stopped me in my tracks.

Slowly and timidly, I turned to look at her. Her stare bored into my soul. "Back to my room," I whispered.

"Don't barricade the door this time," Nora said in an almost too-sweet voice.

With a nod, I bolted back to my room. I could hear her dispensing chores for the rest, but I didn't care. I knew I wasn't welcome anymore, so I did the only sensible thing and ran to solitude.

I arrived in my room and closed the door. *Now what do I do? No books to read, no video games to play, there's practically nothing in here to entertain myself with.* I sat down on my bed, my go-to for a safe place. *How did kids entertain themselves back in the day? I need to find a hobby. No, I need to find a job so that I don't have to owe more time to the military. How do I do that? That should get me out of the house and away from the other kids. But that will put me in contact with the public. How will they react to me? Can I trust myself around crowds of people?* My mind spiraled out of control with questions until I heard a knock on a door.

It wasn't my door that someone was knocking on. I focused on my ears. *These things are pretty cool now that I realize how good they are.* It sounded like Nora had answered the door and was talking to someone. I couldn't quite make out what they were saying, but it sounded like someone was entering the orphanage. Two pairs of footsteps walked to my door, then a knock came.

"We're coming in," Nora warned me before she opened the door. I was sitting on my bed, so I had no reason to react. "Have you calmed down?"

Did she recognize that I needed to get out of that situation? "Yes and no," I answered as I turned to look at the ground. "I'm still a little anxious, but for a different reason."

"And what reason is that?" *A male voice?* A voice that I recognized once I thought about it. It was Phan's. He walked into the room after Nora, flowing robes and all. "Trouble adapting?"

That couldn't be more understated. "I guess," I said as I stared at the floor.

"Let me look at your head first before we try to cheer you up," Phan said as he approached me.

I didn't move. I didn't want to. I just turned my head so that he could see the back of it easily.

He gently grabbed my head and examined it. "Your recovery rate is far greater than it should be at your age. I remember that you have the aptitude for recovery, but there isn't even a scar."

"So what else are you here for?" I sounded more like a brat than I would have liked. *I hate being a kid again. Everything I say sounds worse than how I mean it.* "I'm sorry. I'm not actually sad, just more lost than anything."

I turned to look at him as he released my head. He looked at me just like Nora had last night, before she grilled me about being reincarnated. My eyes grew wide as I turned to Nora and flicked my eyes towards Phan repeatedly. *Hopefully she can see that I need to know if it's okay to tell him.* She shook her head at my look. *I think that means I shouldn't tell him.*

I turned to look back at him, this time with a small measure of confidence.

"How old are you?" His gaze was unflinching.

"Four." I could feel my ears twitching on top of my head and my tail curling around my waist.

"Are you sure?" His eyes narrowed even further with my answer.

I can't break, I must commit. "That's what the stone said. Although I don't know when my birthday is." *Maybe that might distract him.*

His eyes squinted terrifyingly. I subconsciously inched backward on my bed away from him. Without looking away from me, he turned slightly in Nora's direction. "Nora, would you please collect some reading and writing materials from your classroom?"

"You want to teach her in here?" Nora, who had been quietly watching our exchange, quickly straightened her stance.

"Yes, I find that students retain information better if they're in a comfortable setting." His face lightened up. He looked sympathetic now. "She obviously finds this to be a safe place. So, for the first few lessons, we'll be here. At least until she gets more comfortable. She's the only one who hasn't learned to read and write yet, correct?"

"That's correct. That also makes sense. We'll do it your way." Nora sounded skeptical. *What a novel idea, listening to the professional you hired.* Nora walked out of the room, presumably to grab the things for my lesson.

Once she was a short distance down the hall, Phan turned to look at me with the same glare he'd had earlier. "It's safe to talk. What don't you want Nora to know?"

"What?" I stared, dumbfounded.

"It's obvious you're hiding something important." He kneeled in front of me and placed a hand on my knee. "It's okay. I'll guard your secrets." His facial expressions were impossible to read. I could only guess at his mood by the tone of his voice.

"I'm not keeping anything from Nora." *You, on the other hand, are a whole other story. But I'm not going to tell you that.*

"You know I'm here to help you, right?" He sounded sad. "I

know what it's like to be alienated in a place where nobody looks like you."

"You have no idea what it's like to be me." I clapped my hands to my mouth. *I'm acting like a child right now. Stupid hormones. It's got to be hormones. That might also explain my lack of anger management.* I could feel the anger building with each moment. To transform my thoughts, I punched my thigh, trying not to stab myself with my claws. I succeeded, but the punch hurt my hand more than my leg. *Good enough. Now think of waterfalls.* I closed my eyes to concentrate on calming down.

"Excuse me?" Phan took a step back. He wasn't ready for my abrupt display of anger.

I felt a little calmer, but not much. *At least I'm not getting worse.* "I have trouble controlling myself once I get angry." My ears flattened as I kept trying to explain. "I needed to distract myself so I could concentrate on something else." I grabbed the necklace I wore and held it up for Phan to see. "If I get too out of control, this thing will shock me."

"Oh!" *I guess I dumped a little too much information on the guy.* His surprised expression led to one of sadness. "I guess I have some explaining to do, then."

"Explain what?" It was my turn to be surprised.

"I spent much of yesterday going through my collection and found some information about beastkin. I know some things, but I wanted to brush up on everything so I didn't give you the wrong information." Phan looked like he was ready to give a lecture. He stopped because Nora had returned with a portable chalkboard, a book and a small wooden box.

"Don't stop because of me. I want to hear this too," Nora said eagerly. "But I'm hurt that you would start talking about her race while I'm absent." She placed her delivery on the top of my bookcase.

"I was simply trying to get Lucia here to feel more comfortable around me. Then she explained some of her conditions to me." He turned to face Nora and held a hand out to showcase me. "Though I think the necklace you gave her might be too extreme."

"No, I deserve it." I made myself smaller as I sold myself out. "I hurt Oscar, in more than a physical sense, probably."

"The necklace is there in case of an emergency. We've already worked on a code word to try and prevent that from being necessary." Nora's tone sounded like she would keep the necklace on me until I died. *I hope not. I'd like to grow out of it.*

"We'll talk about beastkin after I teach her about writing. I'll come and get you before we talk about her needs and tendencies." He sounded like a teacher who wanted an over-protective parent out of the classroom.

To her credit, Nora moved to leave. "Thank you. I'll see to the rest of the children." She stopped at the doorway before turning to look at me once more. "The door stays open, understand?"

"Yes, Nora," I said as humbly as I could.

Her eyes shimmered as she walked away. *Why is she so sad?*

"Alright, let us begin." Phan grabbed the book and sat down on my bed next to me. He turned to the first page of the book and began his lesson.

18

TOUCH AVOIDANCE GAME

In my previous life, I never learned a second language. But here I am, learning half of one. I've been speaking just fine with everyone. Now all I need to do is learn the written part of the language. This entire world uses one language, so they didn't even bother with naming it. At least it uses the same letters as the English language I know. The hardest part is remembering the extra parts. Learning the letter modifiers was easy. But writing my name won't be as simple as I anticipated. Especially since this stupid piece of chalk keeps falling apart!

I growled as I threw the chalk pieces across the room after I snapped yet another piece. "Why do they keep breaking?" My instincts weren't driving my anger this time. I was honestly frustrated. "First, I learned I can't hold a fork effectively. Now you want me to hold this crumbly piece of chalk? I can't do it." I sat on my bed, pouting, with the chalkboard at my feet.

"Lucia, you need to calm down." *I know I need to calm down. I just can't. No amount of waterfalls will fix this.* "You need to hold it softly." He picked up the chalkboard and tried to hand me yet another piece of chalk.

"I am holding it softly!" I snatched the chalkboard from Phan's hand.

"What's happening now?" Nora stormed in.

"Lucia needs to calm down," Phan pleaded with Nora.

"No, these stupid pieces of chalk need to stop falling apart!" I slammed the chalkboard on my bed. *I'm tired of being humiliated by chalk.*

"Waterfalls," Nora said calmly. Phan gave Nora a look of confusion. "It's her code word to calm down."

"It isn't enough." I huffed. "Every time I grab the chalk, it keeps breaking and making me angry again." I held out the crushed chalk in my hand. *It's just writing my name. I did it countless times in my last life, I had to have. Not that I can remember doing it. It's infuriating that I can't do something so simple. And it's only made worse by how upset I get. Where is all this anger coming from?*

"It's almost lunchtime, so if you help Melody out, it can be a break for you and you can try again after lunch." Nora used her usual sweet voice.

Without waiting a moment longer, I threw myself off my bed and ran out of my room. "I'll take it," I called back as I left those two in my room.

Eleanah was walking into her room with a package. She turned and looked at me as I ran down the hall. I didn't even stop to look at her. *It feels good to stretch my legs. I've noticed that I no longer have any difficulties running or walking. I've adapted to moving around in this body quickly, almost too quickly. With a little effort, I can even move my ears and tail. Maybe this is normal. I don't know or care. Something is finally going right in this life.*

Once I got to the end of the hall, I felt a certain call of nature. Sliding to a stop, not using my claws to scrape the floor, I bolted back the other way and passed Eleanah and Nora, both giving me confused looks. "Bathroom."

"Why is she running?" I heard Eleanah ask Nora as I entered the bathroom.

"When you gotta go, you gotta go," Nora responded quaintly.

After I used the bathroom, I knew I should wash my hands if I was going to handle any food. Also, it gave me the chance to clean the chalk dust out of my fur. I went to grab the wand and looked for something I could use as a sink. The bathtub was my best option. I used a single drop of soap and put the wand in my mouth, and pointed it the correct way. Using the lowest-power word, I washed and rinsed my furry hands. It took much longer to make sure all the soap was out of my fur. Grabbing a towel from the cupboard as I returned the wand, I attempted to dry my hands. *How much water can my fur absorb? If I fall into a body of water, will I be able to swim or will I just sink from all the weight?*

After my hands were mostly dry, I ran out, taking the towel with me. I ran past my room again and threw the towel on the pile of my clothes that I wore yesterday. The chalk pieces I had crushed and thrown around my room were missing, just like Phan. *That's odd. Where is he?*

I kept running through the halls, noticing that my feet didn't make any noise as they contacted the floor. *Even my sharp hearing can barely pick up my steps. My pads cushion my footfalls, so they don't make much noise. I guess I could be quite the hunter or thief. I guess since I'm part wolf, being a hunter sounds more appropriate and legal. One problem: I don't know the first thing about hunting.*

I entered the kitchen and saw Melody humming to herself as she worked. *She hasn't noticed me yet. I don't want to scare her again.* I walked back out of the kitchen and knocked on the kitchen door.

"Oh, who's knocking?" Melody asked as she turned to look at the door.

"I did," I answered as I walked into the kitchen. "You didn't notice me when I walked in earlier. I didn't want to scare you again, so I knocked."

"Thank you." Her voice was soft and kind. "So what are you doing here? Lunch is still a little ways off."

"I'm here to help you." I put on a wide smile.

"If that's the case, then you can set up the table." She looked much more relaxed than this morning.

I assisted Melody with lunch and even learned a bit about how to cook, even though we were just eating the leftover meat from yesterday. They had a strange chest in the kitchen that was full of salt. Melody said that the chest kept food fresh for a couple of days. *I guess since refrigeration isn't an option, this is a viable solution. The meat looks and smells fine.* All the other kids received sandwiches with the meat sliced up for them. They had tomatoes and pickles on their sandwiches, with a side of more strawberries. *Is it strawberry season or something?* I had a pile of meat on a plate.

After we finished the preparations, I sat at the table, ready to eat. Melody told me that Nora wanted everyone to wait until everyone else was at the table before eating. *She's really sticking to the idea that we're a family.*

The first of the others to arrive was Martin. He was sweating, and he smelled of body odor. I smelled him before I saw him. His tan skin was on display as he had on a small tank top. His short, light-brown hair sat ruffled and some of it soaked up the sweat from his brow. I stared at his muscular frame and could guess that he did regular hard labor or worked out constantly.

"What have you been doing? You stink," I blurted out. *I need to stop and think about what I'm going to say. My mouth is going to get me in trouble. Yes, I'm curious what has him sweating so much, but I could have been a bit more tactful.*

"My job." He crossed his arms as he answered. He stopped next to his chair but didn't sit down. "What have you been doing, playing with dolls?"

"Learning to read and write," I said as I answered his stare with an equal stare. *This kid wants to belittle me. Why, is it because I'm a little girl? Well, bring it on, meathead.* I crossed my arms as I stared him down.

"Still learning to read? Ha!" He laughed at me.

Why is he laughing now? I came out here to calm myself down, and now he's riling me up. Fine, two can play this game. "Yes, I am. But what's your job? Stink up the whole town?" *I'm so mature.*

"Very childlike." His face shifted to a scowl. *It wasn't a good insult, but I didn't have a lot of preparation or material to work with. He really stinks, though.* He sat down, calm and collected. "I apprentice at a blacksmith. Not that it would mean anything to you."

"I'm learning to read just like you did at one point." I pointed my finger at him. "You're not better than me at everything. There's something I'm better at than you."

"I learned to read when I was six," he said, his chest ballooning out.

A wicked smile crept across my lips. Martin saw it too, and his expression turned to confusion. "I'm four." I grinned.

"So what? Do you think that makes you special or something?" His cheeks turned red. *Gotcha.* "So if you're so special, what do you think you're better at than me?"

My little win over Martin helped me calm down a bit. My mind felt clearer, but something in the back of my brain wanted me to prove I was better than him. *So he's bigger and older than me. What can I do?*

Something clicked in my head. *He works as a blacksmith, which means he stands around all day using his arms. I'm smaller and have better balance because of my tail. I could outrun him, possibly. It's my best shot.* "I can outrun you in a race," I said with every bit of confidence I could muster.

"I have a better idea." Both of us turned our heads toward the intruder in our conversation. *Melody?* "How about all of you kids play a game of tag after lunch has settled in your bellies."

Martin shrugged, then gave me a steely glare. "Sure, I want to put this impudent pup in her place."

"Well, this *pup* will hunt you down and make you beg for forgiveness." I matched his stare.

"I'm sure everyone else is going to love this idea," Melody chirped happily.

Read the room, lady.

We didn't have to wait long until the rest of the kids filed in. "Lucia and Martin want to play a game of tag after lunch. It would be so much fun if you all joined in!" Melody cheered.

She's way too happy about this.

Eleanah and Evandol both showed their displeasure at the idea by slumping. Oscar had a grin that showed he was up to no good. Molly's eyes exploded with happiness as she turned to look at me. *Am I seeing rainbows coming out of her eyes?* Anna was indifferent. *If we said we were going shopping, she would drag us out of here without lunch.*

"That sounds odd." Nora turned to me and stared.

"Why do you think it was me?" I asked defensively. Her gaze never faltered. I turned away, unable to handle her stare. "Fine, yes, I said something, but playing tag wasn't my idea. It was Melody's. We just went along with it." I could feel her gaze intensifying. *She's going to bore a hole through me at this rate with just her eyes.* "He started it!" I pointed towards Martin.

Nora turned to Melody. "Did he?"

"It was more of a mutual exchange, really," Melody said nonchalantly. *Aren't you on my side?* "But Lucia said that Martin stunk. And to be fair, he does." She punctuated her point with a small sniff and a wave of her hand. *Are you enjoying that fence you're sitting on over there?*

"Sorry for actually working during the day," Martin cut in with way too much sass in his voice. Eleanah face-palmed at Martin's remark. Evandol slapped Marin on the back of the head. "What?" Martin responded to the slap.

"You're right, Melody. This will be good for them." Nora's mom voice was out again. All of us shrank in our chairs. "You all are so full of energy, you need to burn some of it off. After lunch, all of you are going to the courtyard to play a game of tag. No excuses!"

THE BIG BAD WOLF

We all nodded in perfect synchronization.

We ate quietly without looking at one another. *The meat tastes just as good as yesterday. Now I know I'm addicted to meat.* I was the first one done eating and Nora, with one look, told me not to move from my chair. So I sat awkwardly, waiting for the others to finish. I didn't have to wait long.

"Melody, could you please take care of the dishes?" Nora asked in her sweet voice.

"Certainly. I'll be out to watch them play afterward. Is that alright?" Melody asked in the same voice as Nora did.

Nora smiled at Melody. "I was going to invite you to." *Those two going back and forth with that voice are going to drive me insane. They've known each other for too long.* "Alright, everyone, get up and go to the courtyard."

We all got out of our chairs and stood up in sync. Like marionettes, we filed out the side door in perfect silence.

The courtyard was a beautiful sight to behold. *Any dedicated gardener would sell their soul just to see it. I only lost some memories and a body to see this.* Every flower was in perfect bloom, their colors vibrant and arrayed artistically, not a single dead plant in sight. Plants I recognized grew next to others that I had never seen before. There were also a few smaller trees growing and a small fence with vines wrapping around the wood, but it was difficult to see. It looked like a wall of plants to separate us from other buildings.

I stopped and stared. *This looks way different in the daylight. Do I have trouble seeing colors at night? I have to experiment with that later.*

"You're speechless!" Molly said when she noticed I'd stopped. She stood proudly, her chest puffed out.

"I've never seen anything so beautiful," I said reflexively, not leaving my trance-like state. "Who takes care of this?" Molly waved her hand at me. "You?" My mouth was agape with even more surprise.

"Why are you so surprised?" Nora chimed in.

"But, but, but she, she..." I stuttered.

"You, of all people, shouldn't be judging someone based on appearances," Nora said as she crossed her arms and scowled at me.

"Sorry, Molly." My head and ears drooped. *If I want people to give me a chance, I need to give them a chance too.*

"I only accept hugs for apologies." Molly had a smug look on her face.

"I doubt that. You said that just because it's me."

"So what if I did?" Molly spread her arms out wide. All the other kids were watching us now.

"Fine. A short one." *Might as well get it over with. I made my bed. Now I need to lie in it. But first, ground rules.* "Head, ears and tail are off-limits." Molly's left eye twitched, and she lowered her arms slightly. *I figured she would be up to something.*

I trudged up to her, bracing myself for a tackle that never came. Molly held back her enthusiasm long enough to give me a gentle hug. I wrapped my arms around her to uphold my half. Molly wrapped her arms around me. She slowly lowered her hands towards my tail. "Alright, the hug is over." I grabbed both of her arms from below and pushed them straight up.

Molly tried to resist, but I was stronger than her. "That isn't fair! How are you so strong?" She stepped back and stomped her feet in her tantrum. Her arms were at her sides, her fists balled and she glared at me.

"That doesn't matter. Just accept that I am, and always will be, stronger than you." I grinned as I crossed my arms and turned slightly away from her, trying to look cool.

"Don't be like that, Lucia." Nora stepped between us. "She's right, you got your hug. But just like you have an aptitude for gardening, Lucia here has the physical aptitude." Nora stood with her back to me as she addressed Molly.

"She what?" all the other kids shouted in unison.

I cried in pain as the noise assaulted my ears. I could feel their stares. "Stop yelling. It hurts." I continued to hold my ears to my skull.

"You don't get to say that when you're probably the luckiest person in this entire city. How could you get that aptitude?" Evandol was nearly in tears.

I know you were angry with me from before, but you need to chill out. I turned to stare at Nora. "Why did you have to tell them that?"

"Your aptitudes don't need to be a guarded secret." Nora frowned at me.

"Did you just say 'aptitudes?' As in plural?" Martin hadn't lower his voice. *He caught on quickly.*

"Yes, she has the recovery aptitude as well." Nora was now standing between all the other kids and me with her hands on her hips. *I've gone from a pariah to global enemy number one and two. As if my life wasn't already hard enough. Thanks, Nora.* "Well, this is unfair to poor Lucia. You know both of her aptitudes, but she doesn't know yours." She stood to the side and pointed to Eleanah as she looked at me. "Eleanah's is self-control." *That's a broad subject, like mine. But what does self-control amplify?*

Without turning away from me, Nora pointed to Oscar. "Illusion magic." *I knew that one, but I won't steal her thunder.* Then she pointed to Martin. "Ironworking." *Not blacksmithing?* She moved on to Anna. "Conjuration magic." *That's the second magic-related one.*

"What about Mr. Envy over there?" I pointed to Evandol, who pouted harder as Nora shared each child's aptitude.

"The fiddle," Nora said as she clapped her hands together. "He plays the most beautiful music." She stared into the sky with a wistful look in her eye.

A musical instrument? Not just playing music, but with a specific instrument. He's the only one in this group that's so specific. Is there a mix of magic, physical and professional aptitudes?

Nora snapped out of whatever daydream she was having and

13 PITCH BLACK CATS

looked back towards me. "But now with that out of the way, Lucia, do you know the rules?"

"Maybe," I said hesitantly. *Yeah, nobody bought that one, not even me.*

"All brawn and no brains," Evandol quipped.

Anna gave Evandol a quick glare before turning to me. "The rules are simple. We take turns picking who we're going up against. You then have to tag the person you picked. If they tag you, then you pick someone to tag. For our special rules, no touching the building or the flowers. Other than that, you need to touch your opponent with your palm."

"Can I be it first? Please? Please?" Molly jumped up and down with one arm raised.

"What about if you can't catch the person you picked?" I asked.

"When I deem that you can't catch them, I will end the round and you'll be eliminated. Then that person picks someone to tag," Nora said. "Last one standing wins."

"I want to be first!" Molly insisted while still jumping around.

"Fine, you can go first," Evandol groaned as he threw his arms in the air.

"Yay! I pick Lucia." Molly continued to jump up and down.

"We know." Eleanah's tone was almost as bad as Evandol's.

"Go stand over there, Lucia." Nora pointed to a spot on the ground.

I shrugged my shoulders and walked to the pointed location. *I might as well get this over with.*

Molly moved to stand about thirty feet away from me. I could see her shaking as we waited for the go signal.

"Go!" Nora called.

Molly took off as fast as she could towards me, her eyes fixated on me. I stood still, waiting for her to get close to me. *Is that how fast she can run? It doesn't look all that fast. I guess she is still kinda young.* Her legs moved as fast as she could drive them, each step bringing her closer to me.

Just before she was within arm's reach, I extended my arm to catch her.

Her eyes exploded with surprise. She ran into my waiting hand, and I stopped her with far less effort than I was expecting. "What are you doing? You know the objective is to avoid being tagged, right?" She tilted her head to the side as she grabbed my arm.

"I know, but I have a score to settle. And I will not waste any energy beforehand," I said coldly as I turned to Martin. "You know what's coming."

"Yeah, I do," Martin said, unimpressed. He walked to the same starting position as Molly had.

"Ready?" I asked courteously.

"Yes," Martin said coldly.

Without waiting for the go, I dropped into a low stance and charged. Martin never flinched. Nora sounded like she was protesting something, but I was too focused to care. *I just know he has something up his sleeve.*

The world blurred as I ran as fast as I could. *I didn't know I could run this fast.* Surprise showed on Martin's face for a moment as he took a short step back before he raised his left arm. The ground in front of him rose to impede me.

It was my turn to be surprised. *Using magic in a game of tag? I guess they didn't say anything about not using it.* Using the trick I learned in the bathroom chasing the illusion, I dug my claws into the dirt, stopping before the wall, and pulled myself forward as I restarted my charge. As I attempted a second turn, another section of earth rose to block my path.

Fine, you wanna play hard to get? I take your dirt wall and raise you the ability to climb... This better work, or I'll look like an idiot. I turned to the dirt barrier, which was easily twice my height, and jumped onto it and attempted to bury all of my claws into the structure before me.

My relief was almost palpable as my claws held me up.

I drove myself up the wall, always keeping three points of

contact. I made it to the top and looked down at Martin from the dirt wall. The look on his face was worth it.

"Surprise!" I said as I prepared to pounce from my new platform.

Martin punched the section I was on. Everything started shaking as the dirt moved with me still on it. I saw Martin lifting the dirt over his head and planning to drive me to the ground. *Not today.* I leaned back and jumped straight up so that I could land on him. The wall of dirt looked more like a large shield now, and I landed on it on my hands and feet.

Martin tilted the slab towards the ground. I rolled to a four-point stance. *Why do I keep finding myself using my hands for running as much as I use my legs, especially when I take off?*

I charged again. *The distance is much shorter this time, so he shouldn't be able to erect another wall.* I was right; he instead held the dirt shield out to catch me. *I could try to break through it.* I lowered my shoulder and attempted to barge through his defense. When I collided with the shield, it shattered, and I bounced in the opposite direction a couple of feet.

Martin was also knocked off balance and he staggered back a few steps into the still-standing section of the dirt wall.

I rubbed my shoulder to ease the pain even as adrenaline numbed it. *I regret that decision, but nothing feels too messed up, and it's moving fine.*

I charged for the third time and Martin looked at me first in surprise, then frustration and finally determination. He fashioned himself another shield from the wall behind him.

Let's try a different approach. I tried to slide under the shield's guard. He must have expected me to do that maneuver because he attempted to bring the shield down on me, but I cleared it.

Martin realized his miscalculation, and, as I reached for one of his legs, he jumped, using the shield to lift himself higher.

So close, yet so far away. I dug my claws in to slow myself. *While he's still in the air, I can catch him defenseless.* I pounced as soon as my momentum stopped.

I wasn't quick enough.

He landed on the ground and turned with the shield to intercept me. *Come on. There has to be a way around this shield.* I grabbed it, attempting to pull myself around it. *Maybe if I can latch onto it, I can nullify its usefulness.*

Seeing me grab the shield, Martin spun around, trying to dislodge me. I ran to keep up with his turning. I sprinted as fast as I could to overtake the shield. Martin didn't like the fact that I was succeeding, and he turned his shield towards the ground.

I dug my claws into the shield and broke off a handful of dirt.

"Give up," Martin said between heavy breaths.

I came to a full stop and realized I was panting. "This is yours." With his shield still lowered, I threw the dirt I scraped from it at him. He yelled as it hit his eyes. He released his shield and attempted to clear his vision.

I ran up and tackled him.

Both of us tumbled to the ground, with my arms almost completely wrapped around his waist.

As soon as we landed, Martin let out a grunt. "You cheated." He sounded a little light on air.

"How?" I asked between panted breaths. There was no response. *That's right, I didn't.*

I heard clapping from the side, but all I could do was roll off Martin and stare at the sky, exhausted. "Congratulations, you're the first one to tag Martin since he learned magic." It was Nora clapping and praising me.

Do you mean nobody has touched this guy?

"I think I can guess why," I mumbled. Somehow, I found some energy to stand up. I leaned over Martin and stared down at him. "I win."

"Yeah. I guess you aren't all talk after all." Martin smiled. *Is that respect I see in his bloodshot eyes?*

I held my hand out to him. He grabbed it and I helped him stand back up. *Wow, he's heavy.* I turned to see the other kids standing with their mouths wide open. Tired, I walked over to the side, away from the game area and away from the others. "I'm going to lie down for a while," I said as I made myself comfortable on the ground and closed my eyes.

19

SHOCKING CONCLUSION

"Alright, so who do you want, Martin?" Nora asked.

I guess I could at least still listen to what's going on. I am very out of shape. This body was probably never in shape to begin with, being only four years old and all.

"Nobody. I forfeit." Martin didn't sound nearly as tired as I was. "I only went along with this game to put Lucia in her place. But you see how that turned out." *You didn't make it easy for me.* "I'm going to go take care of the pipe in the bathroom now."

"You can go after this is over. You can forfeit, but you're staying. This is a family event." Nora's voice turned serious. *Why does she see us as a family?* "Oscar and Molly will go next. Molly, you need to tag Oscar."

"Okay," Oscar consented.

"Fine. Since Lucia was no fun earlier," Molly moaned.

I told you I wouldn't waste energy on you. And I'm glad that I didn't.

It wasn't long before I heard Nora give the signal to go. I heard all the steps being taken by both kids. It sounded like Molly was having issues deciding where to go. Her complaining of Oscar's magic confirmed my suspicion. I sat there, slowly getting my breathing back in check. Oscar exhausted Molly by hiding which one was the real him. Nora then declared Molly unable to catch Oscar.

Oscar went up against Anna next. Although, from the sounds of it, Anna liked to throw things at Oscar. That match sounded much closer, with Oscar almost as winded as Anna. *Using magic tires you out, apparently.* So Oscar caught Anna, and then it was Anna's turn. She chose Eleanah. There were a few steps before I heard Anna screaming that she had yielded. I sat up as I heard Anna. Unfortunately, I missed what happened as I opened my eyes too late. The only thing I saw was her walking away, rubbing her wrists as if Eleanah had hurt them. With my breathing under control, I was ready to watch the next match.

"Evandol, let's go," Eleanah curtly called out. Evandol merely shrugged.

He shrugs a lot. Does he think he's cool when he does that?

Once they were in the starting positions, Nora gave the signal, and they each charged the other. *What is going on?* I wasn't ready to see the display of martial skills that followed their initial clash. Evandol went for Eleanah's legs in a sliding maneuver. In response, she jumped and did a front flip. She extended a hand down to try and touch Evandol as he passed under her.

He rolled out of reach and to his side, and Eleanah landed effortlessly on her feet. Evandol tucked himself into a ball and rolled to his feet. They turned towards one another and changed their stances.

Eleanah loosened all of her limbs and looked like a marionette. Evandol, in contrast, had his feet just a little more than shoulder-width apart and his arms out with his hands open. Eleanah leaned forward and ran to Evandol with her arms still at her sides. Evandol backed up slowly. Once Eleanah was within arm's reach of Evandol, she raised her right arm to tag him. Evandol sidestepped the arm and reached for it. She pulled it in faster than he could react and reversed her hand.

The scene ended with Eleanah holding Evandol's hand.

"No way," Evandol said under his breath. His confusion quickly shifted to anger. "Rematch!" I flinched from the shout. Without turning away from one another, they both took up their starting positions again.

Nora gave them the go-ahead again.

I was curious about Eleanah. When I stood up, I still felt some fatigue. *I guess I recovered quickly, but I still need to get in shape.* I walked over to Nora and poked her hand with my finger. When she turned to me, I said, "What does Eleanah's aptitude allow her to do? It's another one of the broad areas, like mine, right?"

She turned away from me and back to watching the game. "Yes, it is. She has almost complete control of everything she does. She can control her heart so much that it almost sounds like it's stopped." *That sounds frightening.* "She also has the best balance you'll ever find. She can even write with both hands at the same time." *I know I struggle with writing, but there's no need to rub my nose in it.*

I turned to look at the game, only to see Evandol lying on the ground, face first. He tried to get up, but Eleanah put her boot heel on his spine, right between his shoulder blades.

"Evandol, you're done. Don't hurt yourself. You're so close to joining a company; don't ruin that chance now," Nora pleaded with the defeated kid.

"Fine!" Evandol pounded his fist into the ground. Eleanah removed her foot from his back. Evandol stood up and glared at Eleanah. "One day I won't lose to you."

"Whatever you say." Eleanah's face didn't change. *I think there might be some bad blood or rivalry going on.* "Oscar, you're next." *She doesn't look all that tired either. She must be in really good shape.*

I turned to see that Oscar still hadn't completely recovered. *He won't last long.*

Once they were in the starting positions, Nora gave the signal, and Oscar started walking towards Eleanah. She looked confused, but approached him cautiously. They met near the midpoint, and Oscar reached out his hand and Eleanah took it.

"I guess I lost to Eleanah." *Wait, did he just do the same thing I did to Molly?* "Lucia, you look like you're ready to go." He turned to look at me with a grin on his face. "I have no hope of winning against Eleanah, so I'm just going to try for second place."

"Sure." I replied. *Since he took a lesson from me, I think I should take a lesson from Anna.* I grabbed three stones and put one in my right hand and two in my left. *He might still be scared of me after that incident with the wand. Let's see if I can get him to quit with as little effort as possible. I think I'm going to need as much as I can get against Eleanah.* I took the stone in my right hand and threw it at a tree. The rock whistled as it flew and struck the plant, causing bits of bark to splinter off.

Oscar looked at the impact and slowly turned his head back to me, horrified.

"I'm ready to go when you are," I said, bouncing the two rocks in my other hand.

"I will take third place, thank you." He threw his hands in the air in surrender as he tried to make himself as small as possible.

I tested my throwing arm and secured second place. Now that is killing two birds with one stone.

"Coward," I heard Evandol say under his breath.

"It's alright to be scared," I said in a playful tone, winking at Evandol.

"Stupid wolf ears," Evandol grumbled.

I don't think he likes me very much. I giggled.

"I guess it's down to just the two of us," Eleanah said seriously. Her voice sounded much more mature than I would expect someone with her looks to have.

"Ready?" Nora asked both of us. Without looking away from one another, we nodded. I dropped the stones. *They'll probably be of little use to me.* "Lucia needs to touch Eleanah to win, and Eleanah needs to avoid Lucia to win. Begin."

I leaned forward to charge her, but before I took my first step, a high-pitched noise assaulted my ears. "Ahh!" I clenched my ears. *What was that?* I looked around to find the source. Then I heard it again, this time louder. "Ahhhhh!" I dropped to my knees. I looked at Eleanah and saw she had a finger in each corner of her mouth. "Please stop that. It hurts," I begged.

She made the shrill sound again.

"Aaaaahhhhhh!" Tears started streaming down my face. The pain was more than I could handle.

"Do you yield?" Eleanah asked as she took a few steps towards me. *Maybe I can hold out long enough to surprise her with one quick movement.* Since I didn't respond, she stopped and whistled again. I fell on my back, screaming in pain. "Do you yield?" she asked as she took a few steps closer. Her voice was louder than any other voice I'd heard in this life.

As dumb as this idea is, I have to try it. I could feel my rage building. *I have to stop her from making that noise again. It hurts too much.* "Stop that!" I shouted as I jumped up and lunged for her, both arms extended.

She grabbed my forearms and lifted them up. In one fluid, swift movement, she let go of one of my arms, circled around behind me and grabbed the arm again without me reacting. She stopped me from moving forward and twisted my arms behind my back.

I growled.

"Lucia! No! Everyone, stop!" Nora shouted.

Eleanah made her ear-piercing whistle right behind me. I watched my vision flood with red. *She won't be able to make that sound again when I'm through with her.* I pulled at my arms, growling loudly—

Electricity coursed through my body, causing all of my muscles to seize up, but I wasn't the only one affected. Eleanah screamed in pain right behind me. I don't know at what point she let go, but she stopped screaming. I fell to the ground gracelessly. Once control of my body returned to me, I turned to look at Eleanah.

"What was that?" Her voice was hoarse.

"That's to protect you from me." I sounded much weaker than her.

"I'm so sorry. I'm sorry, I'm sorry." Eleanah crawled towards me and hugged me tightly. Tears exploded from her eyes. She was crying worse than I was. *Wasn't I the one wearing the shock collar and got the worst of it?* She kept sobbing into my shoulder as she held me tight. "I forfeit. Lucia wins." She shouted those two sentences in the middle of her weeping.

"That isn't important right now." Nora kneeled next to us. "She activated the necklace, and now both of you are hurt."

"What necklace? Why would you need such a horrible item around your neck?" Eleanah was still crying, but she at least released me a bit. Her teary eyes were bringing tears to my eyes.

I couldn't look at her, so I stared at the ground. "I asked for this. You're in complete control of yourself. But, unlike you, I can't control myself at all. If it weren't for this"—I touched the necklace responsible—"I would seriously hurt you and be unable to stop myself."

"I will protect you so that this never happens again." Eleanah hugged me even closer this time.

"How about we start with just getting me to bed so I can lie down for a while?" I asked, because my body wasn't moving well. My crying had slowed down. "Could you help me?"

"Of course, your big sister will always help you," Eleanah said with a wide smile.

I don't know about being sisters yet. "Friends?" I asked as she lifted me into a cradle carry. My left arm hung from my side, and it hurt a lot more than my right. Wincing in pain, I lifted it so it would rest in my lap.

"Weren't you listening? We're sisters." Eleanah never wiped away the tears from her face.

I guess she bought into the "this is a family" idea.

"Yes, you two are sisters." Nora tapped my nose with a finger. "And you have two more sisters and three brothers."

I looked Eleanah in the eye. She gave me a soft smile. *Again with this family thing. Yes, we live together, but that doesn't make us a family. We are oly here due to common circumstances. I'm not buying in yet. It's obvious that I don't belong.*

Once Eleanah turned to the door to take me in, I saw Phan in the doorway with his arms crossed.

"We need to talk," he said before he walked back inside.

That doesn't sound ominous at all.

20

WE TALKED

We all filed into the dining room, similar to how we'd walked out. Phan waved for us to all have a seat at the table. Eleanah set me down in my seat and then sat in Anna's seat next to me. I made sure I didn't sit on my tail, but my arm wasn't moving well, and it hurt to try. I felt my shoulder, and something didn't seem right.

"Are you alright?" Eleanah, who hadn't taken her eyes off me yet, leaned in and asked me.

"No, it feels like my shoulder has a hole." I tried to explain the odd feeling. "That and it's hurting a lot now, and it's getting worse."

"Let me see." Phan walked over to me as everyone else took their seats. He lightly grabbed my shoulder and felt it up. He grabbed the arm and rotated it up. "Does this hurt?"

My shriek answered him. *Please don't do that again.*

"It's dislocated," he said with a frown.

I know what that means. He has to put it back. This is going to hurt as much going in as it did coming out. Although I didn't feel it get dislocated. It must have happened while I was shocking myself and Eleanah.

"Anna, can you get me something she can bite down on?" Phan asked.

Yeah, this is going to hurt a lot.

Anna did as Phan asked.

"You can hold on to me." Eleanah moved her chair closer to me and held my other hand in hers. Anna returned with a wooden spoon and handed it to Phan.

"Bite down on this," Phan said as he held the spoon to my mouth.

"Why?" *I've never understood why they bite down on something in all the movies.*

"It will give you something to focus on besides the pain. Also, to keep you from biting your tongue off," Phan stated flatly.

I complied with his wishes. *I'm not ready for this.* "On three." *Don't tell me when it's coming, that makes things worse.* I could feel tears streaming down my face.

"One."

Before I had another thought, Phan moved my arm, and I felt and heard something pop.

I could feel my eyes dilate. Everything stiffened as I waited for the inevitable pain to flood my mind. *Bite down, bite down, bite down.* I bit down as soon as my brain received the pain signals from my arm. It felt like I was being shocked by my collar all over again, but this time it was only in my left arm.

Bite down. I bit down on the spoon as hard as I could. *Bite down, bite down.*

The spoon surrendered to my teeth and gave way. A sharp crack was the only warning I got before I saw two pieces of wood fly off in different directions. I could taste the wood now that it was resting on my tongue.

"Yuck." I spat the splinters out of my mouth. "And ouch! I thought you said on three," I moaned as I turned to Phan.

"I needed you to relax, and if you'd known it wasn't going to happen until I said three, you wouldn't have tensed up." Phan sounded proud of himself. "Although I didn't expect you to bite through the wooden spoon."

"You must have some strong teeth and a powerful bite," Melody said, with a single tear rolling down her face. "I really liked that spoon, too."

"My bad, sorry." I lowered my head apologetically.

Phan cleared his throat. "Speaking of teeth. You haven't turned five yet, correct?" I nodded my head as I turned to look at him. "That means you still have your baby teeth." *Oh, I'm going to go through that again? The phases of awkward smiles and a missing tooth lisp are coming soon.* "You'll need to let me know when your first tooth falls out or all of your teeth start to hurt. Whichever comes first, no exceptions."

"Why?" Nora questioned.

"To avoid any complications. There's a chance we'll have nothing to worry about. So don't worry about it until the time comes."

If Phan's trying to ease my fears, it isn't working.

"But I guess after watching the end of your game, it might be best to tell you what I know about beastkin." Phan moved so that everyone could see him as he sat on the other side of the table. "You should already know that this world has many intelligent species: humans, elves, orcs, dragoons, demons, angels, dwarves, goblins and beastkin." *There are quite a few races.* All the other kids simply nodded in agreement. "This kingdom is almost entirely human and elven, with a few exceptions. Demons and angels don't naturally reside on this plane of existence and have to be summoned here, so don't worry about them too much. But I brought you here to talk about the most varied race, the beastkin." He pointed at me. "Lucia here is one type of beastkin. She is a wolf beastkin with a carnivore diet."

"Is her carnivore diet important?" Anna interrupted.

"Yes, it is. Each beastkin falls into one of three categories: herbivore, omnivore, or carnivore. This determines their

THE BIG BAD WOLF

temperament and sometimes their features. Omnivores are the most human-like. They can be aggressive or passive; you just have to get to know them on a personal level. Herbivores are often very passive and reclusive. Carnivores are aggressive and temperamental, as we have all seen with Lucia here."

Yes, use me as a visual aid, or you could not. That'd be fine too. "Glad to be a convenient example," I said sarcastically.

Phan ignored my comment. "They are the reason beastkin have the aggressive reputation that they have. But the thing about beastkin in relation to their diet is that it often determines their aggressiveness. So if Lucia here was an omnivore, even though wolves are carnivores, she would be less aggressive than the norm. The beastkin that are herbivores or carnivores also always have sharper senses and are more animalistic than their omnivore counterparts."

"Since I have the physical aptitude and am a carnivore, how strong am I going to be?" I asked.

"I honestly don't know. The army will find a way to keep you under their thumb, though," Phan answered. *That was way too blunt. That extra bit about the military worries me.* "The most common beastkin that people have had dealings with are carnivores, since they're the ones adventurous enough to leave the Wild Kingdom."

"Are you telling me that there's an entire kingdom of people just like me?" I slammed my fist on the table. I continued my tirade without waiting for an answer to my rhetorical question. "What am I doing here? Why am I not there with people like me? People who would understand what I'm going through. A place where I might not need to wear a shock collar!" I could feel my mood changing. *Waterfalls, waterfalls. Lucia, calm down, get it under control.*

Phan never moved an inch. "Do you know where the Wild Kingdom is?" he asked. I shook my head. "It's a two-week walk from this kingdom to the Wild Kingdom. Do you know where your village was?"

Again, I shook my head. "But Allen saved me a day away from here."

"It's a four-day walk to the kingdom's border to the north of here, where the orcs likely came from. Do you know why your parents left the Wild Kingdom?" Phan's face never changed as he asked me these questions.

"I don't know anything!" I shouted. "You're not helping me stay calm." I was getting angrier. "Waterfalls!" I jumped from my chair and landed on the ground with weak legs. I collected all my determination and stormed back to my room. As I left the kitchen, I could hear Phan release a heavy sigh. *It's difficult to stomp out of a room to show how angry I am when, no matter how hard I step, I make no sound.*

It wasn't long before I stood in the entrance of my room. *Why is it that every time I get angry, I come here?* I walked to my bed after closing the door hard. I sat down and looked out the window at the sky. *Why can't I control myself? Why do I keep asking myself the same question? I guess I really can't do this.* I heard footsteps coming from down the hall. *What now?* I sat on my bed and waited for whoever it was to pass by. They stopped at my door and opened it, revealing Nora.

"Leave me alone!" I shouted as I stood up on the bed. My tail assisted with my balance as I jumped out the window. *I want to be left alone. I'm tired of being angry because someone did something or said something to me. What did I do to deserve this? I hate being on a hair-trigger.* I ran towards the hedge through the courtyard, where we'd played tag. *Maybe I can hide in the flowers.*

"What's bothering you?" I heard Nora's voice right behind me, and turned to look and saw a cloud slowly dissipating around her.

"Come on, that isn't fair!" I threw yet another childish tantrum. *Stop doing that. You can use magic, and magic is cheating.* "I said, leave me alone." I turned around, ready to run away from her again.

"I won't," Nora said. "Not until you tell me what's wrong."

Defeated, I slumped from my running stance. "I can't do this," I said as I planted my butt on the ground.

"Do what?" Nora walked around in front of me.

"I can't control myself, and I don't think this collar is going to work." Tears welled up in my eyes. "I don't want to hurt anyone, but I can't hold back my emotions. I'm not good at being a beastkin."

"Come here." Nora was sitting in a chair. *Where did that chair come from? That's right, magic.* I complied, and she lifted me onto her lap and held me close. "How old are you?"

"My body is four years old," I said, unsuccessfully attempting to hold back my tears.

"How many kids do you know who are good at being themselves when they're at that age?" Nora used her sweetest voice.

"None." *Every four-year-old does dumb and selfish things. As an adult, your job is to keep them from hurting themselves or someone else.*

"So why wouldn't you be any different?" Nora asked.

"Because I *am* different. I'm not a child in my mind." My crying continued. "I was an adult, and I can't ignore that."

"You're right, you are different. Everybody is different in some way." Nora lifted my chin so I could look her in the eye. "But why can't you be the child you are?"

I don't get it. I knew she could see the confusion on my face. "You were given a second chance at life. Most people don't get to say that. There are even those that don't get much of a first chance. You're too focused on what you were, not what you are."

"What do you mean? Being a beastkin has had its perks. This hearing is cool until someone is too loud or makes a high-pitched sound. The claws are growing on me." I could feel the tears slowing. "All of this fur might be a lot to manage, but I think I can handle it. And the tail is great for balance. But I know nothing about this world."

13 PITCH BLACK CATS

"And being a girl?" Nora's voice dropped just like my heart at that question.

"I don't know." My momentary relief was followed by melancholy. "I don't know if I can be a girl."

"So learn." Nora's voice cheered up. "You're a kid again. Be a kid. Learn everything as a kid should. Run around, have fun, get dirty, get hurt—but not too hurt—fall, then get back up again. Experiment with the world around you. Worry about the things you can change and don't force yourself to be what you're not."

"But I wasn't a girl," I moaned.

"You are a girl now. What is the difference between a boy and a girl, really?" Nora probed.

"How we pee?" I answered tentatively. "And where babies come from?"

"Besides the physical differences. You'll grow into those." Nora frowned. "What's so bad about being a girl?"

"If I'm a girl, doesn't that mean I have to do things like cooking and sewing?"

"Do you like to do those things?" Nora asked with a deadpan look.

"I don't know. If sewing is like writing, that's never going to happen," I said, looking down at my hands.

"Then try them. If you don't like them, then find something else you enjoy doing." Nora lifted my chin again. "There's nothing about being a girl to dictate what you can do or what you like."

Out of options, I surrendered to Nora's idea. "I guess I'll give it a try. Being a kid again, that is." Something felt right about saying that. *I guess I could also join in and drink the "this is one big family" punch.* "You win, Mom."

A tear welled up in Nora's eye as she hugged me close. "Welcome to the family, Lucia." Nora continued to hold me tight.

I returned the hug. *If I'm going to see this as a family, Nora is going to be more of a mother to me than anyone else. Although, something's bothering me now.* "How did you know what to say?"

"This isn't the first time I've had this conversation with someone." Nora gave a slight laugh. "Although the whole reincarnated part was new. The rest, let's just say I had to talk some sense into a certain elven knight."

"Really?" I asked. *That's fascinating.*

"Yes, it's true." Nora released me from her hold. "Are you ready to go back and practice your letters again?"

"Do I have to?" I whined.

"Yes, you're still going to get an education. That I promise." Nora placed her hand on my head and ruffled my hair.

I relaxed and enjoyed the head pat. I leaned back and hugged her again. "Can we stay like this for a little longer?"

"Take all the time you need." Nora returned my hug.

Everything from that moment on felt easier, lighter even.

After I calmed down, Nora sent Phan away as she brought me back in. My consciousness drifted in and out throughout the day. Whenever I looked at the others, something about them felt different.

When we were all sent to bed, I found myself staring out the window again. Something about the moon's presence felt calming.

Learning that I was a girl and then that I wasn't a human but a beastkin, I understood those things. But now I know there's a difference between knowing something and accepting it. Looking back, I feel like I recognized those things about me, but I never dealt with them. Nora made me look at myself and deal with it. But it makes me wonder how many people, out in whatever world they're in, look at themselves and ignore what and who they are?

I curled my tail around and ran my brush through my fur.

I was stupidly stubborn, thinking that being what I am will just become natural all on its own. That's not how it works. Now, I can look at myself and see that I'm a beastkin, and I don't know what that means, but I can figure that out like Nora said. I'm a kid and it's time I accepted it. Just because I'm a girl and half animal doesn't decide for me what I can or want to do. Yes, I have a dietary restriction, but is that any different than someone who was born with nearsightedness or something similar? Everyone can learn to live within their limitations, but I guess people are far less limited than we realize. Because of the one thing that sets us apart, people can adapt.

I smiled as I wagged my tail after I finished brushing it.

This situation is no different. I can't think of myself as a human like in my last life. It isn't that my last life is inconsequential, or dead weight, but more like an old friend who has passed on. Lucia doesn't have to be that person whose name I don't even know. I don't have to be that person whose name I don't even know. The Voice said I could live my life however I want. Hopefully the worst is behind me and I can face this world.

If I'm Lucia, then I will be the best Lucia ever.

I placed the brush on my dresser and crawled into bed.

INTERLUDE: PERFORMANCE REVIEW

A soul sailed off to another world, leaving The Voice alone in the darkness. "I really hope nobody finds out what I did," The Voice said to itself.

Without warning, The Voice felt an overwhelming pressure bearing down on its entire existence. It knew that could only mean one thing: The Voice had been found out, and someone had been sent to investigate.

White, puffy clouds floated in the air as the darkness around The Voice shifted into a large, circular room made of white marble, with swirls of gray and light brown through it. The Voice manifested its position as a simple violet sphere of light.

"Do you know why I'm here?" an echo sounded from the edges of the multiverse.

"Because you want to give me a raise for the good job I've been doing?" The Voice squeaked.

"No. Because you broke the rules. Again!" All of existence shook as The Voice figured out who was talking to it.

"Please, Judge. I haven't done anything too bad this time." The

Voice dimmed its light and cowered to the ground. "I'm trying something different."

"You petitioned for one soul, and one soul you were given." The multiverse ceased its rumbling at the sound. Instead, The Voice felt everything shake within itself as it heard each word. "Yet there is a report that a second soul recently went forth from your realm. It is also stated that you told the first soul that you made a mistake. Is that true?"

The Voice knew that lying to The Judge was a wasted effort. "Yes, but..."

"Don't tell them that. It doesn't matter if you place them in a body different than what you planned. The soul is without form and fills the vessel it is placed in." The Judge silenced The Voice. "Nowhere in your job are you to tell those you send to that little world you had created that you made a mistake. You're lucky that we're letting you continue this little game of yours, so long as the souls you are given do their job."

The Voice cowered against the outer wall even though it knew there was no escape from this trial. "I'm sorry, I couldn't help myself."

"Then after you made that mistake, you grabbed a second soul, one that doesn't meet your limited yet exceedingly specific requirements." The Judge manifested its presence as a beam of orange light in the center of the temporary room.

"It was a soul that nobody wanted. I thought it would be okay to take it." The Voice shook in the presence of such a definitive being.

"These are your forty-first and forty-second infractions. They are both minor infractions, but the quantity is more than enough to warrant action. Consider your performance under review." A cloud approached The Judge. "Tell me why you selected the first soul. And also why you have such a limited soul selection criteria."

"I selected the first soul because I believe every soul is capable of the greatest accomplishments of heroism. It is something I have seen over and over while watching the souls I send to Centari." The Voice was slowly collecting its footing. "I am giving these souls a chance they never had."

"Then you better make sure that these two souls succeed at covering your first major infraction, or all three of you will get relegated."

The Voice shook at The Judge's sentence.

21

THE START OF A SPECIAL DAY

The sun beamed into my room and warmed my face. *Ugh, I guess it's time to get up.* I sat up and rubbed my eyes with the palms of my hands. *I have been a female beastkin child for twenty-seven days now. Alright, let's keep going with day twenty-eight.*

With a heavy sigh, I hopped out of bed. I stretched my back, legs, shoulders and arms before I stripped off my sleepwear and began brushing my fur and hair. *My fur is definitely getting thicker. I guess since the days have been getting colder winter is coming.* After taking my time brushing my fur, I moved on to my hair, but there was a knock at the door.

"Are you up yet?" Eleanah asked from behind the door.

"Yeah." I answered and looked down at my naked body. I dropped the brush on my bed and rushed to get some clean clothes on before Eleanah opened the door. "One second, let me get some clothes on." *Are my clothes getting tighter?* "Alright, I'm dressed now."

"It isn't like I haven't seen you naked before. We have bathed at the same time." Eleanah waved her hand around as she walked in. "What makes you take so long to get up?"

I pointed at my fur. "Do you see this, Eleanah? This takes a lot of maintenance to keep looking nice and knot-free."

"It is looking nice today. Is it getting fuller? Something has been off all week about your fur." Eleanah put her finger to her chin as she stared at me.

"Yeah, it's getting thicker. I guess my fur changes thickness with the seasons." I grabbed the brush off the bed and began working on my hair, which had also grown longer and thicker. *Now that I think about it, my hair is the same texture as my fur.*

Eleanah's face lit up. "Does that mean once fire season comes around, you're going to shed your ice coat?"

Ah, I forgot, again. There is no fall, winter, spring or summer here. They named them differently. Naming of seasons after elements is a little weird, but it makes sense with how it's done. Spring is the water season, summer is the fire season, fall is wind and winter is ice.

I dropped my arms. I felt the dread build as I looked at all of my fur. "You're probably right, as usual. That's going to be awful."

"Dealing with all that fur must be weird." *It isn't weird, it's natural. At least it's natural for me now that I've been doing this for the last three weeks. Since each week is eight days, or one full cycle of the red moon.*

Maybe I should toy with her as punishment. "If you're going to call me weird, then you don't get to be my favorite sister." I crossed my arms and turned away from her.

"Ever since that game of tag, I've been the best big sister to you. Who are you going to get to replace me?" Eleanah had a smug look on her face.

"Molly would. At least she thinks the fur you call weird is cute and cuddly." I gave her a wicked grin.

Her face reddened. "You're just saying that to get me mad."

I giggled. "Is it working?"

Eleanah stuck out her bottom lip as she pouted. "Yes."

"Good. Now don't call me weird." I released my pout and smiled at Eleanah.

We both broke out in full laughter. After we calmed down, I finished brushing my hair.

"You've changed. What happened to you?" Eleanah gave me an inquisitive stare. "Sometimes I find it hard to believe you're just four years old, but then there are times you act your age. What happened between you and Mom after that game of tag?"

"We talked." *That's all you are going to get.* I winked as I walked past Eleanah. "I need to go for my morning run."

"Mom wants to talk to you after you're done. Something about getting a present for Evandol for his farewell party." Eleanah followed me out of my room.

Is that today? I forgot about that. "Okay, see ya later." I waved to Eleanah as I headed to the courtyard. Once I opened the doors to go outside, I closed my eyes. I took a big breath through my nose. *I love the smell of the flowers in Molly's garden. The rancid smell of the city at the same time ruins the mood, though. Alright, time to tire myself out so I can focus on the day.* I leaned forward and took off, running around the edges of the courtyard. *I think I'll try to do twenty-two laps today.* Eager to burn as much energy as possible, I moved from running to sprinting.

The world blurred as I sprinted. I performed my special ninety degree turns, using all of my claws to stop myself before pulling myself forward to resume my sprint. *My mind can't keep up with my running speed. I should only run this fast when I know there are no obstructions.* Feeling the wind flow through my hair and fur, I tried to run as fast as I could within the space available.

After twenty laps, I had to stop. I hunched over, holding myself up by placing my hands on my knees and panting. *That was the same as yesterday. I guess I should be glad that I'm not regressing.*

"Did you enjoy your morning run?" A voice surprised me. I looked and saw that it was Nora. "Do you enjoy running that much?"

"I do. For multiple reasons." I said between panting breaths. "It takes the edge off, relaxes me, and, when I run that fast, it's all I can focus on." I took a deep breath to help with my recovery.

"I noticed that's what you've been doing when you use your code word." Nora walked closer to me. "You thirsty?"

"Yeah."

Nora summoned a cup from out of nowhere, and, with a small wiggle of her finger, water filled it. She kneeled next to me and handed it to me.

I grabbed it with both hands and gulped it down.

"You should slow down. Also, maybe try running around town so that people will get used to seeing you." I emptied the cup and handed it back to her. She took it and stood up. I wiped my mouth with my arm.

"Is that a good idea?" I asked. My breathing was slower, but I could still feel and hear my heart beating quickly. "I don't know how people will react to me. What if they think I'm dangerous or have done something wrong? What if people try to kidnap me?"

"You have a wild imagination." Nora laughed and waved her free hand from side to side. "If you say you're one of mine, I guarantee they will deliver you to the front door. Also, I know that if your running around town becomes a regular occurrence, people will adapt." She patted my head, and I wagged my tail. "However, we need to go into town and pick up Evandol's gift today."

"Is that what Eleanah was talking about? Is that what you wanted to see me for?" I walked towards the door with Nora.

"Yes, but also we'll see if we can find you a job for a couple of days a week." Nora opened the door for me. I walked in first. "We'll go after breakfast. But don't tell anyone where we're going. Got it?" She held her finger up to her lips.

"Right, keep it secret." I nodded. "But is breakfast eggs again? I hate eggs. They don't taste like anything."

"Well, when we tried herbs and spices to flavor them like you

13 PITCH BLACK CATS

mentioned, you got a stomach ache. At least you didn't vomit them back up." Nora continued to usher me down the hall.

"Don't forget the horrible diarrhea." I shuddered as I recalled the memory.

"You never mentioned that." Nora turned and eyed me for a moment before shaking her head. "Regardless, keeping you fed is already costing your entire stipend and then some."

"What can I say? I'm a growing girl," I said, smiling.

"Growing is right. You're on your way to outgrow your clothes by the end of the season, if not sooner." Nora poked my shirt. *I knew they were getting tighter. It wasn't my imagination.* "Next time, I'll tell Anna to make sure you get larger clothes." I followed Nora into the kitchen.

"Did you enjoy your run?" Melody asked as she carried the eggs to the dining room.

"Why is everyone asking if I enjoy my run every morning?" I threw my hands up in the air as I shouted at the ceiling.

"Because you're the only one who has so much energy before breakfast," Evandol spat. "You spend who knows how long brushing yourself, only to get up and run in the backyard." He made a pillow out of his arms that he rested on the table.

"Is that jealousy I hear?" I wiggled my right ear towards Evandol.

"You wish." Evandol turned his head to look away from me.

"Yes!" Molly shouted while she bounced around in her chair.

"Nobody asked you, Molly." Martin glowered at Molly.

Molly just slumped in her chair and pouted.

A lively breakfast today it seems. I took my seat, and we all ate our breakfast. The chatter over the table had been growing a lot lately. *I think the others are getting used to me. They even include me in their conversations.*

As I ate my flavorless eggs, my teeth felt odd. *It's probably just my imagination.*

We talked about the things we'd done yesterday and how

180

some of us were going to miss Evandol. *Not me. I haven't known him long enough for that. I might see him again someday, but I don't feel any attachment towards him.* Nora told us she would keep the chores to a minimum today so we could all enjoy Evandol's day together, but I skipped out on chores because Nora was taking me on a special trip. *Hurray! Chores aren't better in my second life.*

"Why do you get to go out with Mom?" Anna stood in the doorway to the kitchen and pointed a finger at me.

"Because she said so?" I shrugged while holding my palms open and up.

"Where are you going?" Martin joined the interrogation.

"I don't know," I answered. Martin looked at Nora and raised his eyebrows, as if to ask the same question without repeating himself.

"Lucia's diet has become costly. So, in order for her to have any spending money, she needs a job. She also needs to get out once in a while," Nora said, giving me a sidelong glance. "Her being cooped up inside is showing."

"What? I go outside every day." *Why is she being mean to me?* "I've gotten better with my temper."

"So snapping a chalkboard in half and embedding it when you throw it into the wall you would consider doing better?" Nora's look sent chills down my spine. "Or how about the time you threw a plate at Evandol for telling you to slow down while eating?"

"Or that time you clawed my hand," Molly chirped.

"That time you threw me into the laundry washing bin," Oscar moaned.

"I have a perfectly good explanation for all of those. I still hate writing. Evandol said that I shouldn't wolf down my food. It was a terrible pun. I told you not to grab my tail, Molly; it was just a reflex. Finally, Oscar, if you ever come home smelling like rotting flesh and want to hug me again, I'll make you wish that all I did was throw you in some water." I growled at Oscar as I flexed my claws. "Okay,

13 PITCH BLACK CATS

fine, you win! I have anger problems." I continued growling as I pouted. *Great start to the day!*

"That growl is so cute." Molly fawned over me at a distance. That only caused me to growl louder and as fearsome as I could manage. "Okay, that one wasn't so cute. Can you go back to the other growl?"

I stood up and walked out, growling louder with each step. *I can't stand their patronizing. She isn't even considering my feelings at this point.*

I kicked the kitchen door open as hard as I could. The door flung open and slammed into the wall, and it stayed there. *I don't care!* I walked past the door and returned to my room. *Calm down. Waterfalls. It's as if they want me to get angry. They don't have to try that hard.* I slammed my door shut, and I heard a crack as it closed. I stomped silently to my dresser, grabbed my hairbrush, sat on my bed and began brushing my tail. *Here I thought today was going to be different.*

A short time later, there was a knock on the door. "Are you done?" Nora's soft voice called from the other side.

"No!" I shouted. I continued brushing my hair as if she wasn't standing just outside my room. *How thick is my fur going to get? I wonder how well it will hold up during the ice and snow.* After spending more time just brushing my fur, I calmed down enough to acknowledge Nora. "I'm still annoyed, but I feel better now."

Nora walked into the room and examined me. "Good. Are you ready to go into town?" Nora never moved out of the doorway.

"Let me use the bathroom first," I said as I put my brush back on my dresser and stood up.

After I used the bathroom, Nora and I left home. I looked at the streets that I had ignored for the last three weeks. *There are a ton of people out today.* The bustle of everyday life was on display in the capital city. While we walked through the streets, people turned to look at me. Their looks ranged mostly from shock to confusion, but everyone had some kind of look for me. *I guess many of them haven't seen a beastkin before. Well, neither did I before being reincarnated. But I'm a special case.* The crowd's stares and the absurd quantities of sound were almost too much to handle. I latched on to Nora and held her hand the entire time. We navigated through the streets unimpeded until we reached our first stop, a butcher shop.

As we stood near the doorway, Nora turned and looked down at me. "This is where we get the meat to feed your growing appetite."

I wagged my tail back and forth. *This place is going to be my equivalent of a candy store.* "Does that mean I get to go in too?"

"You can come in only if you behave." She lifted a finger and pointed it at me.

"Yay!" *I get to get out of these streets that smell like raw sewage and into a building filled with wonderful meat.* I ran into the building, pulling Nora behind me. Nora's yelp barely registered in my mind as I pulled her along.

22

AN OFFER YOU CAN REFUSE

As soon as the door opened, I basked in the blissful scent of protein. I wagged my tail vigorously. I looked around the storefront but didn't see any meat. It was a small room with a counter and a few chairs set up like a waiting room. Behind the counter was a doorway that led to a hallway. *The meat must be in that direction!* I needed to be careful not to drown in my drool.

A man was standing, waiting at the counter. He was a human, his clothes were clean and his appearance was the definition of prim and proper. Short, neat hair sat on top of his head with a clean-shaven face that was populated with very fine wrinkles around his eyes. *He looks like someone who's important or rich.*

"Well, isn't this a pleasant surprise? Good morning, Nora." He spoke with a dignified yet calming voice. "And who is this dragging you around?" He lowered his gaze to me.

I froze as I stared at him. *Stranger danger.*

"Good morning, Tobey," Nora answered his greeting with an equally high-class-sounding tone. "This is my latest charge, Lucia." She waved her free hand towards me. "Go ahead, say hello," she whispered to me.

I flattened my ears and ran behind Nora. *Why is this guy scaring me?* I couldn't find the courage to greet the man.

Nora turned around at her waist and placed a hand on my shoulder. "What happened to the brave wolf girl with an attitude?"

"I don't know why, but something about him is scary." I buried my face in Nora's dress.

Nora crouched down to my level. "Tobey is a nice man. He runs the delivery services in town and owns many of the trade routes between the villages and the capital."

"I've been called many things, and 'nice' does not come up often." *Why does it almost sound as if he's flaunting that fact?* "I'm shrewd, but I will never renege on a deal." *If that was an honest estimation of himself, can you trust a man who calls himself shrewd?* "What brought you here? Isn't Melody the one who usually sets up the deliveries?"

"I'm out on other errands today besides this one. Despite how shy she's acting right now, Lucia has an appetite we need to feed." Nora stood up and presented herself properly. She stood in a way that permitted me to stand behind her and listen to the conversation.

"Care to explain this one to me? Don't you have a stipend for each child? Why are you ordering more meat because of her?" *I guess I need to get used to telling everyone what a carnivore is, and that I am one.* "I also wasn't aware of any beastkin being anywhere within weeks of Aquittemia. How did you get her?"

"Wait, weeks?" I poked my head out from behind Nora. *Something isn't right here.*

"Yes, it's my business to know about each village close to the capital," Tob ey said. "I don't know of any beastkin villages nearby. So where are you from?" Tobey narrowed his eyes as he glared at me.

I turned to look away. "I don't know." *How I haven't missed saying those words.*

Nora took a step forward. "She received a hit to the head and has amnesia. Allen brought her to me after rescuing her from orcs."

"I heard about the orcs. They say that they were a day away from the capital, just leaving the forest. That is unfortunate for her." Tobey sounded mournful.

Did I pass out for more than a day? How was I even functioning after being unconscious for so long? Is my recovery aptitude responsible? Should I have died? My ears and tail drooped as I let go of Nora's hand. I walked to a chair and climbed into it. I didn't bother to look up and just continued to stare at the ground.

"That answers one of my questions. But why do you need to order more meat? Aren't there cheaper alternatives?" Tobey's voice was softer.

"Because after we met with Phannidoritthin, we learned that certain beastkin can have restrictive diets. Hers is strictly meat-based. I have already asked for an increase in her stipend, but the food will take all of it. We are also out today to find her a job to make some money for her private use." *You're quite willing to explain everything readily, aren't you, Nora?*

"Is that so?" Tobey drawled. *Why do I feel he's looking right at me?* I looked up at him and saw that he was, indeed, looking at me. "So, what can you do?"

"I don't know, but I know I'm stronger than I look and I can run really fast," I said hesitantly.

"Wonderful." Tobey clapped his hands. "How would you like a job from me?"

"What?" I contorted my face in confusion.

"How about you tell me the specifics? Then I'll think about it." Nora stepped in between us.

"Oh, but of course, everything will be done with the approval of the guardian." Tobey bowed towards Nora. "I find myself short-staffed with in-town couriers. One has been very sick of late and the other has taken an apprenticeship under a carpenter."

"So, what do you need me for?" I asked.

"I'm extending an invitation for you to deliver packages and letters to people around town." *So I get a job as a mail-woman?* He stood tall, waiting for my response.

With this, I could make some money and maybe reduce my debt to the kingdom. But there's one huge problem. "I don't know the town very well. I won't know where I'll need to go and could get lost."

"You can learn." Nora turned towards me. "We can get you a map." *I know you trust this guy, but I don't.*

"I'm prepared to compensate for the map. You'll have everything you need and know all that you need to for your job. I find educated employees are far more productive." Tobey extended a hand towards me. "So, what do you say?"

"I want to start her off with only two days a week." Nora stood so she could see both of us. "She still needs to learn geography, how to write and etiquette."

"What do you mean by etiquette?" I asked as I jumped out of the chair.

"You need to know how to behave in civilized company. Your temper tantrums won't fly with everyone." Nora stared down at me.

"It isn't my fault." I crossed my arms and pouted. "Everyone else keeps making me angry."

"If you don't mind my asking, how old are you?" Tobey carefully stepped next to Nora and placed a hand gently on her shoulder.

"I'm four."

"Do you know when your birthday is?" Tobey leaned forward a little more.

"No." I held back a growl.

Tobey looked like he was mulling something over in his mind. "I can agree to two days a week. Come to my office by the northern gate tomorrow. I'll have an employment contract drafted." He turned away from me to the counter, where another male human was standing. *How long has he been standing there?*

Tobey held his hand out to the man behind the counter, who

13 PITCH BLACK CATS

gave him a small cloth sack. I heard the sound of metal colliding as the contents jostled around. "It's a pleasure," Tobey said. "I'll have a cart here in two days with your order." *Ah, he's paying for a delivery. I should have seen that coming.*

"Thank you." The butcher's raspy voice grated on my ears. The man wore a leather apron that had obvious bloodstains on it. His face carried many more wrinkles than Tobey's.

My stomach made a rumbling noise.

"I guess I should deal with my hungry customers," the butcher said. "Nora, who is this?"

I growled. "My name is Lucia."

"I believe that's the attitude you referenced earlier. Until tomorrow, Nora." Tobey bowed to Nora slightly before heading to exit the shop.

Nora turned her attention to the butcher. "I'm here to add more meat to our weekly order. I would like a small increase. I think one portion for every five should be enough." *A twenty percent increase? I'm getting hungrier now.*

"You've ordered way more meat from me than you ever have before. What brought on this sudden splurge of finances? Not that I mind the extra income." The man leaned on the counter. *Of course you have no problem taking our money. Technically it's the kingdom's money, but they will get their money's worth out of me, eventually.*

"Lucia is the cause." Nora waved to me as if she was presenting me. "She can only eat meat, so she's your best customer. It seems her appetite is growing as fast as she is."

"Oh, is she now?" He looked at me with sparkling eyes. "If that was her stomach asking for food, I must oblige. How about something for the road?"

I twitched my ear towards him before bolting past Nora to stand at the counter, which was as tall as me. "For free?" I wagged my tail back and forth as I placed my hands on the counter.

"For my best customer? Sure." He smiled and went to the back. "I'll be back with some nice bacon strips for you to take home."

Bacon? Yes, please! I tried not to drool as I pranced in place. I could hear Nora sighing. "What? I'm excited about bacon!" I turned and gave her my most innocent look.

"I'll have to remember that for your birthday. But weren't you just getting an attitude a few moments ago?" Nora looked tired.

"Isn't the idea for me to not be angry? Besides, if bacon is involved, I'll be happy." I turned back to the counter and wagged my tail more enthusiastically. *In my last life, I loved the taste of bacon. If all meat tastes better to me now, I can't wait to see how good bacon tastes.*

I watched the butcher walk out of his backroom. With a small basket in hand, he walked up to the counter. "One slab of bacon for little miss..." He held out the basket towards me and looked like he was trying to remember something. Before I could remind him, his face lit up as he remembered. "Lucia!"

I snatched the basket off the counter and inspected the contents. Bacon wrapped in a thin cloth sat on a bed of salt. I could smell the bacon, and with one heavy inhale through my nose, I let out a moan as drool slid down my tongue.

"I'm glad it meets your approval." Nora gave me a look that said, *Are you done playing around?*

She turned her attention to the butcher. "How much?"

He looked down at me, holding the basket. *I can do this. I've been practicing.* With all the effort I could muster, I gave him the puppy-dog-eyes look. "That's such a cute face. But I already said that this one is on the house." *Success!*

Nora snapped her attention to me. "You have got to be kidding me," she said under her breath. "I thought Molly was dangerous." I giggled. Nora sighed as she turned away from me. "You have my thanks. I'm sure all the children are willing to extend their thanks too."

Subtle. "Thank you, sir." I grabbed a piece of the belly meat and lifted it. Drool threatened to leak from my mouth at the sight of the mesmerizing piece of meat. My body moved on instinct. I brought the raw meat to my mouth and bit into it.

Nora gasped. "No! Stop!" She reached for my bacon. *My bacon!* I growled as I turned away from Nora and ran from her. "We need to cook it first or you'll get sick!"

I didn't stop chewing the meat. No experience in my first life or this could even compare to what I felt. The chewy texture, the divine taste. My jaw felt strange as I chewed, but I couldn't get enough of the flavor. In my euphoric state, I didn't notice when Nora caught up to me and took the basket from my hands.

"Spit it out now!" Nora demanded.

"No!" I growled with my mouth full of bacon.

She grabbed my cheeks and squeezed, halting my ability to chew my food. "Now!"

You won't take this from me! I growled and swallowed the meat. *What a waste.* I opened my mouth to show her it was now empty.

"Why? What's wrong with you? Why did you just eat that?" She let go of my jaw but kept the basket in her arms.

"I couldn't help myself. It smelled so good that I just had to taste it. That was the best meat I've ever had. Melody's cooking has nothing on how good that tasted." Nora's eyebrows rose. "What's wrong?"

"If you get sick, I don't know what to do," Nora whispered. I heard the butcher whistling as he walked back to his work area. "Did you ruin your lunch with that?"

"Nope. In fact, I'd like to eat all meat raw to see if it's all that good." I wagged my tail.

I watched the tension fall from Nora's shoulders. "We have other things to do besides dealing with your antics. We need to go pick up Evandol's gift." Nora stood up and led me out of my new favorite place in this world.

Nora guided me through the town, holding my basket of bacon away from me. *Don't worry, my precious. Mommy will come to your rescue.* Out on the street again, I was subjected to everyone's stares.

Everyone is making me feel as if I don't belong here. I just want to go back home and enjoy my bacon. Eventually, we found ourselves in front of a shop. The sign above the door read, *A High Note*. I could smell something burning inside.

"Something's burning in there. We need to go get help." I pointed at the building where I thought I could smell smoke coming from.

"Don't panic." Nora pulled me back. "There's always something burning in there." She looked at the door with disgust. "If you can smell it out here, I hate to find out what it would do to you if you go in there."

"What are you talking about?" I asked.

"The owner of this store claims that she works better when she smokes." Nora gave me a serious look. "That stuff is terrible. It addles the brain, and then you get addicted to it. Eventually, it drains you of all ambition and drive, leaving you lazy and worthless. Eventually, you'll do almost anything just to get a leaf."

"But what is it?" *It's good to know that she's against drugs. So motherly.*

"It's called haze. Mostly because when you burn it, the smoke is so thick." I could feel the venom flying from Nora's mouth as she spoke. "It relaxes a person and calms them down. I can understand the use of it in a tactical sense or medicinally, but this use is irresponsible. I still can't fault her for the quality of her woodworking. She's the best in town. I just wish she would stop smoking the stuff."

The burning smell was repulsive. "I don't like the smell. Can I just stay outside? You're going in here, aren't you?" I sneered at the building.

"That's fine. So long as she's done with the order, I shouldn't be gone long." Nora moved to enter the store.

Wait, my bacon!

"Um, do you want to hand me the basket so you have two free

hands to grab what you ordered?" I gave her the puppy-dog-eyes look.

"No. If I leave this with you, it'll be gone before I come back. You'll share this with the others." I deflated at her response. *I had to try.* "Just sit still and don't leave or cause trouble. If anyone tries to do anything to you, don't hesitate to come in and get me. Don't try to handle things on your own." Nora gave me a tender smile. "I'll be quick, so don't worry." She opened the door and out came a heavy cloud of smoke. It looked like fog rolling off the sea onto land early in the morning. It was almost completely opaque, and when it made it outside, it rose slowly to the sky. As Nora walked through the smoke, I could see that none of it was getting within a few inches of her. *She's using magic not to breathe the stuff in? What can't magic do?* She walked in and closed the door behind herself.

23

I'M ADOPTED

Once Nora entered the store, I looked around at everyone staring at me. *Maybe this was a bad idea.* I grabbed the handle of the door in preparation, in case anyone moved close to me. *I know I'm a scared little kid right now. Everyone is looking at me, and they are all adults that are bigger than me. Where are the other kids? Why haven't I seen any around yet? I've seen some babies carried by their mothers, but no kids around my age or that of anyone at the orphanage.*

While I stood in front of the door waiting for Nora, I spotted a girl carrying a backpack and walking towards me. *So kids are around, but why am I only seeing one now?* The girl was human, wearing a simple shirt and pants. She had the same rugged boots everyone else wore. Her blond hair went just past her shoulders. Fair skin and blue eyes were her two most striking features. She kept walking towards me, not looking scared, but more disbelieving.

She stopped about five feet away from me. "Are you real?" her high-pitched voice sang out.

I looked around to see if there was anyone else she could have

13 PITCH BLACK CATS

asked that question to. I tilted my head as I looked at her. "Last time I checked, I was."

"So what are you supposed to be?" She looked like she was studying me.

Does she not know what a beastkin is? "I'm not a guard dog, if that's what you're asking. I'm a beastkin." *I understand the position I'm in and how this may look.* "My name is Lucia. My mom is inside getting something she ordered."

The girl's jaw fell to the ground. "Huh?"

What should I do in this situation? "Let's start with introductions. I gave you my name. So what's yours?" I extended my hand towards her.

"Oh, um, it's Zenny." Her cheeks reddened, and she averted her gaze. *She's shy. That's cute. Oh, I get why people say that about me now.* "I've never seen anything like you."

I chuckled. "I get that a lot."

"You do? I'm so sorry. Please forgive me. I didn't mean any offense." The words flew out of her mouth faster than I could register them. She grabbed the sides of her head with her hands and looked mortified as she stared at the ground.

"Stop that." I ran up to her and grabbed her arms. "I mean, I'm not from around here. Most people in town have never seen a beastkin like me before."

"I'm sorry." She lifted her head to look me in the eye.

"Stop apologizing." I pulled her hands from her head. "Just treat me like you would any other girl your age."

"I'm not very good at communicating with other girls my age, or boys my age, or anyone younger than me, or older than me, or adults." Her voice trailed off. *Okay, so she isn't great at dealing with people.* "I'm always afraid I'll say the wrong thing to someone and that they'll get mad and hit me."

Red flag. "Wait, what? Who's going to hit you?" I tried to look at her face more closely. *Is she the victim of abuse?*

"I shouldn't tell you." *She's shutting down.* "You're going to get angry and hit me, aren't you?"

"Oh, I want to hit something alright, but you're not on the list. Right now, I want to hurt anyone who thinks about hitting you." I held her hand so that she wouldn't run away. *This needs to stop. Now.* "I don't have a problem with hurting people, but they have to deserve it. I will never hurt you."

"So you don't want to hurt me like everyone else?" She finally looked at me again. I could see tears forming in her eyes.

"Just ask my mom. I haven't hurt anyone unless they did or tried to do something to me first." I put on a smile.

"It's true." I heard a voice from behind me. I turned to look and saw Nora carrying a wooden case and my basket of bacon. *How did she sneak up on me? I guess it's hard to focus on any one sound with so much going on around me.* "Although it doesn't take her much to get angry."

"See, my mom agrees." I pointed to Nora with my thumb behind me. "By the way, how long have you been there?" I turned my head to look at her. *I need to know how much she heard.*

"Long enough," Nora answered while giving me a wink.

So all of it, probably. Fantastic.

"That's your mother?" Zenny pointed to Nora. I nodded. "You don't look like her at all!"

I shrugged. "I'm adopted."

"She's an orphan who's under my care." Nora walked up to us. "I believe it's better for everyone to be one big, happy family."

"I wonder what that's like." Zenny lowered her head as she whispered the words.

"What you need is a friend. Lucia sounds like a great candidate," Nora cheerfully suggested.

"You can't do that. That isn't how it works. You can't just tell people to be friends," I said as I turned to glare at Nora. *What is this, some kind of story where if someone says, "Let's be friends," we suddenly are?*

"I knew you wouldn't want to be my friend. Nobody does." Zenny's face darkened as she attempted to make herself smaller.

Now I feel guilty. "I never said that I wouldn't be your friend. It's just that I didn't need my mom to tell me what to do." I tilted her chin up. *She really needs to lighten up.* "Since you know a little bit about me, tell me about yourself and what you're doing here."

"Okay. I just turned seven years old last season. I live with my parents, and my aptitude is memorization." Zenny's voice droned as she answered. "I work for Mr. Tobey as a town courier, and I have a delivery for Mrs. Elasha." She took a couple of steps around me, towards the shop that Nora exited from. "I should get back to work. I have lots of extra stops to make today."

"Did you hear that, Lucia? Your new friend already works where you're going to work."

I really wish you would calm down, Nora. "I haven't agreed yet." Zenny stopped walking as I placed a hand on her shoulder. "If I take the job, would you show me the ropes of where the places are in town? I'm really fast, and if you know where everything is, we could make quite a team."

"That will be up to the foreman to decide. But I don't know if I would do a good enough job." Her shoulders dropped even lower.

She's a veritable beacon of happiness. I put both my hands on her shoulders. "We need to work on your confidence. But I'll start tomorrow. If we use your brain and my brawn, we'll be capable of more than you can imagine." *I know I'm reaching with that one, but this girl's depression is going to become contagious. Should I really be the one playing psychologist now? I want to use her memorization aptitude to learn the town as quickly as possible. I'm hardly qualified to fix her.* "We have to get back home, so we'll leave you to your work. Try to have fun; it'll make things easier, I promise." *I know that it's easier said than done.*

"Goodbye, then." Zenny walked towards the store.

"See ya tomorrow." I waved to her.

"Maybe," she said as she turned away.

Nora and I started walking through the streets back home. "You already made a friend. It was nice to see you care about her even though you had just met," Nora said as she walked beside me. "She sounded like something was bothering her, though."

"It sounds like she's never heard a compliment before." *I really could use her memorization aptitude, as long as it works the way I think it does.* "So, how long until lunch?" I asked as my stomach growled.

Nora sighed. "Do you have any priorities other than food?"

"I like food. And now that I know how good raw meat tastes, I really want some." My mouth watered as I reminisced about the bacon. "By the way, I'm feeling fine. See, no adverse effects from the raw bacon." I stepped out in front of her, held my arms up and did a quick spin to show off.

"I guess you're right. If you were going to get sick, you would have been already." Nora sighed. "But we're still going to cook your meat. We can save the raw meat for special occasions and treats."

I kept my grumbling to an inaudible level.

We navigated the streets quickly. People were still staring at me, but it was getting easier to ignore them.

24

HAPPY BIRTHDAY

We arrived back home just as the sun hit its zenith. Nora walked with me to the kitchen, and we gave the bacon to Melody. Melody asked me to help her, since I was available.

After helping, I hurried to my seat and looked at the buffet of food laid before everyone. There were cooked pheasants, and all but one of them were cut in half vertically. Mashed potatoes sat in a bowl. An even larger bowl carried a mixed green salad with strawberries, onions, some type of nut that was chopped up beyond recognition and little white clumps I couldn't identify. A plate of rolls sat next to my bacon. I shed a few tears that it was cooked. *How could they do that to my perfect bacon? I guess it should still taste good, like all the other meats I've had.*

Everyone passed the food around. Nora placed the whole pheasant on my plate with three pieces of bacon. I dove straight for dessert first, my bacon. With no regard for the utensils next to my plate, I handled the greasy slice of meat with my fingers.

The taste was still divine as the bacon rested on my tongue. I savored every moment as I chewed the meat, ignoring Nora's reprimand about table manners. *It's not as good cooked compared to when it was raw, but it's still the best thing ever.* I noticed all the other kids watching my unabashed display of bliss as I ate the bacon. They all turned their attention from me to the bacon and joined me in eating the bacon first. I could see they didn't understand my reaction until Melody reminded them that my palette differed from their own.

After enjoying the meat, I settled down and joined in the conversation about what was next for Evandol. We talked about which knight company he'd joined and that he was a bit more than a glorified guard. After everyone finished eating, Nora disappeared into the kitchen, only to return with the wooden case she got from the store that was full of smoke. She set the case next to Evandol's chair and returned to her own.

Evandol gave it an inquisitive look, then opened it. He pulled out a violin. *It looks a little smaller than any violin I remember. Is that a fiddle? I don't know.*

As he returned the gift to the case, he thanked Nora for it. He looked happy to receive it. *I guess he really likes to play music.*

Each kid went and retrieved their gift for Evandol. Anna gifted him a carved wooden box. It was about four inches wide, four inches long and three inches tall with an intricate engraving on the top, but I didn't look very closely at it. Martin gave him a dagger without a sheath and called it a "parrying dagger." Molly had knit him a hat, wool socks and a scarf for the coming ice season. *I didn't know she could knit. I wonder if she can sew too?* Eleanah handed him a small bottle with a brown liquid in it. Nora didn't look happy when she saw it, but didn't say anything. Oscar pulled out a sheath that fit the dagger Marin gave him earlier. *Did they work that one out ahead of time? Is Oscar lazy or is getting a sheath not a simple task?* Melody handed him a pouch of coins and said that it was the last of this season's stipend.

Evandol's present parade had ended when I heard a loud pounding coming from the other side of the orphanage. "Hey,

Mom, there are some pounding noises coming from the other side of the house," I said, rubbing my jaw, attempting to ease the pain that was now back. *I really need to tell Nora and Phan about this. It's getting worse.*

"I'll be right back," Nora said as she stood to leave the table. She walked to the front of the orphanage.

Everyone just looked at me, confused. "What? I can hear something. I'm not crazy." Their scrutinizing gazes made me squirm in my chair. I heard footsteps heading our way. "Listen, people are coming this way." *I'm still not good enough to differentiate people based on their footsteps.*

A brief wait rewarded us with Nora walking in, followed by two men. One was Phan. The other was a younger adult. His auburn hair was cut short. It fit with his freckled face. He examined all of us with green eyes that resided on a slightly elongated head. *Did someone squish his head while he was young and it stayed that way?* He looked like a guard, with leather armor, a mace on his hip and a fit physique.

"Sorry to intrude on your birthday party." He bowed and spoke in a scratchy voice directed at Evandol. My ears twitched at the sound. "I just wanted to check up on you and lead you to our training grounds once you are packed and ready."

"I'm here to wish Evandol a happy birthday as he sets out for adulthood." Phan's jovial mood seemed forced. "I take it everyone else is in good health?" *I guess it isn't too bad that he's here.*

"We just finished lunch, and everyone gave me their gifts. I have most everything packed already." Evandol stood up and puffed out his chest. *Trying to make a good first impression?*

I ignored everyone joining in on the conversation. My jaw hurt too much to ignore. As Nora walked by my chair, I hopped out, grabbed her hand and led her away from the table. *I don't need everyone to hear this.*

"What is it?" Nora asked with a concerned look on her face.

"Um, you remember what Phan said about if my teeth hurt?" I

looked up at Nora, holding my hands together in front of me. She nodded. "Well, they hurt. They've actually been bothering me all day. It's just now too much to ignore." I tucked my tail between my legs. *I know I shouldn't be afraid of her reaction. You know what they say, better late than never.*

Nora knelt down next to me. "How bad is it?" She placed a hand on my cheek.

I tapped the tips of my claws together. "On a scale of one to ten, and ten being my collar activating, a four." *That was always the way doctors asked about it in hospitals.*

"Alright, it's good that Phannidoritthin is here, then." Nora smiled. She stood and beckoned Phan over.

He looked inquisitive as he walked to us. Everyone else was still having a wonderful time laughing and talking, but I ignored their conversation in favor of blocking out the pain as much as I could. "Lucia said that her teeth are hurting," Nora said as Phan arrived.

Seeing the color drain from Phan's face disturbed me. Because of the scales, I couldn't actually see the color drain from his face. It was more in his eyes. His look shifted to pity and sadness as he turned to me. He got down on one knee. "Open your mouth, please." His somber tone set off all kinds of alarms in my head, but I complied with his wishes and opened my mouth as wide as I could. He grabbed one of my front teeth and wiggled it. *Are my baby teeth starting to fall out? That's not so bad. But why did he look so distraught when Nora gave him the news? What isn't he telling me?* He moved on to another tooth. That one wiggled too. He tested each tooth, and they all wiggled. "I feared this was going to happen. Nora, when was the last time you practiced holding a person completely still with magic?"

"What?" I shouted.

Nora ignored me. "It's been some time, but I have no problem with it. Why?"

"I can only delay pain, not blunt or prevent it." The sides of

Phan's mouth dropped even more. Nora's face joined him in sadness.

"What's happening to me?" I raised my voice even higher.

"Do you have any pliers?" Phan asked.

Every alarm in my head screamed. "What do you mean *pliers*?" Everyone stopped their conversation and turned in my direction. "What are you going to do?" I pointed a clawed finger at Phan. "Answer me!"

"I have good news and potentially upsetting news." Phan put on the fakest smile I had ever seen. "You've likely passed your fifth birthday. But all your adult teeth are coming in at once, and we need to remove your baby teeth to make room for them."

Everyone in the room held their breath for my reaction. *You need to work on your bedside manner.*

I had only one reaction to the impending pain. *Run!*

"Stop her!"

I got three steps towards the door to the courtyard before Nora grabbed my arm with one hand and tried to pull me towards her. I turned and grabbed her wrist and easily pried myself out of her grip. Even though I reached the door to leave, it didn't budge. I slammed my shoulder into it and felt a strange tingling sensation. All I did was earn myself a bruised shoulder. *Strong, my butt.* Nora and Phan were spreading out to corner me.

"Please, we're just trying to help," Phan said as he extended his arms and crouched.

"Stay away from me!" I bolted for a window and jumped through it. I turned around and headed for the courtyard.

As I entered the courtyard, Nora walked through the door that wouldn't move for me. *Of course, magic.* I growled as the elven woman looked at me. "Lucia, stop running. Please."

Your honeyed words aren't going to slow me down. Without stopping, I sprinted past her and jumped for the window to my room. Before she could follow me, I lifted my bed so it blocked the window.

"She headed to her room," Nora called to Phan.

They're going to corner me. To prove me right, I could hear footsteps running down the hall. I released the bed and shoved my bookcase to barricade the door. After that was secure, I returned to holding the bed to the window. *Nora is likely the one who will reach me.*

Someone stepped up to the window, then stopped. "Lucia, please, talk to me." Nora's pleading voice penetrated my barricade and reached my ears. "You're acting childish."

I don't care at this point. "No!" I pushed on the bed harder. "You're going to pull out all my teeth. I don't want to feel that."

"I'm sorry, sweetie, but Phan says this is for your own good."

I don't remember those words being said. Are you just saying that to make me feel better? Well, it isn't working. "Can you put me to sleep? Or make me not feel the pain?" *Why am I bargaining with her?* I shook my head. "I don't believe it. How can all of my teeth come in at once?"

"It's true," Phan answered from behind the door. "If we don't do this now, you'll be in pain for weeks. And I don't know how it would affect your adult teeth to leave them in. The book says if a beastkin's teeth hurt, then they have to be removed. Admittedly, it is light on details. But finding any books on beastkin is a challenge in and of itself." He tried to push on the door, but my bookcase held it closed.

"What are you doing?" I heard a voice from the other side of the door with Phan.

Eleanah? My hero.

"Lucia needs to have her teeth removed." Phan stopped pushing on the door. "All of her teeth are coming in at once."

"And you're scaring her." I heard some footsteps stomping towards my door. "No wonder she ran. I probably would have run too."

"Listen to me, Lucia." Nora's voice softened as she pleaded. "I know you're scared, but this is for your own good. We will do everything we can to ease your pain, I promise."

"How's that going to happen?" My voice cracked. "How are you going to make this hurt less? Tell me how you're going to do that!"

"I know a way to make it so you won't feel anything as we pull your teeth." To help Phan's argument, the pain in my teeth ramped up slightly. "You'll feel very disoriented while I use my magic on you. But there's nothing we can do to put you to sleep until the pain is entirely gone."

"Of course it's magic," I muttered. *I still can't bring myself to trust Phan.* "Maybe the pain will go away on its own and my teeth will fall out naturally."

"What was that?" Nora asked from the other side of my barricade. "Can you at least put your bed down so we can talk normally?"

"Fine, you can come in, but Phan stays on the other side of that door until I say so." A growl escaped my lips as I turned to make sure the door was secure.

I lowered my bed back to the ground to see Nora standing at the window, calm and collected. After I pushed my bed back to where it belonged, she sat in the window with her back facing the inside. She grabbed the top of the window and pulled herself up and brought her legs in. Her dress didn't move like I thought it would. It stayed tight against her legs, as if someone had helped carry her inside.

My heart pounded in my chest as I stood next to my bed. We didn't say anything to each other as she turned to face me, then just stood there.

"You wanted to talk? Let's talk." My tail lashed back and forth behind me.

"Waterfalls." Nora's voice was crystal clear.

"No." I shook my head. "You need to explain this. Why is this happening to me?" I pointed an extended claw at my guardian.

"Everyone has baby teeth that start falling out when they get to your age," Phan answered through the door.

I could feel the pain in my mouth move up to a six, maybe a six and a half. "I know that!" I turned and faced the door and stomped my foot. It still didn't make any sound, which didn't help me calm down. "But why am I so different?"

"Why are you covered in fur and not scales? Why do fish breathe water, not air? It's just how things are," Phan answered. "No amount of wishing is going to change what's happening."

My gaze fell to the floor as I slumped my shoulders. *I don't want to agree to this. I don't want to. But what if they're right? The pain hasn't gotten better. Actually, the pain is getting worse at an alarming rate.*

"Lucia, if you want, I can stay here and make sure you're alright." Eleanah's voice broke me away from my thoughts.

I looked up at Nora. "I'm scared."

Nora's eyes shimmered as she knelt down and extended a hand. "That's understandable. But it's okay, we're here for you. Come here." She held up her other arm, inviting me for a hug. I accepted the invitation. "I know it can be scary. New things usually are. Not only do you need this, but this could be good for you. Getting your adult teeth is just another part of growing up."

My teeth began throbbing and tears rolled out of my eyes. "Let him in." My voice was barely more than a whisper. *I don't have to trust Phan. I'll trust Nora and Eleanah instead. I hope I don't regret this.* "Let them both in."

Nora only removed one arm, but never looked away. She waved her hand, then I heard the bookcase slide across the floor. The door opened slowly as I heard Phan and Eleanah walk in.

"I take it that you've calmed down?" Phan asked as he peered over Nora's shoulder.

"No. But the pain is getting worse." I wrapped my arms around Nora and squeezed.

"Oh. Easy with the hugs," Nora gasped as she tapped my arms. *I may be a little too tight with my hug.*

"Get her on the bed," Phan said.

Eleanah wrapped her arms around me. As she did, I released Nora and dragged my feet as I walked to the bed. Eleanah didn't hurry me.

"Swear to me you won't interfere. This won't be easy and I can't have you distracting me," Phan said as he pointed towards Eleanah.

"I swear," Eleanah replied quickly.

I think everyone else was too scared to follow. I guess I should be grateful they're not lining up to watch my suffering. But I feel better knowing that Eleanah will be here by my side. "Thanks," I said meekly as I looked Eleanah in the eye.

"No problem. I'll be there for you anytime you need me." She gave me a toothy smile.

"You may sit there," I heard Phan say. Eleanah didn't move from my side as we sat on my bed. "I'll be right back with the pliers. Nora, please get her ready to hold her in place." Phan then walked off.

Nora placed a hand on my shoulder. I looked up and saw that distant look in her eye again. "Are you ready?" I nodded. *Please do this quickly, before I change my mind.*

A tingling sensation spread throughout my body, originating from my shoulder where Nora was touching me, before every muscle in my body shut down. *I assume this is the magic Phan was asking Nora about.* My breathing didn't stop, but I couldn't move my arms, legs, tail, head, or ears. Nora and Eleanah caught me and laid me down on the bed. Eleanah pulled my pillow under my head. My heart raced in my chest as it felt like the world closed in around me. *I changed my mind. I can't do this.*

"I'm going to close your eyes for you. Don't panic. I won't let anything bad happen to you," Nora said as she stood in my vision. She gingerly placed her hand on my eyelids and gently closed them.

This isn't doing me any favors or calming me down. Not that it makes a difference. I can't move anything.

My heart raced even faster with each footstep I heard approaching. "As I previously stated, I can only delay the pain for a short time; to mitigate how long she's in pain, we'll need to work quickly." Phan's flat, emotionless voice filled me with dread. "Open her mouth and prepare to concentrate on holding her still."

A familiar tingling sensation returned as it rang through my mind before everything suddenly became fuzzy and focusing on anything became impossible. I heard voices, but I couldn't comprehend them. It was like I was hearing the third word before I understood what the first word said. My mind was both a fog and a swimming pool at the same time, making me feel like I was floating in nothing while also unable to see what I was floating in.

Without notice, my euphoric state ended, and everything became clear again. The memory of the kaleidoscope of colors I saw when I first arrived in this world flashed through my mind. *Wait, if I can think, does that mean whatever they were doing is done?*

My thoughts couldn't continue as a tsunami of pain drowned everything else out. I did the only thing that I believe anyone who felt that level of pain would do.

I screamed.

And I kept on screaming. I didn't even give any thought to the fact that I could move again until my entire world went dark. I willingly fled to the void of unconsciousness so that I wouldn't feel the pain anymore.

25

SHOW AND TELL

I never want to visit a dentist in this world. I woke up in my bed just before nightfall. The dull radiating pain in my mouth was a stark reminder of my current situation. *Right, even if I got food, how am I going to eat it?* I brushed my tongue across my gums, feeling the absence of all my teeth. *There were teeth there this morning, and now they're gone.*

Feeling restless, I sat up in my bed. I looked around and saw that my bedroom door was closed and I was in my pajamas and tucked in for the night.

I felt a slight rumble in my stomach. *Maybe I can find something, but I won't get my hopes up.* I got out of bed and headed for the kitchen to silence my stomach, stalking silently through the halls. *This is fun, being able to walk around quietly and do whatever I want.*

I made it to the kitchen without seeing or waking anyone, but, once I entered the kitchen, that was no longer the case. Nora stood at the counter with a sad look on her face as she stared at a candle. My stomach growled. *Hush, you're going to alert her. I don't want to talk to her yet. Not after that torturous experience. For my own good, right?*

Much to my displeasure, Nora heard my stomach. "You're awake." Tears formed in her eyes. "I'm sorry that you had to go through that. I promise I'll try to make it up to you."

As Nora took a step towards me, I growled at her. *What could you possibly do to make this whole ordeal up to me?* "I guess I deserve that." She took a step back. *No, you deserve much, much worse. I'll think of something.* "Are you okay? Does it still hurt? Will you tell me what's wrong?"

"That's a major understatement!" My lack of teeth ruined my speech. *You know what? I think I'm just not going to talk until my teeth come in. That should solve that problem.*

"When he said he would delay the pain, I didn't think that you would feel all the previous pain in one moment." Nora was on the verge of crying.

Beg some more and I might think about forgiving you.

My stomach growled again, and she smiled. "You sound hungry."

I glared at her and growled again.

She pulled out half a cooked pheasant. "You haven't eaten since lunch. This was going to be your snack." She pulled a knife out and removed the meat from the bone. I just stood still and stared at her. Once she removed all the meat from the bones, she shredded it into small, thin strips. *I guess since I don't have any teeth right now, I can't chew my food.* "Here, go ahead. It should be small enough for you to eat without chewing. Just take it slow."

Disregarding her advice, I grabbed the plate of shredded pheasant she handed me and shoveled it in my mouth quickly. I swallowed the meat bit by bit. The whole time, I glared at Nora. *This won't repair the damage you've done. But it's easier to think things through now that my belly is full.* I rubbed my jaw in a vain attempt to ease the pain. I didn't chew my food so I wouldn't agitate my gums, but my jaw still hurt.

"I have something that will help with the pain." Nora opened an upper cupboard on the top. *No one has opened that cupboard before.* Inside were a few glass bottles without labels. "I was talking with Phannidoritthin. He said that you're likely five years old now. I know it isn't much right now, but happy birthday." She forced a smile.

Yeah, nope. Please try again later.

"In the future, we'll celebrate your birthday today."

I guess I get to say I'm five now. It was a nice birthday yesterday until Phan decided he was going to pull all my teeth out for my birthday present! I'll deal with him later.

Nora grabbed the bottle with a dark amber liquid, then lowered herself to my level and pulled the cork out of the top. The smell of alcohol assaulted my nose, and the potency burned my nostrils. "This is for medicinal use only." She wagged her finger in my direction. She put her finger on the open end. "Open up, please." She was being extra nice with her requests.

What is this going to do to me? See smells, smell sounds, hear tastes? I'm not sure I want to find out. I shook my head.

"Are you afraid of this stuff?" She lifted the bottle partially while still keeping her finger on top. I nodded. *She can't get into my mouth if I don't talk.* "It's whiskey, if knowing helps you agree to this."

Whiskey? At least I know what whiskey is. Oh, I heard about this. There are some who believe that putting a drop of whiskey on a teething child's gums alleviates some of the pain. I know that whiskey won't actually help. I held a finger to stop her. "No, use ice." I tried to stop her from getting me sick.

She gave me a strange look. "Why do you say that?" She still hadn't taken her finger off the bottle.

"Alcohol doesn't numb pain, ice does." I took a step back to defend myself from her. "It's something I know from..."—I focused on my ears to determine if anyone was close enough to overhear—"before," I whispered.

"What did your old world know, anyway?" Nora said; she sounded condescending.

"We could fly without magic. We could also make it so someone didn't feel pain when you operated on them, also without magic." *That should make her both feel bad and maybe listen to what I say in the future.*

Nora cringed. "Alright, we'll try it your way. I want to learn more about this world you came from. Later, of course." She lifted her finger and resealed the bottle. *Is that regret in her voice?* She put the bottle back where she'd found it. Nora extended her hand to me, and I watched as an ice cube formed in front of my eyes. *I have got to learn magic one of these days.*

It finished forming once it was about the size of my thumb. "Go on, take it." I grabbed the ice cube and opened my mouth to place it on my sore gums. "Hold on one moment," Nora interrupted me.

I stood still, the ice cube slowly melting in my hand, my mouth agape.

She leaned down to get a close look at my mouth. "Your teeth are already breaking through," she said as she squinted at my mouth.

"Huh?" I stared blankly at her.

She summoned a hand mirror with magic. *It's always magic with her. Does she do anything without magic?* "Look here." She put the mirror in front of me so I could look at my erupting teeth. Six little white spots were breaking through the inflamed gum line on my bottom jaw. The same story was playing out on my top jaw. *Are teeth supposed to come in that quickly?* I closed my mouth and stared at the mirror. *They were right! What would have happened if they hadn't removed my baby teeth? Would they come in at the wrong angle? Would I be in pain as they kept growing? There's no such thing as braces in this world, so if they weren't correct from the beginning, they would never be right. But this rate of growth is unheard of.*

"Calm down, your recovery aptitude might be responsible," Nora said as the mirror shimmered before vanishing.

Is she reading my thoughts? They made the best decision with the education they had. But did they really have to inflict that much pain?

Taking a few deep breaths, I calmed down. The throbbing pain in my mouth helped straighten out my priorities. I placed the ice cube on my gums and could feel the relief begin. I relaxed as I moved the ice cube along my gums within my mouth. However, the feeling didn't last long. Soon the ice melted, and it left me seeking more relief. "Another one?" *I guess I can't stay that angry with Nora. But if she tries anything like this again, I will not be held responsible for my actions! Phan, on the other hand, has hell coming his way next time I see him.* I looked at Nora with pleading eyes. "Please?"

"Alright, but it's past bedtime." Nora began creating another ice cube in her palm.

"How about I run a few laps outside first, then a bath and bedtime? I'm not tired right now." *I've been doing a lot of talking since I said that I wasn't going to talk. It isn't a problem since Nora can understand me. Also, who knows, maybe by tomorrow I'll have some teeth already grown in.*

"Alright." Nora conceded to my wishes.

She finished the small ice cube, and I greedily took it and placed it on my gums to alleviate more of the pain. Once my mouth was dealt with, I took off for the courtyard. I didn't wait for Nora to follow me outside. I ran my laps and, afterwards, Nora filled the bathtub for me. During the bath and just before I went to bed, I received more ice cubes to help with the pain, and I got some sleep.

I awoke before the sunrise. I could feel something was off in my mouth. *It still hurts, but not as much as last night.* I moved my tongue to inspect the progress of my teeth. I felt several and nearly shouted. *I need to see this.* After I leaped out of my bed, I left my room and headed for Eleanah's room. *Nora won't give me another mirror after I broke the last one.*

Once I was there, I surveyed her room. Eleanah was sleeping soundly when I turned and looked at the bed. *Good, opening the door wasn't enough to wake her up.* Her small stand mirror was on her desk.

The six teeth that were poking through the gums yesterday had decided that they didn't need to be shy anymore, but weren't ready to reveal themselves completely. My new permanent teeth were nothing like my baby teeth. These teeth were sharp. The front teeth were round and narrow, but I could feel a point on them. My canines were larger and were visibly sharp.

I admired my incisors and canines. Once I looked past the first six teeth, I could see another three on each side growing in also. *How do I have twenty-four teeth already?* I stood there, awestruck, with my mouth open.

I heard a rustling coming from Eleanah's bed, and I turned to see her rubbing her sleepy eyes. "What are you doing in here?" She looked at me.

She isn't at her best first thing in the morning, is she?

"I..." I tried to gather my thoughts. When I looked at the mirror in my hands, everything came back to order. "I wanted to see my teeth. I knew you had a mirror. Sorry, I didn't mean to wake you." I lowered my head.

"Oh, I guess that's alright. I couldn't sleep that well last night after hearing that scream from you yesterday." Eleanah sat up in her bed.

"The one I made before I passed out?" I set the mirror back where I had found it.

"Yeah, that one." I watched Eleanah's eyes go blank. Her personality shifted. "So, your teeth are already coming in? Lemme see." She smiled and patted the bed right next to her. I jumped up and showed her my teeth freely. She stared at them with wide eyes, then shifted her head around as she studied my teeth closely. "They are growing really fast. Does it hurt?"

"Yeah, but less today than last night. The ice helped." *I can talk much better now that I have teeth again. I guess worrying over the fact that I lost all of my teeth so quickly was unnecessary, but the pain was still not worth it.*

"I'm relieved to see you're okay. Everyone said that they heard your scream from across the building." Her voice turned somber again. "Is there anything I can do for you? And what do you mean, 'ice helped?' Didn't Mom use the whiskey?" Her gaze turned to focus on me.

Oh, right, she won't understand that I reincarnated. I need to come up with something. "Everything hurts less when I'm cold, so I thought that if I put something cold in my mouth, it would hurt less. It worked." I smiled nervously. *I hope she buys it.*

"Are you getting your memories back?" She jumped up and grabbed my hands and stared at me with glowing eyes.

"No. I don't remember why I knew that." *Okay, deflected for now. I still have to sell the amnesia act for a little longer.*

Eleanah deflated at my response. "Oh." We sat on the bed together for a while. Neither one of us knew what to do.

Eleanah was the first to speak up. "Are you going to do your morning run now?" She lifted her head at me again.

"No, I have a job that I'm starting today. At least, I think I'll start today," I said with no confidence.

"Where are you going to work? Hopefully you won't be working for a cobbler like me. It's boring and repetitive. Is your job going to be fun? Will you be able to control your anger?" She bombarded me with questions.

"First, I'll be working for Tobey as a courier. I don't know where everything is, and I'm more scared than excited. And what do you mean 'control my anger?' Why do you all always ridicule me there?" I pouted.

"Because you really need to work on it."

"You don't need to keep telling me that." I hopped off the bed. "How about we change topics? I'm kinda hungry. What about you?"

"I guess we can get ready for the day," Eleanah said as she swung her legs off the bed. "Off you go. Brush all your fur. I know how long you take to get all of it done. I'll see you at breakfast." She nudged me to the door.

As I passed the mirror, I smiled at it one last time. Something felt right as I admired my new teeth. *I could get used to this.* I continued to smile all the way to my room. *Pain will not ruin my mood today.*

Everything seemed to have returned to normal again, except for one more empty chair across the table from me. Nora explained to them that yesterday would be my birthday. She said she would make it up to me today. After breakfast was done, Nora and I made ourselves ready to leave for Tobey's office. I enjoyed another stare-filled stroll through town towards the north gate.

26

I GUESS THAT CONCLUDES NEGOTIATIONS

It wasn't long before I found myself in front of a grand brick building that belittled all the surrounding buildings in both size and aesthetics. The face was pristine, and I couldn't find a single deformity or irregularity. Above the wax-coated double door entrance hung a sign that read, *Four Winds Trading Headquarters.*

I guess he is quite the big deal. People entered and exited, and they, like everyone else in town, gave me strange glances. *These people better get used to seeing me around town if I take this job.* We joined the people entering the building.

Entering was shocking. The entire building looked like a giant post office. People were walking up to the counter with papers or packages and leaving with the other. Others walked up with nothing and talked with people at the desk and exchanged bags of money. Behind the counter, I could see what looked like a warehouse and people moving about, but it was hard to get any details while looking through the wooden square lattice structure. The inner walls of the building were wood, despite the brick exterior. I looked around and saw that every piece of wood was also sealed in wax.

I stood staring at everything like a tourist while Nora went to the front desk and asked something. The cacophony of conversations left me a bit disoriented. *Why is it even louder in here?* All the people and things moving around, everyone talking over one another, and the smell of the city all threatened to send me fleeing out of the whole town. Nora saw me still standing and gawking at everything, took my hand and walked me through a door behind the desk.

The noise level decreased drastically once the door closed behind us. A human woman was waiting for us. "Please follow me." Her tone was polite yet direct.

We followed her through the corridor, up some stairs, to a hallway lined with doors. The last door at the far end had a name engraved on the metal plaque: *Tobey Coinwhisper.*

So he has a last name, too. Why do only a few people have last names? I don't have one, at least according to the oracle stone.

The lady led us to the door, stood to the side and waved to the door as if she was presenting it to us. "Master Tobey is expecting you."

Nora knocked on the door before opening it and entering. I followed her closely. *This guy has way too much money on his hands.* Metal chairs with cushions on both the back and seat circled a large area rug with artistic designs of eagles. There was a fireplace with paintings of Tobey resting above the mantel. Bookcases filled to the brim with books lined the wall on our right. Heavy blackout curtains adorned windows that extended from the floor all the way to the ceiling. They were currently tied neatly open to allow the natural light of the day. *Is that a balcony?* A desk made of dark wood shone in a way I had never seen wood shine in this world before.

"How much money does this guy have?" I blurted out.

"This guy has a lot." I heard a familiar masculine voice from yesterday, even though the tone wasn't happy. I instinctively ducked my head and realized I had just thought out loud.

"Please forgive her outburst; she's not acquainted with seeing such displays of wealth." Nora grabbed my shoulders to keep me close to her. *I can't believe I said something so stupid. Me and my impulse control.* "We're here about your job offer for Lucia." Nora carried herself differently in front of Tobey. She held her back rigid, her feet square, and she never removed her gaze from him.

"Yes, I'm glad that you came to negotiate terms." He stood up from his throne. The high-back chair had a padded back and intricate carvings for the back supports and top rail. The chair looked to be made of the same dark wood that the desk was, and it shone with the same sheen. If I saw that chair in a throne room, I wouldn't be surprised.

"Um, yesterday, we met one of your workers, Zenny. Is it possible that I could work with her?" My voice was unsteady as more alarms in my head told me to run. *She was nice enough, and I know she'll be much more of a help to me than anyone else they send to train me.*

"Ah, yes, her." His face soured at my request. "Honestly, that girl should find a new vocation. She isn't cut out to be a courier."

That was blunt. He really isn't that nice. But I can use her. I need to get this guy to agree to my demands. I scrounged up what courage I could find. Straightening myself, I stood similar to how I saw Nora standing. "What if I said I could help with that?" I asked as I extended an open palm towards him.

"And what could you possibly do?" He gave me a stern look as he placed his hands on his desk and leaned forward. "Let me guess, next you're going to tell me how I am to run my operation."

I flinched and pulled my arm back.

"She doesn't mean anything like that." Nora quickly stepped around me. Her voice revealed her displeasure. "They've quickly become friends, and a friendly face will do wonders for her mood."

"I guess I can follow your logic." Tobey relaxed and stood straight up again. "Now, back to the business at hand. I have a standard rate of three coins a day for couriers. I can arrange something so you can work with your friend. You will work two days a week as we agreed yesterday. I will allow Nora to decide those days." He lifted a piece of paper off his desk and began reading it. "This contract will stay in effect until the next water season and then you can renegotiate terms or quit if you would like." He lowered the paper to return his attention to us.

I leaned around Nora. "Can I ask a few questions?" I raised my hand like I was in school again.

Tobey nodded. "By all means. I'll answer any questions you have as well, Nora."

"How long will I work each day?" *It seems like that's something I need to know.*

"From sunrise until the sun is at its zenith," he answered quickly.

"Okay, do you always do contract negotiations at the beginning of the water season?" *It helps to know a few things about workplaces. I don't remember any of the places that I worked or what I did. But I know that vacation time, a 401k and overtime might be things I shouldn't bother to ask about.*

Tobey's look turned from friendly to concerned. "I do them every water and wind season. Why?" His eyes narrowed on me.

"Curiosity." I smiled and turned away from him. "My next question is for you, Mom."

"Yes, what is it you want to know?" She gave me a lighthearted smile as she looked down at me.

"How much do you spend on my food each day?" *I need to know if three coins, whatever they are, are worth it.*

She grimaced. "Seven."

My heart broke when she gave me that number. *Are you saying I'm that expensive? I have to work for three days just to feed myself for one day!* Shaking my head, I turned to look at Tobey. I could see by the look in his eye that he knew exactly what I was going to say next. "Pay me seven coins a day," I said with every ounce of conviction I could summon.

Tobey closed his eyes slowly before opening them again. "I

believe I already stated that all couriers start at three a day. But after hearing about your financial predicament, I can increase it to four. However, I can't show favoritism."

"But I'm not just any courier." *I think I need to find some kind of leverage. The key to any negotiation is confidence. Although I think I need to bluff a bit on this one.* "I have the physical aptitude. I'm easily worth two other couriers. And I can start today, right now, and show you what I can do." I clenched my jaw tight.

Tobey stared at me hard and unblinking. *He's looking for a tell. He thinks I'm bluffing. It is kinda difficult to tell if I'm bluffing since even I don't know if I'm bluffing. If given a chance, I kinda want to see what I'm capable of too.*

"How old did you say you were?" His face didn't move.

"Phan believes she has reached five years of age, considering her recent dental development." Nora placed a hand on my shoulder. I kept my face as still as I could and never turned from the staring contest I found myself in. "She has the physical aptitude. I was there when we read it from the oracle stone."

"So you would vouch for her?" Tobey asked while staring at me as still as a statue. *Does this man ever blink? My eyes are watering.* My heart started racing.

"I do." Nora's tone darkened at his question.

Just as Nora answered him, Tobey relented from staring me down. "I will pay you six. However, if I find that you haven't kept up with your end of the bargain, I will drop your payment back to three and you'll pay me back the difference you received up to that point." His face grew darker.

I guess that's the best I can get. It is a lot closer to what I need.

Tobey spent a moment scratching out something on the paper and writing something else. He placed the paper on the edge of the desk and placed a pen on top of it. "Sign the bottom line."

Nora gently nudged me towards the desk. I never dropped my stoic facade. *His challenging glare is setting something off in my instincts. I want to growl at him and accept his challenge, but Nora will have something to say about that. I need to vent my aggression after we leave.*

I picked up the contract and read it thoroughly, even though it took me a while. There were a few spots I had to reread just to make sure I understood them. Everything he had said earlier was on there. The number three was crossed out and six was written over it in the section that talked about my pay. *I wish all contracts were this straightforward.* Not bothering with the pen, I took a claw to my thumb and gave myself a slight cut on my pad. I placed my thumb on the line he mentioned and put the contract back on Tobey's desk.

The look on his face was priceless. *I think I broke him.* "Are you telling me I just lost a negotiation to a child that can't write?" His jaw was on the floor, and he didn't even try to hide his surprise.

"I know how to write. I'm just not good at it." *That's being optimistic.*

"We are going to work on that, young lady. We can't have you signing everything with a bloody thumbprint," Nora scolded.

I heard a thump and saw that Tobey had dropped himself in his very expensive chair. He started laughing. "Go ask Meline outside to direct you to Decklin," he said between laughs. *Yup, his sanity has gone on vacation.*

After stepped away from Tobey's desk, I noticed that the urge to run away hadn't gone away. Even though I received a higher pay, I never felt the victory of overcoming his challenging stare. I also noticed my heart was still pounding in my chest.

I need to get out of here. I started walking out, and Nora walked with me. When I opened the door, I forced myself to let go because if I hadn't, I would have slammed it so hard that it might have broken. The woman who escorted us here was present. Nora closed the door courteously, and once the door closed, I closed my eyes and tried to envision waterfalls.

"We were told you could send us to someone with the name

13 PITCH BLACK CATS

Decklin," Nora said to the woman who patiently waited for our meeting to conclude.

"Waterfalls," I interrupted. *I need to calm down or I'm going to seek something to rip or break apart.*

"Excuse me?" The woman's voice rose to an irritating pitch. I focused on my breathing and visualizing waterfalls again.

"Please wait. This is important for her." I could hear Nora tell the lady to shut up, although she was nice and polite about it. *I wouldn't have been.*

27

SHOW OFF

The woman led us out of the post office after I took some time to calm down. It worked, albeit marginally. Nora led me through the streets, following the directions Meline had given us. She hadn't given us any street names. Every time we needed to turn, she told us a shop name and a cardinal direction. Nora told me it was standard practice for this entire city to have shops on corners. Residencies weren't allowed at corners unless it was a three-way, then that rule got an exception. *Now that I need to find my way, I should start paying attention to where I'm going instead of just following others.*

The directions we followed led us to a small house. There were hundreds more just like it on the street. It was a quaint wooden dwelling with a single level and a few windows. We walked to the door and Nora gave it a knock.

I heard loud, uneven footsteps approaching. The door opened and revealed a man. I had to suppress a gag at the sight of him.

He was wider than he was tall, and I could smell him. *Ugh, could you please bathe more often?* He reeked of body oder that he failed to cover up with an equally horribly smelling perfume. His unpleasant smell went along with his greasy, thinning hair, which he had combed over in a fruitless attempt to mask his balding. He looked like the stereotypical unscrupulous merchant who would sell his sister if he had one. He wore a brightly colored green coat. He wore nothing but bright-colored clothes.

"Good morning. It's a pleasure to make your acquaintance. I'm Decklin." He spread his arms out like he was going to hug Nora. "I never thought that I would meet you in person, Nora."

Why does this guy know who she is? Is he a stalker? Did someone tell him to expect us, or is she just that famous?

"It's good to meet you too," Nora answered politely. "But the one you should greet is Lucia here." She held me with a hand on each shoulder in front of her.

"Hi." I waved at him. *Please don't touch me.*

He turned his attention from Nora to me. I could see the surprise on his face. "Oh, uh, a beastkin? Uh, well, I guess good day to you, little one," he stammered. *What kind of greeting is that?* "Did you need something from me? It looks like you aren't here to send a package or a letter."

"You're right. I'm here to start working." I tried to put on a big smile, not showing any teeth. *Don't scare the man...yet.* "Is Zenny here? I was told I could work with her. She's going to show me the ropes and where everything in this city is."

"Huh?" He responded by staring at me slack-jawed.

I guess that was a bit much all at once.

"Is it alright if Lucia goes inside?" Nora asked as she nudged me into the building.

Decklin closed his mouth and shook his head. "Yes, please, come in. If Zenny's delivery went smoothly, she'll be here shortly."

Nora stopped me before I entered. Her face was serious. "Now, I want you to behave. But, most importantly, I want you safe. If anyone causes you trouble, if it's Decklin here, someone on the streets, or a person you're making a delivery to, I want you to run away from them and find me. Do not, under any circumstances, handle it on your own." She kneeled down and grabbed my hands in hers.

I think this moment is usually the part where I'm supposed to be the clingy one. Not the other way around.

"I promise, Mom, I'll behave." I gave her a sincere hug. Nora returned the hug, and we embraced until Decklin cleared his throat. "Don't worry, I'll be back for lunch." I gave a toothy smile and a thumbs-up.

I entered the building as Nora watched me. I watched her as the door closed, and I think I saw a tear roll down her cheek. *She really acts like she's my mother.* Keeping a respectable but comfortable distance from the smelly man, I followed him as he gave me a quick tour of the place and gave me the short version of what they expected of me. *It's an easy enough job; just grab a parcel and deliver it. Because someone already paid for the package, I just need to make sure it ends up in their hands or in the hands of someone close to them. After each delivery, come back and get the next one. I just have to try to get as much done each day as I can. There will always be more tomorrow because of the staffing shortage. Right now, we're one of two operating outposts, as he called them.*

As we were going over the final bits of information, Zenny arrived. "You actually came," she said under her breath. *She doesn't know that I can hear that.* Zenny stared at the ground, shifting from one foot to the other.

I ran up to Zenny, leaving Decklin behind. "Of course I came. I said I would." I sounded as cheery as possible. *Hopefully I didn't scare her with that.* "Oh, by the way, these things on top of my head are my real ears and they are extremely good at picking up even the slightest sounds. So please don't yell or make any loud noises." *I hope that my olive branch helps her open up.*

"Oh." *She closed up even more. Come on, work with me here, girl.* "I'll just get another package and go."

"Hold up." I put a hand on her shoulder. "I think we need to change things up a bit for you."

"What do you mean?" She looked at me with wide eyes.

"Yes, what do you mean?" Decklin echoed. I ignored him.

Is that fear or hope I see in her eyes?

"Remember yesterday when I said that I needed you to help me learn where everything is in town?" Zenny nodded. "Well, how about we make a system for us?" I grabbed her hand and attempted to lead her to the deliveries yet to be made.

"I don't know what you mean? What's a system?" She looked at me, confused.

I get it. She's only seven. If she knew about systems and efficiency, then that would be strange. Just like what I'm doing right now. Decklin is probably looking at me with his jaw on the floor right now. I turned to look at Decklin and found that his jaw had found its new home, firmly in contact with the floor.

"Decklin, do you by chance have a spare map?"

My question snapped him out of his stupor.

"Yeah." He walked over to a cupboard and pulled out a piece of paper. I stared at his jacket as he extended the map to me. *Now that I think about it, I haven't seen many clothes in bright colors. Nora has several colored dresses, as does Anna. But Eleanah and the rest of us have mostly gray and dull-colored clothes. Most people I've seen wear brown, tan, gray, or black.* "Here, take it. You need it?" His hand was shaking.

I grabbed it gingerly, trying not to touch his hand.

"Yes. Thank you." I gave him another closed-mouth smile. I took Zenny's hand and dragged her to the back with all the packages. As we were about to leave his view, I turned to tell him one last thing. "Don't worry about us. I have my secret weapon here." I pointed to Zenny. *If he can unscramble his brain enough to say anything, I wonder what he'll tell Tobey.*

Once we were no longer in view of Decklin, Zenny stepped in front of me. "You can't talk to the foreman like that! He's in charge and can make it so we don't get paid."

You're worried about your pay? Sorry, kid, I'm about to throw you for a loop.

"Don't worry about him. I'll make sure we both get paid." I gave her a thumbs-up. "Listen, I have a plan and I need you to trust me on this one. Okay?" *I need her to follow my instructions over his if this is going to work.*

"I can do whatever you need me to do. But I wouldn't get your hopes up. I might not be that good." *There's that ray of sunshine I missed.* She was looking back at the ground, avoiding my eyes.

"I plan on using your memorization aptitude and my physical aptitude together," I whispered. "You have the locations of everything in town memorized, correct?" She nodded. "See, you're already perfect for the job."

"But I'm slow and I can't carry heavy things," she whined.

"I don't need you to worry about delivering packages." I held up a finger.

"I thought I was a courier. Isn't my job about delivering packages and letters?" She looked at me with teary eyes.

"I have a more important job for you. Don't worry about the foreman or anybody else. What they don't know won't hurt them." I gave her a sly wink. "All you need to do is direct me through town and give me directions to where everything needs to go. I'm faster than you, and I can run through town even faster if you give me directions." *I'm trying to cheer you up. Accept my praise!* "You're the perfect one for the job. Nobody else can do it like you. You can write, can't you?" I realized I should have started with that question. *Whatever. If she can't, she can at least point it out on the map.*

"Of course I can write. Why? Can't you?" Her face showed small signs of her sadness leaving her.

"I can, but I stink at it and it makes me so angry that I snap chalkboards in half." I released a low growl. *That is going to be a sore spot for a long time.*

"You mean I can do something you can't? I can be useful?" Her voice sounded like it was about to break.

Got her! Now to reel her in.

"Absolutely! If I'm honest, there are a lot of things you can do better than me." I held my arms out like I was displaying her to herself for a moment before returning them to my side. "Where do you get this idea that you're useless?" *I don't know if I should ask this now or wait. But she might answer since she's the happiest I've seen her yet.*

"My father keeps saying that I'm useless, and he says my mother is just as bad." She turned her head away from me as she stared at the floor and crossed her legs.

"Does your dad drink a strange-smelling drink, stumble around a lot and slur his words?" *I hope the answer is no.*

Zenny tilted her head to the side. "Slur his words?"

"His words run together and sound weird when he says them." *Please say no.*

"How did you know?" Her face never changed.

Well, that explains everything. Now what? I guess that's a problem for another day. At least now I know her father is an alcoholic. I can't solve every problem. I'm supposed to be a kid.

"Don't worry about that. Let's concentrate on work right now. I have to make a good impression on my first day, after all." I put a smile on my face and hoped it would grow on her.

"So, what do you want me to do?" She gave me her wide-eyed look again.

Okay, there is definitely hope in her eyes. "We need to pick a package, determine where it goes on the map and then you have show me how to get there." I picked up the closest package. It was a small box, about the size of a book. "This one will make a great start."

She read the paper that sat next to the package. "Okay, that one goes here." She put her finger on the map near the center of the city. "We're here." She pointed to a building near the northeast corner of this round city.

"Okay, that isn't that far, I think." I grabbed her backpack. "I'm going to use this. Is that alright?"

"But what am I going to use?" She looked at me with sadness.

You weren't paying attention earlier, were you?

"You aren't going to use anything. You aren't going to leave here," I said in a rough tone. "Your job isn't to deliver anything. You're going to plan out where each package and letter goes, then write the directions on a piece of paper so I can read them." I picked up the map. I tried to memorize what route I needed to take.

"Okay, but how many do you want me to do? And where am I going to get a pen and paper?"

She's calmed down some but is still sweating the small stuff. She's at least looking me in the eye now. "Do as many as you can. I'll be back before you know it. I'm sure if you asked Decklin nicely, he could get you a pen at least. If you need to use the paper with the details on it for the directions, go ahead and do it," I said before setting out. *I hope I didn't forget anything. If I did, I hope she can figure anything else out.* I placed the box in the bag and put my arms through the straps.

I walked past Decklin as he sat at a small desk facing the front door. "Off to your first delivery? Why isn't Zenny going with you?" He stared at me, perplexed.

"She and I have a new way of doing things. I deliver and she navigates." I smiled warmly at him. "Don't worry, I'll show you this will work better than anything before."

"Are you serious?" he whispered.

"I am. Watch me leave. You'll see something really cool." I waved at him to follow me as I headed out.

He got up and walked to the doorway behind me.

I walked to the street and saw that there was room to run, but not sprint my fastest. *I need to avoid running into people. That would cause unneeded complications.* I turned to look at Decklin and saw his bored face. I winked at him and took off. Everything blurred, but I could make minor adjustments to avoid colliding with someone. My tail acted as a rudder and I made my perfect ninety-degree turns when I needed to.

Nora was right, I needed to do this. This is way more fun than running in the courtyard. I feel like this is a game. How fast can I go and not hit someone? The feeling of the wind through my fur is fantastic. If this city didn't stink, then this would be perfect. Now to concentrate on getting to my destination without getting lost. It looks like people are making way for me. How nice of them! That makes things even easier. This is the final turn and it should be the third building on the left.

28

I'M GONNA TELL MOM ON YOU

That was a nice little old lady. I guess I shouldn't have worried that everyone was going to be racist towards me. Maybe they're the minority and most people just don't know what to make of me since they've never dealt with a beastkin before. I turned and ran back. There were a lot more people out and wandering about now. I found that most people gravitated towards the sides of the street, leaving the center as my path of least resistance. I had to go a little slower for two reasons. First, I was getting tired. Second, people weren't moving out of the way as much. *I need to remember to do my longer deliveries in the early morning when I have more room to run and more energy.*

I made it back to the outpost and walked in. I panted heavily as I took a moment to recover. *Okay, that was longer than I anticipated. I really hope I can get in better shape with this job.*

"Wait, you're back already?" Decklin stood up from his desk. "I know I saw you take off with a sprint, but did you really sprint there and back already?"

"Yeah, and I just need a moment to catch my breath before the next delivery." I took deep breaths, fighting to fill my lungs with air.

"Which package did you take?" He looked at me with concern.

"A book for a little old lady by the name of Alison. She was friendly too," I said, trying to stand straight again.

"What's wrong with you, child?" I flinched at his loud voice. "What good are you if you only make one delivery a day? We're backlogged and need to catch up. Then you say that Zenny doesn't need to do any deliveries and you come back looking like that after your first delivery..." He never lowered his volume. I was covering my ears to lessen my pain. "I have half a mind to tell Tobey..."

"Shut up!" I screamed. *You need to stop talking and give me a chance to explain.* I saw Zenny run into the room. "I have the recovery aptitude. Give me a few moments and I'll be ready for another delivery. I know what I'm doing," I growled.

"Who do you think you are to tell me what to do?" His volume dropped, but his aggression rose. "I'm in charge here, not you. You will do what I say, when I say it and how I say it. Is that clear?" Decklin stomped his feet as he took a few steps towards me.

Didn't this guy just stand there and watch me implement a new system for Zenny and me to work with? Does he think he needs to assert his dominance over me? Is he afraid of a five-year-old? Dude, get your priorities straight.

"No." I stood up straight and stared at Decklin.

"Please don't do that." Zenny, finally driven to action, ran up to me. "Don't argue with the foreman. If you go away, how will I be useful?" she pleaded, with tears forming in her eyes.

I looked at her with wide eyes. *What have I done?*

"But he started it. He was yelling at me first." I pointed at the disgusting man. *Did I just rationalize and explain myself to a seven-year-old?* "He's wrong. If he was paying attention, he would notice that my breathing was already slowing down. Even adults can be wrong."

"Didn't you say you had the physical aptitude before? Physical or recovery, which one do you have?" Decklin took another step towards me while pointing his finger at me.

He heard that?

"Both. I have them both." I growled at Decklin again.

"Two?" Decklin stopped dead in his tracks. His tone lost all aggression and returned to a normal level. "Impossible."

"You shouldn't lie like that." Zenny grabbed my hand with both of hers.

"I'm not, though." I looked at Zenny, then turned my attention to Decklin. "It's improbable, not impossible." *I get it, having two aptitudes is a rare occurrence, but why do people keep having that reaction?* "I hate having to keep explaining that."

"Implob, inrobable, in..." Zenny's tongue fumbled around.

"Improbable." I corrected the girl. "It means unlikely or not common."

Zenny's eyes went wide while she gawked at me.

Decklin's face shifted. It looked like he was thinking about something. "Whatever, get back to work. It won't be long before your work for the day is over." He walked to his desk again. "I need to send a report saying that some work was done today."

He isn't angry anymore. It sounds more like he has something else on his mind and he's going through the motions right now.

His sudden mood shift once he learned I had two aptitudes doesn't sit well with me. But I can't do anything about it. Besides, I have to get back to work. I've had enough rest.

"Let's get back to work, Zenny." I grabbed her hand and led her back to all the packages we needed to deliver. "Do you know which ones are closer to where we currently are?"

"I think I can find one or two that are nearby. Why?" She walked over to a larger square cube, grabbing the map along the way.

"There are a lot of people in the streets, which makes it harder for me to run. We can save the longer deliveries when there are fewer people on the streets earlier in the morning." I followed her to size up the package.

"How are you getting all these ideas?" She read the paper lying on top of the box. She turned to me and pointed to a spot just a few streets down. "This one goes here, to a man named Hermon. This is heavy. We may need to get a cart for it."

"I guess you could say that I think differently than other people." *I can't tell her all my secrets yet. Especially here, with Mr. Suspicious being too close for comfort.* "Watch this." When I lifted the box, it was heavier than I expected, but I could manage. I left poor Zenny to wonder at my strength.

I walked towards the door and noted Decklin's surprised face when I passed him. *Believe me now? Do people have a habit of lying about their aptitudes? Although he did accept that I had two a little too quickly. Something feels off about that man.* I followed the simple route I'd seen on the map, carrying a box a little more than half my size down the populated streets. People stared at me with curiosity. *I'm glad they have a new look for me. If I saw someone my size doing what I'm doing right now, I might have the same look. I can't run with something this big compared to me. Finally, my destination. Good, this thing was getting heavy. I might be strong for my size, but even I have limits.*

I completed my delivery, and the trip back to grab another delivery went without incident. *It looks like I have time for one more before I'm done for the day.* I grabbed a letter and instructed Zenny to prepare for tomorrow before going home. I made my delivery quickly, dodging through people and moving as quickly as I could. Once I made it back to report the success of my task, I saw Tobey standing at the door, talking with Decklin. *Well, this can't be good.*

Tobey turned once Decklin nodded his head towards me. "Three deliveries, even after a late start. And one delivery was halfway across town," Tobey said. He was staring me down again. I stopped with plenty of distance to run away if I needed to. "You didn't tell me you had two aptitudes."

"You never asked," I replied sarcastically.

"Alright then, you want to play that game?" He glared at me. "Come inside." He stepped to the side of the door.

"Actually, I'm quite alright out here." *I smell a trap, figuratively, not literally. Although I might be able to smell some traps now. Food for thought, later.*

"Do you wish that all passersby hear your secrets?" He waved his hand to the crowded street.

"You assume that I have secrets and that I would tell you if I did. Which I don't." I watched Tobey turn redder. *Angry people make mistakes. But I don't want to argue with him again.* "How about I just get my pay and we go our separate ways?" I held out my hand.

"If you don't tell me what you're really doing here, I'll keep your pay." He held a small leather pouch and gave it a quick shake.

"If you don't pay me, I'll just tell my mom." I folded my arms and stood defiantly. "I did my job and I deserve my pay. And if you think you can catch me before I get back to the orphanage, I'll tell you now, you will fail." I returned his angry glare. *Time for my poker face again.* I flattened my ears, then started flicking my tail back and forth.

I could see the gears turning in his head. *Did his eye just twitch?* "You get half. You worked half of the day." He never took his eyes off me as he pulled three coins out.

"She gets paid how much?" Decklin screamed.

I guess he didn't know how much I was paid.

Tobey walked up to me without blinking and held his hand out with the three coins. I extended my open hands to catch them as he dropped them. Once I safely cradled them and closed my hands, Tobey grabbed one of my wrists with the other hand. A smirk grew on his face.

I growled. "Let go," I said as menacingly as I could. I then bared my now very sharp teeth at him. The corners of my vision started turning red.

He flinched at the sight of my teeth and let go of my wrist.

I took off for the orphanage as fast as I could. I even accidentally bumped into several people, but I could still keep going in a mostly straight line. People parted and created a path for me once I started pushing. I continued all the way home. I burst through the door. "Mom!"

"What?" I heard someone running from the hall. I ran towards the voice. *It sounded like Nora, and that would likely be her running this way.* Once I saw Nora and the giant ball of fire floating in her hand, I panicked. I scraped my claws through the floor to stop myself, then turned around and sprinted towards the classroom.

"Lucia, where are you going? What's wrong?"

I stopped as I got to the door. I turned and saw that the fireball was gone. *She needs to stop running around corners with such dangerous magic active. She's going to scare me to death with that.* "It's Tobey," I said while panting heavily.

"What did he do?" I saw her get angrier with each word.

"What's going on here?" a third voice called from the front door. I then heard another set of footsteps heading our way. "Nobody move!"

"What?" Both Nora and I stopped and turned to look at the third voice.

It was a male in heavy plate armor—a familiar, gleaming white suit of armor. He stood with his face covered in a helmet and his sword drawn, and held it out to the two of us. "Nora and the beastkin kid. I'm glad you're okay. Where did they go?" He sounded like he was on a mission.

"Who?" I asked.

"The intruder. Which way did they go?" He took a few steps in, but his head was looking everywhere.

Wait, that plume on his head looks vaguely familiar.

"There's no intruder, Allen." Nora stood relaxed.

I knew it.

"That's good to hear." The knight sheathed his sword and took his helmet off. Allen's kind green eyes kept surveying the room. "I was worried given the number of missing persons cases that have been coming up. Why did your door just fly open?"

"That was me." I timidly raised my hand.

"Yes, please explain why you just ran in here screaming for me. What did Tobey do?" Nora turned to look at me.

"After I delivered my last package for the day, he was waiting for me. He and Decklin were talking, and he wanted me to tell him my secrets." *Wait, keep a tight lip on my secrets. Allen is here. I have to remember that.* "First, he wanted me to go into the building alone with him and Decklin, but then we argued in the street. I demanded my pay because I wanted to get away from him as quickly as possible. He gave me three coins because he said I did half a day of work. But then he grabbed my wrist. I bared my teeth at him, and he let go. Then I ran all the way here." *There weren't any secrets in that. Besides, Allen is an upstanding citizen, so he can vouch that I didn't do anything wrong.*

"You work for Tobey, as in the owner of all the major trade caravans in the capital?" Allen's voice rang with confusion.

"Yes, today was her first day," Nora answered without even looking at Allen. "Come here." She held her arms out for a hug. I walked over to her, ready for a hug. "It's okay, I've got you now. You're safe," she said in a quiet, motherly voice.

My heart rate lowered substantially. *I didn't even realize I was so worked up.*

"I don't think I should work for him anymore." *I know I need a job, but I really want nothing to do with that guy anymore. He reminds me of the mafia of my old world. I almost feel bad about leaving Zenny with them and all the work again.*

"Shh, it's okay. I'll go talk with him after lunch. He won't dare touch you again. Not if he wishes to live." Her voice was icy at the end. She kept hugging me until I pushed her away.

"So, other than to play hero for me again, are you here for any reason?" I asked Allen.

"I was just about to leave for a mission. I'm likely going to be gone for a several weeks, but I wanted to see how you were settling in before I left." Allen lowered his voice as he talked to me.

"You came to see how Lucia was doing?" Nora asked as she stood up. "You really gave me a tough one with this girl."

"So your name is Lucia?" He gave me a warm smile. "I think it suits you."

Nora walked over and closed the door to the outside.

I had a pleasant time talking with Allen just before lunch. He told me he was on a mission to defend some villages at the border of the nation. According to Allen, the goblins were getting aggressive again. Apparently, every couple of years or so, the goblins would decide to leave their desert homes to raid other kingdoms. Sometimes they would attack the elven or the dwarven kingdoms, but they preferred to attack the human kingdom. Their favorite tactic was to attack just before the start of the ice season. Allen made a comment that the goblins must know that our kingdom's troops move slower while the snow falls.

Nora interrupted my impromptu military history lesson to tell me lunch was ready.

So far, there are the wild and mostly chaotic beastkin, the murderous raiding orcs, and now jealous goblins. This world is not a friendly place.

29

WAR HERO

We wished Allen a fond farewell. Then, Nora and I had lunch with everyone else. I got to have a raw beef steak. Everyone gave me looks of disgust as I tore into my meat with absolute delight. *Raw meat just tastes better.* The other kids all ate a little lighter lunch than usual. *I wonder what their problem is? Their meat is cooked. Okay, I should try to act a little more civilized. If I didn't know that I could handle raw meat, I would have likely been put off my lunch too. But it tastes so good. And the way my teeth shredded the meat was perfect. Have I been slowly getting more animalistic the longer I'm in this body? Should that be bothering me? I mean, if the shoe fits. But do I want to wear that shoe? I think I need some time alone to get my thoughts together.*

After everyone finished eating, we cleaned up the dishes from lunch and I asked Eleanah to use her mirror again.

My teeth had grown since this morning and the three teeth growing in the back were just as sharp as the others. But they looked like they were going to be more triangular in their shape. I bared my teeth in the mirror just like I had done to Tobey, and I grinned even wider. *That is a brutal smile. I need to make sure I don't bite my tongue or cheek. That would hurt a lot.* But as I continued to smile in the mirror, I couldn't suppress the feeling of pride welling up from inside me.

Nora, true to her word, left to talk to Tobey. I cleaned the entryway, which was more about washing the floor of the entryway and hallway. I got the brush and bucket, filled it with water and began scrubbing the floor. The brush was at the end of a long handle, so I wasn't scrubbing the floor on my hands and knees. I had some time to myself to think about what I wanted to do about Zenny. I finished just as Nora returned. She had a satisfied look on her face.

"What did you tell him?" I stared at her, my tail wagging behind me.

"Don't worry about that." She cheerfully walked towards me. "Just know that if he does anything to any one of you kids, he will beg me to kill him." Her smile made my heart skip a beat.

Good, that guy needs to be brought down a peg. "Um, about that, though," I said meekly. "I still don't want to work for him, but now I don't want to leave Zenny alone. That isn't a good job for her, and I don't know what he'll do to her if I'm not around." *I guess she really has become a friend. She looks up to me, and it would be irresponsible to leave her.*

"You want to get out of the contract you signed?" Nora asked me.

"Yes, and I think Zenny needs to get out of hers too." *I think I have a plan.* I shifted my feet before I continued. "As much as I don't want to go back, I will, one last time."

"What are you planning to do?" Nora gave me a concerned look.

"I'll take Zenny out on a delivery with me, and we just won't go back," I said as I planted my feet firmly. "After we get back, I'll ask you to take us job-hunting the next day." *Tobey will probably be very mad at us for abandoning him.*

"I'll help you if this is truly what you wish." Her voice was sorrowful. "I don't agree with abandoning him like that. I'll tell him it's your last day while you're working. He'll let you go."

"Also, there's another thing." I grabbed my necklace.

"What is it, sweetie?" Nora put her arm around me.

"Can you maybe take this thing off?" *I think I have a handle on things now.* "Before you say anything, hear me out." Nora said nothing, but kept looking at me. I took it as her permitting me to continue. "When Tobey grabbed me, I felt I was about to activate the necklace. If it had activated, he could have kidnapped me far easier."

Nora sighed. "If it had activated, you would have had to attacked him and been in trouble. Do you really think he wanted to kidnap you?" I nodded. "But you're right. I never gave it any thought to what would happen if it activated outside. Seeing the state it leaves you in, activating it could cause worse things to happen." She placed a finger on her chin.

"I know. But I'm getting better at controlling myself." I turned to look up at Nora. "Even if I'm not perfect, I want to be able to defend myself or others. And I don't think that I can do that with this thing on me."

"Hmm, what if we changed what it did once you would normally activate it? I'd still feel better with something keeping you from losing control." Nora tapped her finger on her chin. "Any ideas?"

"Anything that doesn't leave me incapacitated would be a good start." *At some point, I need to learn how to fight. Let's start with just being able to fight. What can magic do?* "Can you use this thing to find where I am?" *If I can't get rid of it because she wants insurance, maybe I can try to use it.*

"I think I can try something with Anna's help." Nora was still pondering all her options. "I know I can have it notify me once it activates."

Good start.

"Can you make a loud, high-pitched sound with this thing?

Maybe not high-pitched but definitely loud. And what about a sudden bright light?" I asked. *All it needs to do is disorient those around me, so if I need to flee, I can. Also, if I know it's coming and I'll be able to prepare myself. I'll probably recover faster from it than everyone else. If I need to fight, I can use it to get the jump on my opponents. A personal flash-bang would be invaluable. But it might not be as good since I'm wearing it.*

"That's oddly specific. What do you hope to do, blind and deafen everyone around you every time you get angry?" Skepticism filled Nora's voice.

"That's exactly what I want to happen." *I'm glad she figured that out.* "If I get into trouble, it should be enough for me to snap out of it and run away to safety. And if you can get it to let you know when it activates, you can come and get me, if needed."

"Sometimes I forget you're more than the child you appear to be." Nora chuckled. "I'll attempt to make something more manageable. Until then, you are to practice your letters."

"Do I have to?" *I hate practicing writing. I know I need to know how to do it, but it's just so hard.*

"Yes, young lady." Nora placed both hands on her hips. *She's not leaving any room to negotiate. Or is she?* Nora leaned forward and reached around the back of my neck. With a warm tingling sensation, I felt the necklace leave along with Nora's hands.

"Can I at least have a pen and paper instead?" *I've seen some pens. They won't break when I hold them.*

"Find Eleanah. She can teach you how to use a pen properly." She waved me off. "If you break a single pen, there will be consequences. Do you understand?"

I nodded my head stiffly. *She can still scare me. Is that something all mother figures can do, or is that just because this lady has the power to incinerate anyone she wishes?*

Eleanah wasn't hard to find. She was glad to have an excuse to get out of her combat training today. *She might be outstanding at fighting, but she doesn't enjoy it.* We walked into the classroom together, and she pulled paper, a pen and ink out of the supply cabinets.

"So Mom wants me to teach you how to use a pen. Why? You still can't write with a piece of chalk. This is much more difficult." Eleanah set everything up on a table for me.

"I can't write with chalk because I can't hold it without breaking it," I said as I sat in the chair. "I don't think I can break the pen."

"I guess that does make sense." She grabbed a chair to sit next to me. "So what were Mom and you talking about in the hall earlier?"

"I don't want to work for Tobey anymore." I lowered my head. "But I made a friend while working today. I don't want her to work for him, either."

"My little sister made a friend? Who is she? And why do you not want to work for him again?" She placed a hand on my shoulder. "What happened?"

"He scares me. And I'm afraid that he wanted to kidnap me." I sat staring at the blank page before me.

"Mom won't let anyone kidnap you." She grabbed me and forcefully hugged me. "And if anyone does, they'll find a one-woman apocalypse headed their way."

"Is she really that powerful?" I looked at her face. "Could she truly dissuade everyone?"

"I guess nobody told you yet." Eleanah gave me a gentle squeeze and then released me. *Will I finally learn who Nora really is?* "About thirty-five years ago, there was a war between Rophmna and Brentiveil. The dwarves had perfected a new style of ballista for the war, and it was a war we were losing badly."

"Why did the war even start?" I interrupted, a little too eagerly.

"Why do any wars start? Because someone was envious or angry with someone else. Nobody knows, and it doesn't matter." She looked at the table sadly. "This country is always at war every ten or so years with some kingdom or another. Then there are the constant orc war bands and goblin invasions, too." *This kingdom is in perpetual war! The prophecy from the oracle stone said that there would be a lot of blood in my future. This isn't looking good for me.* "But back to the story. As I was saying, we were losing until a small knight company of misfits, designated as specialists, was deployed to destroy all the dwarves' siege weapons. They were seven extremely skilled individuals, including our mom."

"I knew Mom said that she was in a knight company, but she wouldn't tell me any details." *I remembered what she said when I learned her last name.* "Does this have to do with why she has a last name?"

"It does. She isn't very fond of this part of her past. She set fire to all the siege weapons during the siege of Argenbeuge." Eleanah's eyes glimmered as she spoke. "Her companions fought off all the enemies to give her the time to complete her magic. All the records say that she summoned a massive storm to block out the sky for miles. Then she called down the lighting and struck each ballista. Once they were all destroyed, the enemy morale was broken, and, when the hail started, they broke ranks. She almost single-handedly ended that war."

"So Brentiveil and Rophmna signed a peace treaty?" I asked. *She can summon a literal storm. I guess that makes sense with the last name, Stormleaf.*

"It wasn't a peace treaty, more of a cease-fire." Eleanah shrugged. "If they signed a peace treaty, then they would have a harder time trying to start a war any time they want. The kingdom drafts us into the military out of necessity. On the bright side, once our service is up, we don't need to pay taxes for the rest of our lives. Why do you look so sad suddenly?"

"Do you remember your prophecy when you used the oracle stone?" I asked with a worried look.

"No. I was told that it was mostly guesswork." Eleanah tried to sound chipper, but I could tell there was still some reservation in her voice.

"Mine said that there was going to be a lot of blood spilled in my future, either small amounts constantly over my entire life or all at once with a massacre. And with being forced into the military for possibly fifteen years in a country constantly at war... I don't know what to do." It was hard to stay calm with all the bad news I was getting. *Do I run? What will that get me? Do I just live in the wild? Will I spend my entire life just surviving? Do I try to find the Wild Kingdom and hope that other beastkin treat me well? Do I work with the devil I know, or attempt to brave the unknown world?*

"If you're worried that you'll do a lot of fighting, don't. Most wars are just a bunch of posturing and vying for positions." She returned to hugging me. "The things you need to worry about are orcs, goblins and dires."

"Dires?" I flicked my ears up and turned one towards Eleanah.

"Dire beasts is what they're actually called, but most people call them dires for short." She released me and I turned my head towards her. "They're uncommon, but a problem that knights need to take care of from time to time. They're the most dangerous animals you'll find."

I guess that means going through the wild is almost guaranteed suicide. With wandering orcs and these dire beasts, I'm going to stay right here. I don't stand a chance out in the wild.

"How can you say all this with such a calm attitude?" I slumped in my chair, feeling more drained than after my morning run.

"The world has always been like this. The world is what it is. I can't change it, so I'll do my best just to live in it." Eleanah put on a smile. *I guess since this is the only world she has ever known, this is all normal for her. I'm definitely not on Earth anymore.* "You're too young to worry about this stuff anyway. Aren't we here to practice your writing?"

So much for procrastinating. "Nora wanted me to make sure I know how to write my name so I don't sign anything with blood anymore." I relayed what Nora had said after I negotiated with Tobey.

"We can't have that, now can we?" Eleanah pulled the cork off the pen and put it in my hand.

I had seen pens at a distance, but holding one made me wonder how it worked. It was a triangle-shaped metal tip that was attached to the wooden handle. It looked like there was a thin tube coming from inside the pen to rest on the metal. The tube looked like it was filled with what I assumed to be black ink. I flicked the tube with the back of my claw so I wouldn't cut it. It flicked back into place after bending slightly.

"The most important thing about using a pen is holding the point at the right angle." She grabbed my hand and manipulated the pen so that I held it at an angle and carried on about how to use the pen for the rest of the day.

30

SAVING ZENNY

Alright, I can do this. Just go in there, get a delivery, get Zenny and get out. Simple. I stood across the street from the outpost that I worked at. The morning sun barely crept over the horizon. *Hopefully Zenny is already in there.* I grabbed my newly enchanted flash-bang necklace and stared at the building with trepidation.

Testing the necklace was painful, but not nearly as debilitating as the shock-collar version. It took a lot of work, but I summoned that rage-like state on my own. It also seemed that I had control for a split-second. But once it activated, blinding light and a loud bang snapped me out of it. Nora said that she'd modeled it after the effects of a lightning bolt hitting the ground at three hundred and sixty inches away, without the shock wave. *I have to remember that there's no measurement of feet in this world. It seems awfully inefficient.*

My walk into the building marked the beginning of my mission. I opened the door and walked right in. Decklin was sitting at his desk. "You came back? You have some nerve." His voice was as sour

13 PITCH BLACK CATS

as his scent. "Hurry up and get to work. And tell me where you're going when you leave so I can keep track of you."

"I'm not here for you. My mom is going to talk to Tobey today and end my employment contract." I didn't even bother to hide my agitation. "Zenny, are you here?" I turned my head to look for Zenny.

"Whatever," Decklin grumbled as he went back to his stack of papers.

"Yes, back here."

I followed the voice into the other room. As I walked by Decklin, I growled at him and flashed my teeth. They looked like they had finished growing during the night, and something about seeing them felt right. Eleanah had to pry the mirror from my hands while I admired them.

When I saw the glimmer of fear in Decklin's eyes, I had to suppress a laugh. I left him to find Zenny hard at work sorting all the deliveries.

"You came back!" She turned to see me, eyes wide and with an unusual bounce in her step.

I'm going to cause all kinds of problems for this girl. "Yeah, for you," I said. *I'm not looking forward to this part.* "So, what do you have for me this morning?" *I have to keep up the act until I get her outside with me.*

She brought the map to me. "That barrel there needs to go here." She pointed to a barrel then to the map. The place she pointed to was straight down the road from here. "Then we have—"

"The barrel will be enough for now. It's this one, right?" I interrupted her. I pointed to a barrel large enough to fit the two of us inside of it together.

"Okay, if you want to do that one, you can. It's really heavy." She glanced at me skeptically.

"You said that you have a cart you can use?" Zenny nodded. "Then help me get it out the door and onto the cart." *Alright, that*

THE BIG BAD WOLF

should get step one done. My heart was picking up pace and my tail flicked back and forth behind me.

The two of us turned the barrel on its side and rolled it to the front door.

"What? Not strong enough to lift a barrel?" Decklin's voice called out to us. "Where are you taking that?"

"This is going to Nick's," Zenny answered immediately.

"Just don't come back exhausted again." Decklin sounded like he was scribbling something as he spoke.

I growled and stomped my foot to dig my claws into the floor. When I dragged my toe claws back, they tore up the wood. *Leave me alone.* The two of us made it out the door with the heavy barrel.

"Alright, now that part's done. You want to show me the location of this cart you mentioned?" I shouted it so that I knew Decklin heard me. I then slammed the door shut.

"The cart is around the back." Zenny started walking to the back of the building. I grabbed her shoulder to stop her. "Eh, what is it?" She turned to look at me, confused.

"We won't need the cart." I wagged a finger. "I was just saying that to get you outside with me."

"Why? We could just talk inside."

"Because I don't want Decklin to hear us talking." *Now I hope she'll follow me.* "I came back for you. I don't want to work for Tobey anymore."

"But what do you want me for?" Zenny stared at me, unblinking.

I hope I can phrase this right. "I think you should quit with me. Tobey doesn't think that highly of you, so he won't miss you, and this way we can find something that suits your talents better." I smiled at her.

"I don't understand." She looked like she was about to burst into tears again.

I continued to roll the barrel on its side. "Let's start by rolling this down the street to where it needs to go. I know I said that you wouldn't need to go on any deliveries with me, but, just this once, come with me."

"If I go with you, will you explain everything to me?" She walked to stand next to me, ready to push the barrel.

"Not everything, just most of it," I said, smiling at her without showing my teeth. *I don't want to scare her.* We rolled the barrel slowly down the street. Fewer people were moving about as the sun was still rising, just as I predicted. "Was Tobey here when you left yesterday?" *I need to figure out what time she left there yesterday.*

"He had just arrived and asked where you were. I told him that you were out on a delivery and would be back soon." She kept pushing the barrel. I was holding my speed back so that we would go at a pace that was comfortable for her.

"When I arrived, he and Decklin were talking," I said. "Then he asked me some personal questions and was aggressive. He didn't like that I wasn't answering them." I had to push a little softer because we were slowly veering off course.

"What kind of things was he asking about?" She eyed me eagerly.

"I think he thought I was sent to infiltrate his business to learn his secrets. He's too paranoid for his own good." I gave a slight laugh. Zenny didn't laugh with me. She just stared at me with a blank stare. *Moving on.* "But then he grabbed me and acted like he wanted to kidnap me. So I ran away from him and told my mom about him."

"Who's your mother, exactly?"

She met her, but I never introduced her. "My mom is Nora Stormleaf. But she doesn't tell people her last name," I said pridefully.

"That was *the* Nora Stormleaf, the one who runs the orphanage?" She stopped pushing the barrel and stared at me.

"I thought she mentioned that I live at her orphanage," I said as I caught the barrel. "Is there another orphanage in town?"

"No, I just didn't think about it. When you said that you were adopted, I thought of something else." Zenny lowered her head and looked at the ground.

"It's okay." I put my hand on her shoulder. "Do you think of me as a friend?"

"I don't know. I've never had one before." She turned to look at me.

"Will you leave Tobey and go with me?" I needed to get us back on track. "We can find you something better than a town courier." I started pushing the barrel again.

Zenny noticed and resumed helping me. "I guess I could. You said that Tobey really doesn't want me. Could I still be useful to you if I'm working for someone else?"

"You'll probably be more useful working for someone else, and be useful to many more people too," I said with as much enthusiasm as I could.

"I can?" Her eyes lit up and glistened in the morning light.

"Yes, you can, but only if you come with me and leave Tobey." *I know this is manipulative, but it's for the greater good, or her greater good at the least.*

"I'll go with you, then," Zenny said as she looked down the street.

We're close to our destination. It should be okay to send her off to the orphanage. "We're close enough. I know the rest of the way to the delivery. I want you to go to Nora's orphanage and wait for me there." As I stopped the barrel, I put a hand on Zenny's shoulder. "You know where that is, right?"

"I know where everything is in this town." Zenny's eyes were still shimmering.

"Go ahead and go. Who knows, I might even beat you there." I gave her a smile and a wink.

I watched Zenny walk off to another street. *She'll be fine. Now I've got to finish this delivery. Someone paid for it, after all. They shouldn't suffer from Tobey's actions. He just needs to find more couriers. Now I can see why that person left to be a carpenter.* I kept pushing the barrel and reached the destination quickly now that I could go at my pace and not Zenny's. I rolled it to the front door of a building that looked much like the others in the city, only larger. With a bit of effort, I stood the barrel back up so that it wouldn't roll away.

I knocked on the wooden door and waited. A short time later, a man opened it. He was rotund, dressed in red overalls with a slightly balding head and a large, white, bushy beard. He smiled as he saw me. "Oh, are you a new courier?" His voice was deep, yet happy-sounding. I couldn't help but want to like him. *Although there is something about his appearance.*

"Hi, my name is Lucia." *I should be professional even though this is my last delivery.* I stood up straight and put on a smile. "But, to be honest, this is my last delivery. I'm not going to be a courier anymore."

"That's sad to hear. You were able to get this to me by yourself. That's quite a feat for someone so young." His rosy red cheeks only made his smile even more friendly. "Do you want to help me bring this in? I know you've already done enough as it is, but I'm not what I used to be. Getting old makes everything more difficult." The man opened the door wide as he stepped to the side.

"Sure, I could help you. What is it, anyway? It's quite heavy." I tilted the barrel over again, but this time I tilted it into the doorway.

"It's just some things I need for my business." He pulled the barrel as I pushed. "I'm a toy maker, you see."

Wait, toy maker? An old guy with a white bushy beard in red that makes toys... Santa?

As I pushed the barrel into the building, a room full of shelves greeted me. Each shelf was full of all kinds of different wooden toys. There were horses, unicorns and some had people riding on said horses and unicorns, just to name a few. They were all painted in bright colors and in extreme detail. The guy helped me set the barrel back up, and I looked around the room with my mouth wide open.

I spun around as I looked at everything. "You made all these?"

"Yes, do you like them?" He stood next to me. "Would you like one?" He waved his hand out to present them all to me.

"I couldn't possibly take one. I don't have any money to pay you." *Besides, I don't know which one I would even want.*

"Nonsense. Think of it as an extra payment for bringing the barrel into my home." He laughed. It was a deep, heartfelt laugh that was almost contagious. "So, what do you like, Lucia?"

I don't know if I want a toy. My mind has kinda grown out of that stage. I know I said that I would try to be a kid again, but I still lost that childlike imagination to be able to play with toys like a kid again. But I guess I can't leave that question unanswered. "I like meat." I looked at him and gave him a forced smile.

"Ah, yes, I should have expected that answer from a carnivore beastkin." He gave me a look. It was a look that showed he knew I knew a better answer than that.

I look like a kid, so everyone will expect me to act like a kid. I admit, I act like a child occasionally. But that just goes to show that there are some aspects of everyone that they never really grow out of, doesn't it? "You know I'm a carnivore?" I looked at him with surprise.

"Of course, I've seen many beastkin back in my day." *So, Santa isn't from around here. But what is he doing here and not some place hidden? I should stop projecting my fantasy onto this guy.* "I saw your teeth when you smiled, and when you said you like meat, it made it obvious." He smiled as he started walking to a shelf near the door. "A good little girl like you probably likes a nice unicorn. This one here will do." He picked up a beautiful unicorn. It was a very light gray with a black mane and tail. The hair looked realistic, and the horn was bright yellow.

As he turned around, the front door flew open and two men walked in. I couldn't see their faces past their hoods, and they wore masks that covered the bottom half of their faces. All of their clothes were black and dark gray.

"Nothing personal, Nick. We're here for the beastkin." One of the men pulled a sword from his hip and stabbed the old toy maker through the heart as he was still grasping the toy unicorn.

They wanted me, and they killed Santa because he was here with me. I'm going to kill them! I could feel my rage building. Before I could make a move, the other man ran up to me and swung a club at my head. Everything went dark.

31

FIRST BLOOD

This is a familiar feeling. There was a lot of pain originating from the side of my head where the guy hit me with his club. Everything was white, and I could hear and feel a ringing in my head. *Still not any better the second time.* Just like the first time, I couldn't move my arms or legs.

My vision shifted to black, and I opened my eyes. My head was still sore and I could feel the ringing, but it was steadily subsiding.

Everything was clearly lit. I saw a ceiling and more walls with shelves full of toys. These toys were unfinished, disassembled or not painted. *Am I in the toy maker's basement? Oh no, the toy maker. They killed him.*

I looked around for any signs of my attackers and saw several tables full of different pieces of toys and wood-carving tools. All the tables were pushed to the walls to clear the center of the room. The walls held many lit candle sconces, giving plenty of light to see things clearly.

Two men who looked identical to my attackers were standing in the center of a strange drawing engraved into the floor. *I guess since all I saw was their eyes and clothes, they could be actually anybody.*

What are they doing? I've never seen symbols like the ones on the floor before now. It looks like they are going to perform some kinda ritual. But that's not a professional opinion.

What are they using to mark the ground? I could see a small urn in the hands of one of the men. The plain clay pot was spilling forth a reddish liquid that sizzled against the cobblestone floor. I smelled something acrid. *It smells like someone's vomiting up rotten food. Are they using acid to etch the symbol into the ground?*

I continued my inspection of the situation by looking at myself. I was lying on the ground with my hands and feet bound. *Being tied up after getting your head hit isn't exactly fun. I hope this doesn't become a pattern in my life.* The rope tied my legs, and I saw it was just a simple bundle around my knees. *I guess since I really don't have distinguishable ankles they went for the next best joint.* They had tied my hands behind my back, and I could move the knot under my legs to bring my hands out in front of me. *Being this flexible is quite handy. They didn't even bother to gag me. Is this amateur hour for kidnappings?*

Now I need to decide what to do. Do I sit and see what they're up to? No, I think it's a better idea just to cut myself loose and leave through the hatch up those stairs. I think I might be able to outrun them. Worst-case scenario, I make it to the street by the time they catch up to me, and then the people in the street will see and react, I hope. Now I should be able to cut myself free with my toe claws and quietly make my way to the door and make a break for it.

I changed my sitting position to allow myself to have enough leverage to cut my hands free. *Now that I'm in full control of my body, keeping me held captive is going to be a much more difficult task for everyone else. Those orcs had it easy. Although, if I got out, I wasn't going to make it far with them. I would have died much sooner that way.* I shook my head free of my distracting thoughts and proceeded with my plan, cutting my hands free with the claws on my toes and stood. *They may be shorter than the ones on my hands, but they're still just as sharp.*

The two wannabe kidnappers were still concentrating on making whatever it was they were making. *This is my chance to get out of here.* I walked silently over to the stairs. I walked as close to the sides of each step as possible to prevent any creaking noises. When I reached the door, I found something I hadn't planned for.

They locked it.

"Where'd she go?" I heard a voice call out.

"I tied her up, just like you told me to." The other voice was similar to the first, but he talked slower.

"Ho, trying to escape, are you?"

I turned around. *Now that I can see his face, I wish I couldn't.* It was full of acne scars and a patchy attempt at a five-o'clock shadow. "Who are you, and what do you want with me?" I flexed my claws, ready to do something. *I don't know what, but I can't just sit here and let them do whatever they want. They just killed a guy.* "And why did you kill Santa?"

"I don't know any Santa, but poor Nick was in the wrong place at the wrong time." The guy shrugged. "We were ordered to make sure there were no witnesses. Besides, we couldn't have him running to the guards while we were working. And I sure wasn't going to carry him down here."

But you didn't knock him out first. You just killed him. "I don't know what your job is, but if you let me go, I promise I won't tell anyone that I've seen your ugly mugs." *Where did that come from?*

"Are you calling me ugly?" His brown eyes nearly bulged out of their sockets.

My impulse control still needs work.

The other man walked up. His face was almost identical to the other's, but, instead of scars, it was full of acne and he had some dark blotches on his skin. *Are they brothers, or maybe twins?* "Mother always said that we were her handsome sons." His slow drawl caused my ear to twitch.

"Of course she would say that—she's your mother." I covered my mouth after I realized I'd thought out loud again. *Stop it! Don't* anger the killers. Something isn't right here. When I met Nora for the first time she nearly terrified me. The same was true for Phan. Even Tobey caused a reaction from my instincts. But these two don't. "But is there any chance you have the key to this door?" I used a sweet and innocent tone. "If I don't get home before lunch, my mom, Nora, will come looking for me." *I dropped Nora's name because she said if I was kidnapped, I should say I was hers and they would just let me go. Time to test that.* I walked to the base of the stairs.

The one who spoke normally pulled a simple brass key from a pocket on his pants. "This key?" I nodded. "I don't know who this 'Nora' is. But if she's looking for you, we need to hurry this up."

There goes plan A. The whole idea hinged on them knowing who Nora is. Are they not from around here? More importantly, now what do I do? I continued to think of any possible way out of this kidnapping until the uglier brother stepped towards me.

"Hi, I'm Signet." He still spoke slowly while he waved his hand at me.

The guy holding the key slapped Signet on the back of the head. "Don't introduce yourself to the person you're going to sacrifice to the demons. That's morbid." He returned the key to his pocket.

Sacrifice? Demons? What?

Signet held his hands up in surrender. "Mom always said to introduce yourself to strangers."

Alright, one is an idiot and the other is still under evaluation. But as things stand, he isn't much better.

"Just grab her, you idiot." The keyholder shoved his brother towards me.

"You're going to sacrifice me?" I asked while tucking my tail between my legs. "Why?"

"Them's the orders we have." Signet sounded sad about doing this. *Can I use that?* He reached his hand towards me.

I guess I don't have time to think of a plan. I need to defend myself now. Once I activate my necklace to alert Nora, she'll come running here. Once Signet put his hand on my shoulder, I growled.

I turned my head and bit down on his forearm, hard. I could feel my teeth digging down deep into his flesh through the clothes he wore.

With a scream of pain and surprise, he tried to pull his arm away from me. I only bit down harder and I reached out with my claws further up his arm. He swung his left arm around and hit me in the face. The blow dislodged me, but I took some of his arm with me. *I just bit a guy. Where did that come from? My teeth really are dangerous.*

"She bit me! She bit me, Cereb!" Signet hunched over, clutching the arm I'd bitten.

"Quit being a baby. She's just a little girl; how bad could it be? " He walked around to look at his brother's arm. He turned to look at me once he saw the wound I'd inflicted. I could see the fear growing in his eyes. "What kind of monster are you?"

I spat out my souvenir, a small chunk of skin and cloth. "Yuck! You taste like dirt." *When was the last time you had a bath?* "And I'm not a monster, I'm a beastkin." I lowered myself and charged him.

Time for some payback.

I didn't want to just defend myself anymore. Now it was personal. They'd attacked me, kidnapped me, planned to sacrifice me and insulted me, and they were going to pay the price.

And the price was blood.

Cereb didn't sit idly while I charged him. He drew the sword from his waist and attempted to cut my head off at the same time.

That's a sword. Avoid the sharp end! Whatever possessed me to charge him forced me to duck under the blade. It was easy to do with how slow it was moving.

Even though I dodged the sword, his knee headed for my face. I couldn't dodge out of the way, and, for some reason, I opened my mouth to bite his knee.

His knee collided with my teeth, and he yelped in pain.

I stumbled backward, a little disoriented and with my teeth

13 PITCH BLACK CATS

hurting. *Okay, that wasn't a good idea.* I could see his pants soaking up small patches of blood.

I looked at his brother and saw blood pooling underneath him. *That's a lot of blood. He doesn't look too good, either.* Cereb charged at me this time. He lunged with his sword outstretched. I sidestepped the thrust. *People don't usually move this slowly right? He has a weapon and I don't.* I looked down at my claws. *No, I have three weapons, my teeth and claws. I just have a shorter reach. But if I can get closer, he won't be able to swing his sword at me. I can handle his punches and kicks somewhat, at least.*

As I stepped towards him, he quickly changed his stab to a swing. I was fortunate enough to get inside his reach so that he only hit me with the cross guard of the blade. I clutched the side of my head where his weapon hit me, at about the spot where a human's ears would be if I had them. *That hurts.* My sight swam from the blow, but the outer rim of my vision leaked red. *What is it with people and hitting me in the head? Stop it!*

I was still clutching my head when his left hand struck me in the face. I stumbled over to Signet.

"Grab her and hold her still." Cereb was angry and was nearly shouting.

"It hurts." Signet was crying. He put his bloody arm on my shoulder as I stumbled over to him, then grabbed my hair with his uninjured arm.

"I know it hurts. Hold her still and I'll make her pay for it!" Cereb was winding up to stab me.

Do not grab my hair. "Let go of me!" I screamed as he yanked my hair just behind my ears. I reached up with both hands and raked my claws through his good arm. His scream was identical to when I bit a chunk out of his other arm.

He released my hair and shoulder simultaneously and reeled in pain. I dove to the side to avoid the incoming sword. I tried to roll and stand up, but I only accomplished the feat of sitting on my tail. "Ow."

I saw Cereb kneeling down next to his brother. A large pool of blood was growing around him. Signet's face was extremely pale, and he wasn't moving much, but I saw his chest still rise and fall sharply. *He's losing a lot of blood. I probably cut an artery.* I looked closer and saw Cereb's sword was embedded in his brother's gut.

"I'm scared. Help me, please." Signet's voice was weak and his breathing was slowing.

"I'm sorry. I didn't mean for this to happen. It's all her fault," Cereb said as he watched Signet's chest stop moving. "This was supposed to be an easy job. 'Just kill the girl and summon the demon,' he said. 'She won't be a problem for you two.' I'm going to kill Decklin when I see him again." His voice was soft even for a whisper.

Decklin?

Cereb stood up as he extracted his sword from his brother's body. Slowly, he turned to look at me. "You killed my brother, you monster! Why don't you just die like you were told?"

Hearing his words unleashed something in me. "I told you I'm not a monster!" My vision filled with more red after each word. "I'm a beastkin!" With the last word, my vision went completely red and my necklace activated.

I closed my eyes in time, but the explosion's sound was unimpeded. I reflexively clutched my ears from the pain as I fell to my knees. Everything was silent except for the constant ringing in my ears. I opened my eyes and saw Cereb flailing around. I couldn't hear him screaming, but I saw his face, and his mouth was wide open. His hands were covering his eyes. The sword was on the ground next to his feet.

My vision was no longer red, but I was still angry with him. *You kidnap me, tie me up, plan to sacrifice me to a demon, try to kill me and then call me a monster! I don't think I have ever agreed more with my instinctual rage than I do now. If anyone is going to die, it's going to be you.*

I stood up and walked over to him. My steps were unsteady, but

I used my tail to keep standing upright. He was still holding his eyes, but he wasn't thrashing around as much. Just as I stood before him, he removed his hands from his eyes and looked at me. I don't know how much he could see, but his face turned to horror as I placed my claws around his neck and dug them in. He desperately clamored to grab my arm, but once he did, I pulled back, leaving five blood-red gashes in his throat.

His blood flowed like a river down his neck. He grabbed at it, struggling to stop the bleeding and keep his precious blood in his body. It was hopeless. I watched as his mouth moved, but I couldn't hear any sound come out.

I, however, was not satisfied.

Growling, I jumped on his chest, brought him to the ground and savagely tore into his chest, slashing my claws across him repeatedly.

I don't know at what point my emotions turned from unhinged rage to pure joy, but they did. A sense of pride welled up within me as I looked down at the bloody remains of Cereb's chest cavity. *That is not the feeling I expected. But I feel much better now.*

I looked at the two people I had just killed. *Certain onlookers could see this as murder. But it was self-defense. A bit of overkill there at the end, though.* I went to the pocket I'd seen him take the key out of and retrieved the key I needed. *I need to get to Nora to explain everything.*

When I stood up, I noticed that I no longer heard the ringing noise from when my necklace went off, but a slow, steady clap. *Weren't there only two kidnappers? They're both dead right next to me. Who's clapping?*

A deep rumble of a voice spoke behind me. "Marvelous. Just marvelous."

I slowly turned around. A male humanoid stood in the center of the symbol that was now glowing dark red. He only wore a smile, and that smile had teeth that looked a lot like the teeth of an orc. *That close-up visual of them when I first woke up is forever imprinted in my mind.* His skin was the color of the blood that I was now standing in. A pitch-black segmented tail, like that of a scorpion, extended out behind him and curled upwards. He had clawed hands that were as black as his tail. They were similar to my own, just without being covered in fur. His feet were massive hooves attached to the legs of an extreme bodybuilder. All of his muscles looked like they belonged to a world-class weightlifter. His towering stature was crowned with four pitch-black horns. Two horns curled up, growing from his forehead. The other two started from the back of his bald head, wrapped around and continued for several inches past his face.

He continued slowly clapping as he walked over to a table, cleared it with a swipe of his tail, and sat down on it.

I'm going to die, aren't I?

32

KILLING SPREE

I stood still, petrified by fear. *That has to be a demon.*

The demon watched me with an appraising look. "I have been summoned many times, but this is the first time I've had such a spectacular show. Usually, I'm summoned by a group of people all dressed in the same boring black robes. It's always kill these people, destroy that town, bring down that kingdom." He sat there talking like we were old friends.

"Are you going to kill me?" I squeaked.

"Do you want me to?" His voice hardened.

I shook my head slightly.

"I'm in a good mood with your display of rage. It's been a long time since I last saw a beastkin. It's good that none of you have lost your touch."

Is he talking about me tearing apart Cereb's chest? "Why are you here? How are you here? I don't know how to use magic." I took a few small steps towards the door. *If I want to take off running, I need to get out of this puddle of blood first.*

"What are they teaching kids these days?" He shook his head as he pointed to the symbol etched into the ground. "You see that summoning glyph on the ground there?" *So it is actually called a glyph.* I nodded slowly. "It was useless until blood was spilled on it." I looked at the puddle I stood in. It had grown to the point where it was touching the glyph and some of the blood was even filling the engraving. "Your little display of rage made sure I was summoned."

"Are you a demon?" *I know the answer, but I hope he can give me a bit more to work with. And I need to buy time for Nora to get here.*

He stood up and slammed his tail on the table he was sitting on. It shattered into dozens of pieces. I jumped, slipped on the blood and landed just on the edge of the pool. He bared his teeth at me for a moment, then relaxed. "Here I am, being kind and civilized, and you go and say something like that. But judging by your reaction, you didn't know what you just did. Is that correct?"

I shook my head enthusiastically. *I'll agree with whatever you say, mister.*

"Calling a sin like me a demon is such a barbaric description. You see, I am a sin of wrath. Do you enjoy it when someone calls you an animal?"

"I'm sorry. I didn't know. But I see your point." *Am I agreeing with a demon? Is that a bad thing? Aren't demons a great evil? He's acting civilized, with the lack of clothes being the exception.* "But what is a sin of wrath? Is that supposed to mean something?"

"Do you have a name, little beastkin?" He cleared another table before sitting down on it. This time, I could hear the wood groan in protest.

"Lucia." *Was that a good idea? His conversational attitude is odd.* I stood back up.

"Well, Lucia, since I'm in such a complacent mood, I'll tell you." His face carried little emotion. "The infernal plane is home to the fallen and sins such as myself. Then there are the riders, and finally, the demon lord who rules everything."

It's the demon lord looking to invade this world. I almost forgot that the whole reason I was even sent here was to stop him when he invades.

13 PITCH BLACK CATS

"I guess talking about each one of those isn't going to happen." *I don't want to push his boredom to the point of making him mad. Keep him calm. Nora should be on her way since my necklace has activated. She'll know what to do in this situation.* "Thank you for answering one of my questions, but could you answer my other question?"

"Are you telling me what to do?" He looked and sounded agitated.

Wait, I need to calm him down. How do I do that? I flinched. "I just want to know what you want to do now." The words flew out of me faster than I could think them.

"My job," he said nonchalantly. I looked at him from behind my arms with anticipation, hoping he would elaborate. "I'm here to slaughter everyone within the city walls."

That's not just casual information you can just share like that. Didn't he complain about doing that kind of job when he first started talking to me? "If you don't enjoy doing it, then don't do it," I said in an optimistic tone. *I'm inside the city walls and I don't want to die.*

"You thought I was complaining earlier? Let me correct you. Just because I have a limited skill set and my jobs are almost always the same doesn't mean I don't enjoy them." He smiled, showing all of his razor-sharp teeth. *Well, there goes that idea. I'm going to die.* "I'll give you a chance." He stood up calmly. "I like you, little girl. You're welcome to join me. There's a lot of rage in you yet, and I would like to see it. Or you can sit and watch, it doesn't matter to me." He started walking to the door.

I instinctively backed up to the wall. *Is he going to let me go? Just like that?*

He walked up the steps, and each step complained as he climbed them towards the door. With a simple push, the door flew open and off its hinges. He continued on his way, leaving me standing in the basement alone with the two corpses.

266

I looked down at the key still in my hand. *This is useless now.* I threw the key towards the bodies.

What should I do? I couldn't keep him here until Nora arrived. I can't fight him; that would be suicide. Could he kill everyone in this town? If Nora is still here, she could fight him. But what if he gets the jump on her?

I racked my brain to figure out the best course of action, but screams interrupted my thoughts. *He's started killing people in the street.* I ran up the stairs and followed the screams to the front door. I made it to the first room where I entered through. Santa—*I actually think his name was Nick*—was still lying face-first on the ground with a small pool of blood around him. *I'm sorry you got caught up in whatever this is. At least I made the two who did this suffer. Although I released a demon as a result. How am I going to fix this?* With a heavy heart, I walked outside.

The demon hadn't wasted any time in getting to work. Blood, bodies and severed limbs already filled the street. People ran screaming away from the sin of wrath that I had released.

The demon followed the crowd, using his multitude of natural weapons to kill anyone he could reach. People were ripped apart by his brute strength, impaled by his tail and crushed under his hooves.

I could feel a slight rumble in my stomach. *Why is this sight making me hungry? No, I don't have time for this. I need to fix this.*

I turned around to look in the other direction of the people fleeing and saw that some were standing still. They weren't civilians, as they wore leather armor and wielded maces or swords. *The guards? Do they think they stand a chance against that thing? It's their job is to defend the town, isn't it? Maybe there are enough of them to kill him.* I watched as more guards gathered together and the remaining people fled past them. They shouted and charged the demon.

The demon turned to look at the source of the shouting, and I shuddered at the sight of his malicious grin. *He's enjoying himself.* One thing was certain: *They're all going to die.*

The group of twelve guards charged the demon with either ignorance or misplaced bravery. The demon jumped up just before they engaged one another. He landed on a poor soul who didn't get out of the way fast enough. The demon grabbed two guards by their heads, one in each hand. His tail stabbed into the shield of a guard, piercing through to his arm on the other side. The guard yelled in pain as two heads of his companions popped like grapes in the demon's hands.

The other guards began swinging their weapons at the demon. While the maces did no visible damage to the monster, the swords cut into his flesh, but I doubted they were deep wounds. *This is hopeless. What have I done? Stop thinking like that, Lucia. There has to be something I can do.*

I looked around to see if I could think of anything to do to help. All the pedestrians had fled the street. *Come on, I need to think of something.*

The sin of wrath lifted the man he'd pierced with his tail and bit down on his neck, removing the head as the demon jerked back. The demon opened his mouth and sent the severed head flying as an ax came down on his tail. The weapon cut off a good third of the appendage. Blood poured out of the demon's wound.

His blood is the same color as mine.

As the demon roared in pain, the remaining guards and I all covered our ears.

Ahead of me stood what was possibly the largest human I have ever seen; he held the ax responsible for nipping the tip of the tail. The man wore a chain-mail shirt with an animal hide to cover the rest of him. He wielded a huge double-bladed ax in his hands. The head was as wide as his torso, and the handle was as long as his leg.

The demon swung one of his claws at the man's chest. The warrior leaned back out of reach, then stepped forward, swinging his ax low at one of the demon's legs. The demon reached down with his other hand and caught the ax by the handle in mid-swing. Grinning, the demon stared the man down.

The other guards began swinging their weapons again. Those who had maces traded them for swords from their fallen comrades. They had similar results from the last time, but at least this time they all left a mark. One guard got a lucky stab in the back of the knee on the demon's trailing leg, burying his sword deeper than anyone else had done so far.

The demon let go of the ax and turned on the man who stabbed him. He shoved a clawed hand through the poor guard, and the man's bowels exited out the back on the monstrosity's fingertips.

The large human used the opening to bury his ax into the spine of the demon, who howled and turned around so fast the man lost his grip on his ax.

He didn't cut deep enough to sever the spinal cord. Did his ax get stuck in a vertebra? Why am I still standing here watching?

The demon grabbed the human's neck and roared in his face, then lifted the man off the ground.

I heard a whistle before an arrow embedded itself in the demon's chest. The demon unceremoniously dropped the warrior to the ground.

Another arrow struck the monstrosity's shoulder. We both looked for the source of the projectiles, and I saw an elven archer with another arrow nocked.

"You lot, go and get reinforcements," the large human commanded the guards with a hoarse voice. The guards that were helping scurried off as they obeyed his order.

Why did the demon let go of the man? He could have just killed him and moved on afterward. Wait, every time someone has done significant damage to him, he turns his entire attention to them. Can we use that?

The demon charged the archer, who was slowly backing away and releasing more arrows.

I took a step forward, and then every muscle in me locked up. My body wouldn't move. I could feel my heart pounding in my chest. Every warning my instincts could give me screamed that I shouldn't move towards the demon again. I wanted nothing more than to run away from him. So I started running, but I stopped after a few steps. *Maybe I can distract him so the ax guy can get his weapon back.*

"Hey, you big stupid demon!" I waved my arms as I yelled. *Among all the stupid things I have ever done, this might be the one that takes the cake. But I have to help. This is my fault, after all.*

"You?" the demon called out to me. I questioned all of my second life's choices. Every alarm in my head went off and blocked out any thought that dared manifest. "I let you live and this is how you repay me? If you want to die, then so be it!" He took a single step towards me before I took off sprinting. "Get back here!"

I didn't turn around to make sure the demon was following me. *This was a stupid idea!* I heard something whistling, and I turned to see the ax flying towards me. It didn't spin, but the massive blades at its head were coming right for me.

I shrieked as I dropped to my knees and curled up in a ball. There was a gust of wind followed by the sound of a heavy clang behind me. I looked up and didn't see the ax anymore. *I'm alive?* Even though I didn't see a projectile ax, I did see the hulking demon charging towards me.

The demon stormed towards me, continuing right past the human the ax belonged to without acknowledging him. The warrior picked up a sword and sliced in an upward motion across the back of the monster's leg. *Why don't you just kill him?*

The demon's attention turned from me to the man. The demon was still standing, but he was favoring his right leg. He retaliated by swinging his tail stump around to pen the man in and brought his left claw towards the man's face.

The man raised the sword. Claw and steel collided, but the demon sliced through one of the man's wrists, cutting off his right hand through the bone. When the man recoiled, the demon hit him with his knee.

The human tumbled back a ways before stopping. Arrows

found their way into the demon's back once again, and he went back to charging the archer.

Where is Nora?

Blood poured from the stump where the man used to have a hand. *He's probably the best chance I have at getting out of this alive.* I ran to one of the dead guards and removed his belt that held his sword, then over to him and grabbed his stump.

"What are you doing? Who are you?" he grunted.

I think he might have gotten a few broken bones from that kick.

"Saving your life." I wrapped the belt halfway up his forearm. "This is going to hurt, but you at least won't die from blood loss." I tightened the belt as much as I could. The man held back his complaints as I tied it off. "Have you noticed how he keeps changing his focus once someone hurts him or makes him angry?"

Recognition flashed across the man's face as he nodded. "It's been leaving me alive when it could have easily killed me."

"How well can you use your other hand?" I looked at the stump. "I have a plan." *I don't know how long that archer will be able to keep him busy.*

"I can use it fine, but I will be less effective." He winced as he held up his hand. *I would say you would be half as effective, but now isn't the time for jokes.*

I pointed to the archer that was still backing away from the charging demon and firing arrows at him. "You and that archer guy need to keep trading his attention until my mom gets here."

"What does your mom have to do with this?" He narrowed his eyes as he glared at me.

I stared at the sin of wrath. "My mom is Nora Stormleaf. She can kill him, I know it."

"While I would like to agree with you, kid, I don't think they know your plan." He pointed to a group of men and women in black leather armor. Hoods covered their faces, and they wielded a complete assortment of weapons. *I forgot that several knight companies inhabit this town.*

They charged fearlessly, shouting all kinds of battle cries. Once the first person struck the demon, his attention shifted to the crowd of people attacking him. All of their attacks hurt him, but two of the company died in the demon's retaliation as he flailed his claws around.

Even with two cut down by the dangerous claws, the men and women pressed on.

"You want to play games? Fine, I'll play games with you," the demon roared in frustration. Suddenly, flames engulfed the area around it.

People were running and screaming while on fire. Those not caught in the conflagration backed up, attempting to shield their eyes from the light. Slowly, everyone watched as the flames receded and shaped into the body of the demon.

The demon laughed. "The time for mercy has passed." His voice sounded like a roaring inferno. *I think we have officially pissed him off.*

Now what do we do? I stood up, trying to remember where Nora would be. *Tobey's office! She was canceling my contract. The north gate, where is that? Conveniently, the sun rises in the east in this world too.*

I looked at the sky and saw black storm clouds. *Wasn't it sunny this morning? This is going to make finding north much more difficult.* I took off running in the direction I thought was north, towards the archer and as far away from the burning demon as I could. Neither acknowledged me as I ran past them.

As I ran down the street, the sounds of screams lessened with each stride. I kept running until I heard a familiar voice. "Lucia!" I turned to look down a street I wasn't going to turn down and saw her. Nora's hair defied gravity, and her whole body glowed dimly. Little blue sparks periodically jumped from her hands.

I went to her, ignoring any instinct telling me to run. "You're safe, thank goodness." Her face softened, and she jogged towards me. Her surrounding glow dissipated.

33

NO MORE BLOOD

"Demon!" I shouted as she ran towards me. *Is this the same magic she used in the story Eleanah told me?*

"Demon? Where?" The glow from earlier returned.

"This way!" I shouted. "It's fighting some people right now."

Nora didn't ask any questions and followed me down the road back to the fighting. I had to slow down some so that Nora could keep up. *All this running and fighting is exhausting.*

I knew we were close to fighting because there was a charred corpse lying in the middle of the street ahead of us. *What happened to the archer guy?* I stared at the burnt body closely as we ran to it. A curved charcoal stick rested in its hands. *I think the archer guy is toast. Does that mean the demon killed everyone already and moved on?*

We arrived at a shallow lake of blood and bodies, some burnt and others torn asunder.

"Get behind me," Nora said.

I followed her order, but I continued to survey the massacre before me. I saw the corpse of the large man I'd tried to save. He was torn in half at the waist. *I'm sorry I took too long.*

"The demon is loose," Nora said sadly. "I have to find it and kill it."

I concentrated on my ears to see if I could hear fighting, screaming or anything that might help me locate the rampaging monster. I heard some faint explosions. "That way. I think it went that way." I pointed in the direction I estimated the sound came from. "But I'm not very good at figuring out which direction things are happening yet."

Nora dropped to a knee next to me. She hugged me. "You've already done more than should ever be expected of you." *I haven't told you the whole story yet.* "I'll go find and kill the demon. You need to head to the orphanage and get everyone out. Then head for the south gate away from this demon." She leaned back and held my shoulders while looking at me.

"What if it moves again? I can help you track it." *This is my fault. I need to help make this right.*

"I'll be fine. This isn't the first demon I've had to fight." She put on an obviously forced smile. "Go and take care of your brothers and sisters." She shoved me in the direction of the orphanage. "The fight will be too loud for you to handle anyway."

"Okay, but home is that way, right?" I pointed in the direction where she'd pushed me.

Nora stood up and started walking in the direction I said the demon could be. "Yes, head that way as straight as you can. I'll come back for you all."

I guess we should evacuate. The way Nora was talking, she made it sound like it would be a destructive battle. I won't be any help in the fight, especially now. I started running back to the orphanage, zigzagging through the streets until I recognized the street I was on and corrected my path.

When I got to the orphanage, I was exhausted and panting heavily. "We need to leave, now!" I used whatever breath I had left to shout. *It's been a long day and I still need to get everyone to the south gate. I hope one of the others knows where that is.*

Eleanah, Melody, Martin, Anna and Molly started running to the front door. I waited to catch my breath. "Why? It's almost lunchtime," Melody said as she walked around the corner. She gasped and jogged towards me. "What happened to you? Come here, we'll get you cleaned up."

"That will take a long time to explain. But we have got to go now." I was still panting, gasping for air.

"What's the rush? What's wrong? Why do you look like you've been running all day?" Anna asked as she and Eleanah continued to my side. "And whose blood is this?"

I gave up trying to stand. "There's a demon in town, killing everyone." *I'm too tired for this. I can't keep going.* "Nora told me to get everyone and then we would head for the south gate away from the fighting."

"You look drained. Rest up for a moment and let us know when you're ready to go." Eleanah sat next to me. She looked around the room. "Alright, since Oscar is already out of town working, we can leave once Lucia has had a moment to rest." She returned her gaze to me. "Whose blood is that?"

I'm surprised Nora didn't ask me about all the blood.

"It's a long story. But if you're worried that any of this is mine, the answer is no." I could see the blood drying. *That's going to take a long time to get out of my fur.* "Does anyone have something I can drink? It will help a lot."

"I'll be right back." Melody walked back to the kitchen.

"Is there really a demon in the town?" Martin asked, his concern obvious. "How do you know?"

"Again, that's part of the story. I'll tell you all of it once Nora is here and can hear it too." *I really hope she wins.* "But I saw it, and watched as it killed dozens of people effortlessly."

"You watched?" Martin's voice rose.

"I couldn't do much else. Believe me, if I did any more than what I had, I'd be dead right now." *Do you think I enjoy watching people get slaughtered like that?* I flicked my tail around behind me.

Melody walked around the corner, carrying a cup of water. "She's right, Martin. She did the right thing by running to Nora and away from the demon. Here you go." She leaned over to hand me the cup of water, and I drank it eagerly. "If it had been a fallen, it would take only a few guards to bring it down, and there wouldn't be much of a fuss. It sounds like someone summoned a sin, and those can only be brought down by the strongest of companies."

"You know it's a sin?" I asked once I had drained the contents of the cup. "He said he was a sin of wrath."

"You talked to it?" Martin screamed.

I rubbed my ears to ease the pain. "Stop yelling," I growled. "I'll tell you the whole story later. But I think I can manage now. We need to head to the south gate." I stood up.

"What about everyone else in town?" Molly spoke finally.

I think she's too young to know what to do in this kind of situation. "I guess we can shout down the street telling people to head away from the west gate." *I never thought about everyone else in the town.* "But we need to keep moving. If someone doesn't believe us, we go on."

"Why are you so mean?" Molly looked at me, scared.

"Nora told me to make sure you all leave. I'll do that. I don't care about anyone else. We'll give them a chance, but I don't want to die because of their stupidity." *I really don't want to die again. It was bad enough the first time.*

"Eleanah, can you make sure Lucia can keep going? Martin, carry Molly," Melody directed.

We all left the orphanage together, and Martin led the way, carrying Molly on his back. Eleanah walked beside me while Anna and Melody trailed behind us as they shouted at all the houses to head for safety. As we walked, droplets of rain fell from the sky at a steadily increasing rate. Eventually, the south gate came into view.

The rain turned to a downpour from the dark clouds overhead.

As we looked around, we noticed large smoke clouds over sections of the city. They were even getting close to where we were standing. *The demon is headed this way, isn't he? But why?* My tail wrapped around my leg.

There was an enormous explosion on our right. A wooden building broke apart, sending burning chunks everywhere. We all shielded our faces from flying debris.

The demon walked out of the wreckage, staring directly at me. "Found you." The roaring inferno in his voice caused all my instincts to shout at me to run. He stood tall, but the flames were smaller than before. Steam rolled off his body as the rain continued to batter his flames. "I gave you the chance to join me, but then you insulted me. And now you're helping others run away."

Why is he here? How did he find me? "Why are you after me?" I shouted.

"Because, little beastkin, you have earned my wrath."

If a being known as a sin of wrath tells you that, there is only one appropriate response to the situation. Panic!

He stomped the ground, ready to charge me.

"Run!" I shouted as I pushed Eleanah towards the gate away from the demon. "Get out of the city!"

The next thing I knew, something erupted behind me. I could feel an immense amount of heat on my back as I sailed through the air. My arms and legs flailed as I tumbled to the ground. I landed awkwardly, and I heard something snap in my leg.

A wall stopped my uncontrolled roll. Pain wracked my entire body as I lay on the ground, immobile as I screamed.

"Run, run as fast as you will. For it is you I will kill." The demon taunted me like a cat playing with its food. I couldn't open my eyes as tears poured forth from them.

"Lucia, no!" I heard Eleanah scream. "Mom, it got Lucia!"

Nora's here? Am I going to be saved? A bright flash of light preceded a loud bang. I could do nothing about the ringing in my ears, but I could still hear myself screaming in pain. I wailed, unable to move or alleviate my discomfort.

"Go, all of you! Get through the gate! I'll take care of Lucia!" I heard Nora shout.

"But she's hurt," Eleanah cried.

"Go!" Nora shouted once more.

More bright flashes and explosions erupted around me. They threatened to destroy my hearing for good. Each flash shook the ground, sending more pain through my body. After an uncountable number of flashes, they stopped for a brief moment.

"I'll remember you, mortal." The demon's voice was weak, and it no longer sounded like there was a fire surrounding me.

"Good, then you'll remember to run." Nora's voice was icy. Then the world convulsed. I felt my voice failing with how much I was screaming. The rain cooled the burns on my body. I stopped screaming, but only just.

"Shh, it's okay. It's over now. I've got you." Someone was hugging me gently.

"It hurts so much." My voice was hoarse.

"I know. Just don't move. I'll cool your burns." Nora was on the verge of sobbing, too. I could feel a cooling sensation on my back.

I slowly opened my eyes as the pain subsided. It felt extremely tender. *I think I have some exposed nerves. How badly was I burned? Is my leg okay?* I slowly lowered my head to look at my legs. The bone between my ankle and knee was bent in a new direction. I felt my heart drop and my face fill with despair. *Yeah, that isn't supposed to bend at all!*

Tears started flowing from Nora's eyes. "Yes, your leg is broken. I'll have to set the bone so that I'll heal correctly."

Those words struck fear into my heart. "I know it's going to hurt, but I need to do it." Nora caressed my cheek before moving a few strands of my hair out of my eye.

"No." *I've had enough pain in the last few days to last me a lifetime. I don't want to feel this.* "I can't, I don't..." I couldn't finish my sentence as my voice failed.

"What? It's okay; take your time. You don't what?" Nora's face was still red as tears flowed down her cheeks, but she sat close to me, trying to comfort me.

The pain in my leg made it impossible for me to relax. "Me, sleep," I whispered. *She should understand what I want. I don't have it in me to get more than a few words out at a time. But I just can't seem to pass out.*

"Sleep?" Nora gave me an inquisitive look. She thought for a second before her face shifted, as if an idea had just popped into her head. "I'm sorry, but not here."

I opened my mouth, but no sound came out. More tears flowed as I slammed my eyes shut. *I wish I could pass out now. Why don't I pass out?*

From behind Nora, I heard Martin. "I think she wants you to knock her out first."

Yes, that's it! Please!

"I know, but not here. We'll do it back at home. I'll keep your leg from moving so it doesn't make things worse." Nora placed her arms under me. I felt a strange sensation in my leg, but it was hard to say what it was because of the pain.

Once I was off the ground and in Nora's arms, my back felt cold and hot at the same time. *I'm really messed up right now, aren't I? My back is burnt to a crisp, my left leg is broken, I don't know how many bruises I have decorating my body, my hands and feet are soaked in blood, there's probably some blood around my mouth now that I think about it and I'm extremely filthy. All before lunch, too. I guess I'm going to miss lunch today. I think this might be my worst day ever. Can I please be unconscious now?*

People were filling the street as we walked by. The other kids were falling in behind Nora. Nora turned around and gave me a view of a crater in the middle of the street. In it was the corpse of the demon, a monumental spear of ice impaling him. *Wow!*

13 PITCH BLACK CATS

Our little procession through town was slow, but unhindered. I closed my eyes, hoping I would pass out, eventually. I didn't. Everything seemed to move slower with every painful moment. I don't know how long I listlessly stayed wrapped in Nora's arms, but, eventually, she carefully placed me on a table. *I don't remember anyone opening a door.* When I opened my eyes, I saw that we were in the classroom. *So close to passing out on my own.*

Nora looked me in the eye with sadness. Eleanah moved in front of her to hug me. "I'm sorry. Please don't be mad at me."

Why would I be mad at you?

"It's okay, Eleanah. She asked for this," I could hear Nora whispering to Eleanah.

"I know. But that doesn't make it any easier. I don't want to do it," Eleanah said, about to burst into tears. But with that sentence, I could feel a hand on the back of my head as everything faded to black.

34

DAMAGED

I woke up in my bed to the sun shining in the window. *How long was I out? Everything felt weak, but I could finally move. Improvement already? I'll take it.*

I sat up slowly. My back wasn't hurting nearly as much, and my leg itched something fierce. *It's healing. I hope.* I looked down at myself and saw that I had bandages wrapped around my entire torso and my shoulders. There were also two bandages on my left arm and one on my right. *It looks like I may have had some cuts too.* I wasn't ready to remove my sheets to see what I looked like below the waist yet. I inspected my left hand because I saw two of my fingers were tied together. *Did I break a finger too? How am I still alive? There's no blood in my fur either. I guess they bathed me.* I looked at the back of my arms to see if my fur was burned off, but it wasn't. However, I could tell that the area close to my shoulders was shorter than it should be. *Not as bad as I was expecting. But the fur on my back is going to take some time to regrow. That's going to itch terribly.* The back of my head didn't have any signs of injury, and my face felt fine too.

Time to inspect everything else. I removed the sheets, expecting things to be far worse than I had originally determined. *It's not too bad.* My left leg was in a splint and that was it. It was the most obvious injury, other than the burns on my back. *I don't know how long that's going to take to heal, but it's going to make it difficult to walk.* There was more singed hair on my tail, but it was mostly untouched. *I really want to see the extent of the burns on my back. But I'm part wolf, not part owl. I need a mirror.*

I slowly moved my legs to the edge of my bed. *Nothing hurts too badly right now, but I don't want to make things worse.* I looked around my room and saw a pair of wooden crutches propped up next to my dresser within arm's reach of my bed. *I guess someone was thoughtful.* I grabbed them and attempted to see if it would work for my size. Instead of adjusting the size of the bottom half of the crutch like the crutches from my memories, I would move the crossbars so they sat correctly under the armpit. There was also leather wrapped around the foot to provide better traction.

I grabbed the crutches and carefully stood up, avoiding putting any weight on my broken leg. My hands had difficulties grabbing a section of wood I assumed was a handle, but I could manage.

I looked out the window to see where the sun was. It looked like it was rising. *I think I slept until the next day. I need to get some food in me. It's still early. Maybe everyone's still eating breakfast.* I grabbed some clothes and gingerly dressed myself. *I'm down a shirt and skirt. They were probably too damaged or soaked in blood to salvage.* Slowly, I limped my way out of my room and headed down the hall towards the kitchen.

I heard talking in the kitchen. *So everyone is eating breakfast. I guess that they didn't think that I would be awake now.* Taking small steps and making sure I had plenty of traction, I eventually made my way to the kitchen. *It sounds like they're finishing up with determining who does what. They didn't give me anything. I don't think I'll be much help for a while.*

I carefully pushed my way through the door. As I did, I saw Melody carrying the plates from breakfast. "You're awake!" she shouted.

"Not so loud, please," I grumbled. "Is there any food for me?" Even though my stomach wasn't rumbling, I knew I was hungry.

"Sorry." Melody flinched. Nora and Eleanah walked into the kitchen as Melody apologized. She turned to Nora. "She's finally up. Do you want me to give it to her?"

"Of course, she earned it," Nora said while smiling at me.

Earn what? What am I getting? My tail wagged in anticipation of being rewarded, though I didn't know what for.

"Go and sit at the table. I'll bring it to you." Melody went to set down the dishes she was carrying.

Eleanah ran up to me. "Here, let me help you." She prepared herself to carry me. She squatted down so that she could give me a piggyback ride.

"Okay, I hate using these things already," I growled.

"Martin worked hard to adjust those for you," Eleanah said in a cheerful voice. I leaned forward and wrapped my arms around her shoulders and lifted my legs. As my legs swung to her side, she grabbed them in her arms and stood up.

"They're nice, but it's hard to hold one with my left hand." I waved my fingers that were splinted together to accentuate my point.

"I guess you're right," Eleanah begrudgingly agreed as she carried me to the table, leaving my crutches behind.

I'll have to ask someone to grab them later.

All the other kids were done with their food and were still standing around the table. They all gave me apologetic looks. *I don't look that pathetic, do I?* Eleanah sat me down carefully, then turned around and gave me a look similar to the one Nora used when I had done something wrong.

"What?" I asked.

13 PITCH BLACK CATS

"You have a story that you said you would tell us," Eleanah kept her gaze on me. *Wasn't she happy to see me up and moving?* "Why did you come in here covered in blood that you claim wasn't your own? Why did that demon say the things it said?"

"If you aren't ready, we will wait until you are," Anna chimed in. "I'm amazed that you are moving *At least one of you is on my side.*

The look Nora gave me was the same one Eleanah was giving me. *I'm not getting out of this, am I?* I looked at the table and breathed a heavy sigh. "I guess I need to start from the beginning. It started just as I made the delivery that I brought Zenny along with me on." A realization exploded in my mind. "Wait, what happened to Zenny? Did she make it here? Why was she not here when I arrived?" I sat straight up and started looking around in a slight panic.

"I sent her back to her home so she could eat lunch. She said that you were going to meet up with her here." Melody walked in carrying something on a plate that smelled heavenly. *Raw meat?* "I told her you'd go see her when you got back. When you came back, you were yelling that we needed to leave, so I never thought to mention it. I hope she made it home alright."

"I don't know where she lives, though." The sight of raw meat left me conflicted. *Zenny could have been hurt or worse yesterday and here I am, excited about the prospect of eating raw meat.*

"She said that you would say that and asked for a map so she could draw where she lives for you." Melody chuckled at my worry. *I'm honestly starting to like Zenny.* Melody arrived with the plate and presented me with several pieces of raw bacon. I didn't wait for her to retract her hand before I reached out and grabbed a piece. "She lives near the east gate, by the way." Melody smiled.

She should be safe then.

My guilt dispersed, tail wagging, a smile on my face, eyes closed, and, with my teeth chewing through the bacon like they were made for this, I was the perfect picture of delighted. I continued to single-mindedly consume and enjoy my treat. Nobody interrupted my meal, leaving me in a cloud of true bliss. I was enjoying myself so much that after I had eaten my last piece, I absentmindedly grabbed at the plate, believing that there was still one more piece. When my hand grasped at nothing, I stared at the dish, longing for another piece.

I looked around and saw everyone was once again sitting in their seats, patiently waiting for me. Melody, Anna and Molly were all smiling at me. The two boys looked at me with amusement, as if my eating was entertaining to watch. Nora and Eleanah softened their looks, but, once I glanced at them, I could feel that they wanted me to continue with my recollection of yesterday's events.

"After I sent Zenny here, I completed the delivery to Nick, the toy maker." I lowered my head. *This isn't a happy story. I really hope Zenny's alright.* "He was such a nice guy. After I helped him bring the barrel in, he wanted to give me a toy. Before he could do that, two guys barged in. One stabbed him in the heart, and the other hit me in the head and knocked me out."

"You're really good at getting your head hit, aren't you?" Oscar quipped.

"Shut it!" I snapped at Oscar. *Calm down. Just because he's right doesn't mean I need to bite his head off, literally or figuratively.*

Oscar flinched. "Sorry."

I continued my story. "I woke up in the basement of the toy maker's shop, tied up. I cut the ropes with my claws to try and escape. They did nothing right away because they were using some kinda liquid to engrave something into the floor. A glyph? I think it was called a glyph. Anyway, they noticed I had escaped my bindings after I found out that they had locked the door. They then told me they were going to sacrifice me to summon a demon. One of them said they were ordered to by Decklin. Then... then I killed them both." A strange feeling of pride filled me when I admitted it. "I did it to defend myself," I blurted out.

Nora's eyes shimmered with moisture. "I understand. I'm sorry

I wasn't fast enough to save you from them. When did your necklace activate in the fight?"

Is she blaming herself because I killed those two? "Near the end." The feeling of pride returned. *Why am I so happy that I killed people? Shouldn't I feel sad that I ended a human's life?* "It only activated because one kept calling me a monster. I'm beginning to question how right he is." My head dropped with my mood. *There's something very wrong with me.*

"You did what you had to do to survive. You shouldn't feel ashamed about that," Martin said tenderly. "But how could you possibly kill two adults?" He gave me a hard look.

"Martin!" Nora scolded him. "Now isn't the time." She then turned to me with a soft look. "It's alright to feel sad about what you did. Killing someone doesn't make you a monster. If it did, I would be one of the most dangerous monsters in this entire kingdom."

"That isn't it." I watched as everyone looked at me, bewildered. "I don't feel sad that I killed them. I'm happy that I killed them. I enjoyed ripping that man's chest apart. And when I left the basement and saw the carnage the demon caused, I wasn't sick; I was hungry! That's why I feel like a monster!" My voice broke as tears formed in my eyes.

Everyone stared at me. *They see me as a monster, don't they?* The kids all exchanged glances with each other.

Nora slammed her fist onto the table. "Enough!" she bellowed, but not loud enough to hurt my ears. "She is still a part of this family." She turned to look at me. "Do you want to kill anyone else?"

"No, I don't want to kill anyone." I couldn't hold back the tears anymore, and they flowed as I closed my eyes. *I'm scaring myself now.*

"We'll figure this out together." Nora's tone quieted down. "But I expect each of you to treat her the same way you would treat anyone else. Understood?" I heard no replies over my sniffling. I heard Nora get out of her chair and walk over to me. "Come on, you still need to rest up. We'll look at your wounds and get you taken care of." She lifted me out of the chair, and I grabbed onto her as she put her arm under my legs to hold me up. "Molly, please take Lucia's crutches to her room for her."

35

BEDROOM BOREDOM

Nora carried me to my room and sat me down on the bed. She gingerly removed the bandages from my back. "It looks worse than it is," Nora said with a hint of happiness.

Is she forcing herself to sound happy to make me not panic? I grabbed Nora's arm. "It's just the two of us. You don't need to sugarcoat it for me. How bad is it, really?" I looked at her seriously. "Can you get two mirrors so that I can see?"

"It really is a lot better than I would have expected. You heal quickly. I have to go and get the ointment. I'll see about getting a mirror too." Nora stood up from inspecting my back as I released her arm.

"I was wondering, since I'm on a no-walking regimen right now, could you teach me different things about this world?" I asked just before she reached the door.

"I have a few things I want to look into today. Once I see to them, I'll bring Phan when I can. He can teach you something new." Nora gave me a warm smile.

"Why do you keep telling him to teach me? Isn't there someone better?" *After what he did to me, I want to pull his teeth out. I still haven't forgiven him, and I won't ever forgive him.* I could feel myself tense up. "And why don't we have a real doctor? He isn't one, he's a librarian."

"Why are you so angry with him?" Nora stopped and looked at me.

"Why? Why? Let me pull all of your teeth out and see how you feel!" I bunched my blankets up in my hands, claws shredding them. My tail thrashed from side to side.

"First off, calm down. Waterfalls." Nora stood unfazed by my display. I started my usual meditation, attempting to calm down. It worked a bit, and as I returned to my sitting position, Nora picked up where she left off. "I don't blame you for being upset. But we had to do something. I couldn't just watch you suffer."

"I know. But there must be something that can make it so that I can't feel pain or put me to sleep where pain can't wake me up." I folded my arms and stared at Nora accusingly.

"I'm sorry, but the substances that I know that can do that were developed to kill. If I were to use any of them on you, you probably wouldn't wake up. Even with your impressive recovery aptitude. We talked about that." Nora stood unflinching. I cringed. *It still didn't help the situation.* "I'm sure that Phan knows of many more that I don't. But I also believe that he would have used them if he could. We told you that."

"Then you should have knocked me out like you did when you were going to set the bone in my leg." I never gave up on my stare.

"We didn't knock you out." Nora relaxed and turned back to the door. "You passed out on your own. Eleanah couldn't do it. Besides, I'm not in the habit of knocking children out. I've caused enough pain in this world already." Her voice dropped lower the more she spoke. She opened the door and walked out. "I'll be right back."

I sat alone in my room, brooding. *I don't care what reasoning she wants to give. That was the most painful experience of my two*

13 PITCH BLACK CATS

lifetimes. Granted, one is still short, and the other has many holes poked through my memories of it.

It wasn't long before Nora returned with Eleanah's small desk mirror and a small jar that had a sweet smell emanating from it.

"What's that I smell?" I closed my eyes and tried to focus on the scent and attempted to find anything in my shoddy memory banks that would be relevant.

"I believe Midas called it aloe vera." Nora scrunched her face with discomfort. "I learned it from the one who had your job before you. It does wonders on burns." She held up the little mirror for me to look at my back.

"So this Midas, was he from my world?" *How much did he lose on the way here?* I looked at my back with the mirror Nora gave me while she held another mirror in her hand. I saw a mixture of red, pink and white spots. The pink looked like skin that was still recovering from the burn. The white patches I saw were dead skin. And the red was where the burn was worst. None of the patches were large, but there were a lot of them.

After Nora let me look at the condition of my back, she placed the mirror on the dresser. "He never said." Nora turned it back on me. "But where are you from?"

"Earth?" I asked, puzzled. *She did say she was interested in the world I was from.*

"Well, welcome to Centari." Nora held her arms out for a hug. "How do you like it so far?"

"Honestly?" I put a finger to my chin. *How do I answer this politely?* "Since I arrived, I was turned into a little beastkin girl, captured by orcs, subjected to racism, drafted into the army, beaten up, painfully shocked multiple times, dislocated a shoulder, kidnapped, almost sacrificed to a demon and nearly killed by said demon." I paused for dramatic effect. "I'd say it's a solid one star so far. I would not recommend it."

Nora stood dumbfounded. "One star?"

"Out of five. It was a common measurement used to rate things in my old world," I said with a wave of my hand.

Nora sat next to me. "When you focus on all the bad things that have happened to you, of course you will have a low opinion." She opened the jar of aloe vera and scooped a small amount onto her fingertips. It was a thick blue substance that overwhelmed my nose. *Isn't aloe usually white?* "What about the new family you joined? What about the friends you made? The joy you feel when you run around? The taste of raw bacon? A second chance at life? Do those mean nothing to you?"

She applied the strange ointment to my back, and I jumped slightly, unprepared for the chilly feeling mixed with the stinging sensation when she first touched me. "Sorry, it'll feel cold."

I settled down and prepared for it, and, when she applied it a second time, I didn't move. The cooling sensation felt slightly familiar, but I couldn't pinpoint why. "I understand that a second chance at life is a gift that shouldn't be squandered." I lowered my head and let my ears droop. *This is a depressing topic, and it's one I don't want to continue.* "So, what are you going to do while you're out?"

She finished applying her medicine to my back. "You don't want to keep talking about it? If that's what you wish." She closed her jar and stood up. "I'm going to go see the summoning glyph that brought the demon here. Also, I want to see the two you killed. I need to take Anna's conjuration teacher to look at the glyph too." She wrapped new bandages over my burns. "And I'm going to drag Decklin to court and watch him get executed."

If there was a person who could out-wrath a sin of wrath, it would be this woman. I looked at Nora, confused. "Why were you the one who killed the demon? Aren't there other people who can do that in this town?" *She can't be the only one that powerful.*

"There are usually many more." Nora had a thoughtful look in her eye. "But yesterday all of them had left to deal with their missions. You might be on to something. It's too convenient that the day after everyone who can bring down a demon leaves town to deal with the goblins, a demon is summoned."

"But why did they try to use me?" I made myself smaller.

Nora's eyes grew with my question. "A great question. I will pry the answer from Decklin by any means necessary." I could see some of Nora's hair defying gravity. "Please stay in bed and rest. I'll take care of everything." Her voice was full of anger.

She gives me a hard time with my anger-control issues. She treats me like I'm her child. If someone wanted to hurt my child, I would hunt them down and tear them to shreds. Kill them, and I mean kill them. You know what? I think in this life I would tear them to shreds. Although I have to have kids first. That will be a topic of discussion for many years down the line. I'm still just a little kid.

Nora left my room during my little dive down a mental rabbit hole. *She took the mirror with her. This is going to be very boring until my leg heals.* I lay down and relaxed as much as I could. The splint that held my leg bones immobile was constantly on my mind. I tried to avoid lying on my back so as not to disturb my burns. I started counting sheep in an attempt to bore myself to sleep. It didn't work. *Maybe I should ask if someone has a book I can read. Who's walking around right now?*

I got up and used my crutches to make my way slowly out of my room. Once I opened the door, I saw Melody walking with Zenny coming from the front door. "What are you doing here, Zenny?" I stood in my room's doorway.

Melody waved to Zenny as she said, "I thought I could cheer you up. You looked sad when you were using your crutches. So I went and got your friend Zenny. You sounded very concerned for her safety too. So I thought if I brought her here, she'd cheer you up and you'd be able to relax."

"You were worried about me?" Zenny sounded happy. But her face turned worried once she looked at me more closely. "What happened to you? You look terrible."

Thanks, I feel terrible.

"How about you go with her into her room and you can have all the girl talk you want?" Melody gave Zenny a slight push in my direction.

I moved to make room for Zenny to enter my room. She entered and gave me a sad look before walking immediately towards my bed. She started making my bed by spreading the sheet out so that it was flat and fluffed my pillow and placed it in the center at the top. I stared at her.

"You shouldn't leave your bed in a mess like that," Zenny said sternly. "And why are there so many holes in it?"

"Why? Once I sleep in it, it'll be a mess again. Besides, that's the third sheet I've had in three weeks." I started making my way back to my bed again. "I keep tearing holes in them with my toe-claws."

She looked at my feet. "Oh, I would never have guessed that would be a problem for you." *That's only part of the list. The first time I rolled over on my tail while I slept was a real eye-opener. I haven't made that mistake twice.* "You don't wear socks to bed? Don't they get cold?"

"My feet are covered in fur. So no." I looked at her, eyes narrowed. I sat on the bed, and Zenny joined me, looking despondent.

"Being a beastkin must be useful." She looked at her stocking-covered feet, kicking them back and forth.

"I'm not going to lie, it has its advantages," I said, admiring my claws and licking my teeth. "But it isn't all sunshine and rainbows over here, either."

"What do you mean?" She turned to look at me.

"I have way too much energy. It's almost killing me not being able to go out and run right now." I pointed to my broken leg. "I also have an expensive and very restrictive diet. And there are times I just want to break something or hurt or even kill someone. Also, there's the destruction of bedding while I sleep." I pointed to the bed, and the two of us giggled.

"You're weird." She tilted her head to the side and stared at me. "Why didn't you come here yesterday?"

I waved my hands towards all my injuries. "This is what happened." *The confusion on her face tells me I need to tell the whole story.* "You know how we were delivering a barrel to Nick yesterday?" She nodded. "Once I completed the delivery, some guys decided to kidnap me and kill Nick..." I recounted the rest of my story until the moment I passed out. Zenny stared at me, unblinking and completely silent. Once I was done, I sat still, waiting for a reaction from her.

"Does it hurt?"

I wasn't expecting those to be her first words. "Right now? Not really, it's mostly uncomfortable." I sat motionless as I answered her question.

She leaned forward and hugged me. Her arms wrapped around my neck and never touched my back. "I'm glad you're alright." Her soft voice trembled slightly.

I returned her hug. *I don't know what's going on right now. She seems to need this, so I'll just go with it.* "Sorry about making you worry." *She isn't crying, but I can hear her heart slowing down. I didn't realize that she was that worked up about what happened to me.* "I'll be okay after taking some time to heal. Do you know of anything I can do while I'm forced to stay in bed? Are there any books I can read?"

"You like to read too?" She released me and sat up. There was a twinkle in her eye, just like when she asked if she could be useful to me. "I love to read. Especially stories where the hero saves the princess." She bounced as she sat on my bed. "What are your favorite stories?"

That doesn't surprise me. "I don't actually know of any stories." I gave her a sheepish grin. "Actually, I don't know if I'll like any stories, but since I can't do much, I thought I could give it a try."

"You've never read a book before?" Her excitement evaporated as she looked mortified. "But didn't you say you knew how to read and write?"

"I do, but I don't remember anything from before a few weeks ago." *I guess I haven't told her about my amnesia yet.* "I probably should tell you that I became an orphan a few weeks ago. I have no idea how long ago it was since some details aren't adding up right now, but that isn't important. What is important is that my first memory is of waking up in a village being raided by orcs that took me captive."

"You don't remember anything?" Her eyes grew wide.

"Nope, not a thing." *Let's continue to leave out the whole reincarnation detail. Not that it's that relevant anyway.*

Zenny just sat there. *Is she feeling pity towards me? It's hard to tell.* I could hear footsteps coming down the hall. *It sounds like several people are walking, although it's hard to tell how many.* It wasn't long before the door to my room opened and three people walked in. Nora, Anna and someone I'd never met before. *Is that Anna's conjuration teacher?*

36

MAGIC 101

An elf stood in the doorway dressed in silk robes. He had long, curly black hair just past his shoulders, and his brown eyes gazed out from an angular face that was tipped by the sharpest nose ever. His skin was almost chalk white. *When was the last time this guy got out and saw the sun?* His robes didn't hide that he was bony, but he didn't look unhealthy either.

"So, this is your newest addition." He gave me a harsh look. "What happened to her?"

"She was injured in the demon attack yesterday," Nora said with a slight grimace. She turned to me. "What is Zenny doing here?"

"Melody thought that bringing her here would cheer me up," I said with a shrug. "It worked, I think. I had someone to talk to." Zenny's face filled with a bright smile.

"As long as you take it easy, it's fine." Nora sighed. "Since I can't find Phannidoritthin at his home and nobody has seen him, I've asked Folmas here to teach you in his stead." She waved to the elf standing next to her.

Anna walked up to me, holding a familiar unicorn toy. "We found Nick. He was holding this. Does it mean anything to you?"

She presented the yellow-horned toy. There was no hint of blood on it, not even the smell.

My heart sank. "He was going to give that to me as a reward for helping him." I saw everyone else lower their heads sadly. Everyone except Folmas, who, for some reason, looked out the window in my room.

"Then you should take it," Nora said while lifting her head. "A child's happiness was all he ever asked for."

I grabbed the toy and held it. *I promise that nobody will ever suffer for my sake again. One death because of me is more than enough.*

"Now if you are done, Anna, make two copies of the glyph we found and try to translate what you can." Folmas's tone brought everyone's attention to him, and Anna gave a slight bow before leaving my room without a word. "What do you want me to teach her, Nora?" Folmas crossed his arms.

Does he see this as a chore?

"Since nobody can find Phannidoritthin, and you wanted someone else to teach you so badly, Lucia, why don't you tell us what you want to learn?" Nora turned her attention to me.

There's something I have always wanted to know about since I learned it existed... "Magic. Can you teach me magic?" I asked eagerly. My tail hit Zenny, who was sitting on my bed with me. "Oh, and can Zenny stay too?"

"I have one student already. I'm not taking up another, especially one so young." Folmas waved his hand dismissively.

"You can teach her about magic." Nora glared at him. "I agree, she shouldn't learn how to perform magic. For the time being, that would be..."—Nora paused for a moment—"unsafe." *Why is it bad for me to learn magic now?* "And if Zenny would like to stay, she may." She smiled at Zenny.

"If it isn't a bother." Zenny made herself as small as possible while looking at the ground.

"If you need someone to set the foundations correctly, I guess I will do it." Folmas relaxed a bit. "It will be better than letting that backward-thinking doctor fill her head with misconceptions."

Is he talking about Phan? Why doesn't he like him? I know why I don't.

"Is there anything you need?" Nora said to Folmas. She sounded a little annoyed.

"Nothing is necessary." Folmas stood before the two of us sitting on the bed. "I expect the two of you to pay attention. Save all of your questions for the end. I will not be interrupted. Is that understood?" His tone was abrasive to my ears, but I nodded my head. I assumed Zenny had done the same, because our teacher took a deep breath before he began his lecture.

"Magic is categorized into four major schools: manipulation, conjuration, enchantment and necromancy. We will start with the one you need to know the least about. Necromancy is illegal in every kingdom. It is one of the few things everyone can agree on. Every time someone has attempted to perform necromancy magic, it has led to entire sections of kingdoms being left lifeless for several years. If you see anyone ever practicing it or studying it, report them to the nearest officials, or, if later in life you are the official, arrest them on sight. If they resist, it is generally accepted to kill them." *Zero tolerance for necromancy. Got it.* "Hopefully you never experience any necromancy magic, but know that those that practice it often manipulate souls and corpses to nightmarish effect. All of it is unnatural and perverts the natural order." I could see the metaphorical venom dripping from his lips.

"With that unpleasantness finished. On to the second school, conjuration." I watched our instructor relax. "Conjuration is my specialty. To perform conjuration magic, one must first learn the glyphs associated with it. Glyphs are the crux of conjuration magic. One mistake with a glyph is all it takes for your magic to turn from success to failure. Many similarities are shared between conjuration and enchantment. Most of the time, people limit the possibility of conjuration magic to the simple summoning of mundane objects. While I must admit the transportation of living beings is met with a disturbing mess, it is capable of much more." The two of us sat still like good children watching the elf's ego swelling with word. *If it grows any more, Zenny and I will be crushed to death.*

Nora cleared her throat and gave Folmas a look that screamed, *Get on with it!*

Folmas shivered before turning back to us. "But as I was saying, you can summon demons or angels. Now I know what you are thinking. If summoning living creatures results in the grim death of the summoned, then how do demons and angels survive? See, there's been speculation that demons and angels live on different planes of existence—"

"Enough!" Folmas shut up and flinched as Nora stomped her foot. I tried to hold back a giggle, but failed. Zenny just stared at the elf, unblinking.

"Sorry, that is a more advanced topic. Let's just say that's how the magic works for now." Folmas flinched as he took another step away from Nora. He collected himself as he gave Nora a sidelong glance. I raised my hand and waved it back and forth. "What are you doing?" The elf glared at me once he saw me.

"I want to see some magic." My tail slid across the mattress as it wagged behind me.

"Can you show us?" Zenny asked with bated breath.

Nora clapped her hands. "That's an excellent idea, Lucia." She walked over and placed her hand on Folmas's back. "Keep it simple for the kids, please." The smile on Nora's face was almost terrifying.

I'm glad that she isn't giving me that smile.

Folmas's tongue and jaw refused to move as he looked around the room nervously. Sweat slid down the side of his face. "I-I need something to use as a demonstration." The man's voice cracked.

I held out the toy unicorn in my hands. "You can use this."

Nora's eyes looked like they were glowing as she watched Folmas grab my toy. Sweat soaked his face as he kneeled in front of us. *Is Nora making him nervous? Not so tough now, are you, tough guy?* Something about watching him melt under her gaze felt satisfying.

Folmas held one hand flat with the unicorn resting on its side. He placed a finger on the toy's front shoulder. "This is what a glyph can look like." Where his finger touched the painted wood, it glowed softly, leaving an oddly shaped wolf head outline. "This is a temporary glyph for this demonstration only." Folmas sounded like he was straining to carry something as he placed the toy on the floor in front of me. "Don't touch it." The elf stood up and started breathing heavily as he walked to the far side of the room.

Zenny and I stared at the glowing glyph as the toy rested on the floor. Zenny and I leaned closer, and, as we did, it looked like the world around the unicorn started folding in on itself. The head and tail turned inwards towards the glowing outline Folmas had drawn with his magic. Everything pulled to the center of the toy until it was nothing more than a gray line. I blinked and then it was gone. I looked around the room to see if I could find it.

Folmas held out his hands, and in them sat my toy unicorn.

"Are you done showing off?" Nora smirked as she grabbed the toy from him. As she placed it back in my hands, she smiled. "He won't admit this, but creating a visible glyph of pure magic takes a lot out of you, even a temporary one."

Folmas stood back and panted as he wiped his face with his sleeve.

"That was cool." Zenny's eyes nearly bulged out of their sockets as she watched Nora return to her post by the door.

So did he just fold the fabric of space? Is that the correct way to describe what I just saw?

Folmas took a deep breath and straightened his back. "Since I alluded to enchantment magic earlier, how about we cover that next?" Nora gave him a nod. "Enchantment magic is most often practiced by dragoons and dwarves. It is similar to conjuration, in that the magic is more permanent. Where conjuration uses large,

THE BIG BAD WOLF

complicated glyphs, enchantment uses small, simple runes. Enchantment is no less complicated than conjuration because, just as changing the spelling of a word can change its meaning, using runes in a different order can have drastic changes. Enchantment is known as the most dangerous of the schools of magic because if you don't get it perfectly correct, it will literally blow up in your face." Folmas rubbed his cheek. *Does he have a bad memory of enchanting something?* "The dwarves found that gold is the best metal to use for enchanting, but they have to create an alloy with either platinum or copper to make it more durable. It doesn't work as well as pure gold, but it takes more than someone with a strong grip to remove the rune that way."

I grabbed my necklace.

"Yes, that necklace is magic." Nora stepped up to me. She knelt in front of me and covered the gem on the necklace with both her hands. "If you would like to see the runes, I can show them to you."

I shook my head. "Not really. But the wands are an enchanted item too, right?"

"Yes. Please wait for me to return." Nora walked out and Folmas, Zenny and I all stared at each other in silence until she returned.

She entered with a wand in hand. "These are a special case since I made them with kids in mind." Nora stuck her fingers into the wand and pried it open like a banana peel. "Here are the runes, nice and safe."

Nora turned the wand sideways and showed us the hollowed-out center. Inside were silver shapes and designs I couldn't begin to describe.

Zenny reached out a hand and brushed the runes. She jerked her hand back and giggled.

"I used silver since it's more available in this kingdom. And since it's covered, you kids have to break the wand to ruin the enchantments." Nora smiled as she folded the wooden rod back to its original state. "Your necklace's runes are woven into the threads

13 PITCH BLACK CATS

of the necklace and engraved in the center of the gem. It's common practice to place runes somewhere where they won't be disturbed through normal use. Breaking the magical item often will result in an explosion of magic. It's very difficult to know what will happen in such instances, so try not to do it."

"Yes, all those things are important, but let us continue," Folmas said. "The last school is the catchall: manipulation. Manipulation has many subcategories to it, like illusion, healing, elemental, material and plant. Most of the time, when you see someone showing off with magic, it's manipulation. You can't create something out of nothing, even with magic. You can change the shape, temperature, whether something is a solid or liquid, and you can stimulate growth or impede it."

It looks like manipulation magic has to follow most of the rules of physics, but it bends them quite liberally.

"Manipulation differs with conjuration, enchantment and necromancy another way too." Folmas gave us a serious glare. "While you can be skilled in each of those schools in their entirety, with manipulation you can't. Most people find themselves only able to focus on one or two aspects of manipulation magic. Also finding anyone who can use more than one school of magic is rare. Nora here is the exception. She is one of a few who can practice all schools of magic. But her most prominent school is manipulation. Since you were so quick to volunteer me to demonstrate conjuration, please give the kids a show." He waved his arms to lead Nora to the center of the room as he took a few steps towards the corner of my room.

Nora smiled politely as she took center stage. She held out her hand and waved it around. Water materialized around her hand and circled around her wrist like a big wet bracelet that wouldn't touch her. With her other hand, she touched a finger to the ring of water. It froze immediately and began plummeting to the ground. Nora caught the ring before it hit the ground and offered it to us.

THE BIG BAD WOLF

I grabbed it and it didn't feel cold. It felt nice. My tail started wagging behind me again and I unconsciously hugged the icy ring.

"That isn't the reaction I expected," Nora whispered.

"I don't know, but something about the ice feels right." *It's impossible to put into words. Why do I want to hug ice? I think my instincts are looking for something cold, but why?*

"Sorry, honey, but that's eventually going to melt. It's still just ice." Nora extended a hand to me.

I looked at Nora's hand, then at the ice in my arms. My shirt was starting to feel wet, reinforcing Nora's words. I slowly extended the ring of ice and hung it on Nora's hand. Something felt missing in my heart when I released the ring. I had to suppress the tear forming in my eye as I watched the ice evaporate. *Why was that so difficult?*

"I wonder if you're a wolf who likes snow." Zenny reached out and rubbed the fur on my arm. "It's so soft. Maybe it will keep you warm in the ice season."

I shrugged. "Probably. That's why I have it, I think."

"Hopefully you'll be on your feet by then." Nora chuckled as she stood up. "But remember, you need to rest for now. And take it easy after the day you've had."

Folmas cleared his throat. "Yes, we were lucky to have Nora react so quickly to the demon yesterday. If she hadn't, many more lives would have been lost."

All the lives lost were my fault. Guilt gripped my heart tightly. I held the toy unicorn tightly as a reminder that Nick was killed because of me.

"Don't concern yourself with what happened yesterday, Lucia." I looked up and saw Folmas looking at me. "You defended yourself from those two who sought this city's destruction. The glyph was primed to be activated by anyone's blood. But I must say that if that was truly your handiwork, you must learn to control yourself better, or you will never find yourself a student of mine."

I don't care about that.

"I think that is enough about magic for now." Nora quickly

stood between the two of us. She gave the male elf a stare that melted his courage. "How about we end this lesson and prepare for lunch? Zenny, I hope you had fun, but it's time for you to head home."

Zenny lowered her head while blushing. "Is it alright if I come back with some books for Lucia to read?"

Nora turned her head to me and looked at me inquisitively.

"What?" I shrugged my shoulders while looking as innocent as I could.

"You're welcome to come anytime you want." Nora extended a hand to Zenny. "I'm sure Lucia would love your company."

"You mean it?" Zenny grabbed Nora's hand and jumped off the bed. When she looked at me, I nodded. "I'll bring you all my favorite books, Lucia." She skipped as she walked out of my room, heading for the front door with Nora walking with her.

Folmas was about to follow them out the door.

"One moment, Folmas." I held up my hand to stop him and placed the toy unicorn on the dresser next to my bed. "I have a few questions first."

"If I must, I will answer them." He sighed as he turned to face me.

"Why, if necromancy is so bad, even bother telling us about it?" *Telling people something is forbidden often has the opposite effect on them.*

"It serves as a warning. Ignorance is no excuse in the eyes of the law." *Calm down, grumpy. But he isn't wrong.* "As I stated earlier, if anyone in this world sees you perform necromancy, they will not hesitate to brand you as a menace to all life. The elves of Osarin have special teams they send out to hunt anyone suspected of necromancy. We have, on occasion, assisted those teams with one or two of our own."

Okay, onto a happier note. "You were rather vague about manipulation magic. Could you tell me more about it?" Folmas

THE BIG BAD WOLF

started looking at me strangely. *Oh no, I'm doing it again. I'm supposed to be a child. I can't ask complicated questions.*

Folmas began speaking without changing his expression. "Most people are familiar with manipulation of the basic elements: fire, water, earth and air. There have also been mages who have manipulated metal and wood too. I don't understand most of the specifics of healing magic. It has been explained to me as using magic to accelerate natural healing in a specific area. Illusion is more complicated to explain. So if you don't understand it, don't worry. It involves forcing something you have seen to be seen by everyone. You can also do the same for sound."

I have a simpler theory: You're manipulating light. I sort of figured that out with Oscar's little displays.

After I nodded, Folmas relaxed. "I am well aware of Nora's favorite use of manipulation magic, her so-called summoning of water. I will tell you right now, she isn't summoning anything. She's simply making it rain in a small area."

She's pulling water from the surrounding air and condensing it. That makes sense. I guess I'll learn more when I learn how to perform magic.

"Also, the demon told me that because of what I did to the one guy, I guaranteed a sin of wrath was summoned." I folded my ears back.

"That makes sense. But after seeing the bodies, if they had sacrificed you, the result would have been the same. Your wrathful spirit would have drawn it anyway. It's troubling news that it took any interest in you."

I looked up at Folmas and shivered. "How did— How do you know that?" My heart started beating faster against my ribs.

"A demon on the mission he was on would not have just left you there. There is something special about you, Lucia." Folmas placed a finger on his chin as he watched me. "I can't put my finger on it, but it makes me want to keep a close eye on you." *Please don't.* "But I know Nora will take good care of you. Regardless, you really should let that entire incident go. One as young as you will be better off forgetting everything."

Would you look at that? He isn't completely heartless. But no, I will never forget what happened. Nobody dies because of me again. "Thank you. I'm going to go eat now," I said as I grabbed my crutches.

I ignored him as I set out on my—much harder than I would like—trip to the bathroom. Folmas left the room before me, so I watched him as he left, and Nora watched me as I entered the bathroom. Once my business was done, I exited to find her still standing by the door. She gestured to the kitchen wordlessly.

I broke the silence between the two of us. "So, how powerful are you?"

"Back when I was in the mercenary company at my peak, there were four of us at about the same level of mastery over magic. But that was years ago, and I haven't been as strict with my practice." She had a distant stare as she answered. "One was a human who has likely passed away by now. A high elf with whom I fought to a stalemate in a duel. And a dwarf named Boulderchip. His brother was in our company. He hated violence so much that he left his kingdom once they went to war with our kingdom. Nobody has seen him since. There was also a dragoon named Zorgintenthed, but he moved to the crown of the world to make oracle stones."

I nearly stopped walking. "Why did he do that? And how do you know that?"

"He wanted to be left alone and was tired of people asking him to join their kingdom." She placed a hand on my shoulder and led me towards the kitchen.

"How do you know that?" *That seems like too personal of information to just know.*

"I met him," she answered. "He told me when I met him at the crown of the world."

"You went to the crown of the world?" I stopped. "Isn't that a big mountain?"

"Yes, and I went once and never again. I hate the mountains." The look of displeasure on her face was obvious. "All that climbing in the cold makes it worse. Don't get me started with the cold."

I resumed my limp to the dining room. "You don't like the ice season, do you?"

"Of course not. It's the worst season by far." She chuckled.

But it's looking like it'll be my favorite season.

37

ANOTHER INNOCENT DAY

I yawned as I stretched in bed. I sat up, rubbing the sleep out of my eyes. *Time to give this another try.* I removed the splint from my leg. I set it on the ground and stood up. The lack of pain was a welcome change. *After two entire weeks of waiting for my leg to heal, I'm finally free of this splint.* I took a few light steps, expecting some sign that my leg wasn't finished healing yet.

"Finally!" I shouted in triumph. *I'm going to go for a run. Not too fast, I don't want to break it again.* I quickly got dressed and didn't bother brushing my fur yet. I ran out of my room and almost made it to the front door.

"Where do you think you're going, young lady?" a voice called as a door opened and closed.

I stopped my dash through the orphanage. *Why did Nora have to stop me?* "For a run," I answered meekly.

"No, you're not." I turned and saw Nora standing behind me, hands on her hips and a scowl on her face.

"But, Mom," I whined. "Can't you see my leg is completely healed? I've been dying to run for two weeks now."

"I know, but if you go out and re-injure yourself, I'll lock you in your room for another two weeks until we know for a fact that you aren't going to hurt yourself again." She raised her voice, but not loud enough to cause me to feel pain. *She has gotten very good at hitting that limit and stopping.*

I stood up straight. "What if I have a clean bill of health? Do I get to go for a run then?"

"You and your bargaining." She shook her head.

"Well, I've gone through acceptance, depression and anger. Maybe I'm in denial right now and I'm moving on to bargaining next." I grinned.

Nora released a heavy sigh. "Fine, but if Salien says that you need more time, you'll be carried to your bed, where you will stay until she says so." She walked up to me and leaned over me.

"It wouldn't be so bad if it wasn't so boring!" I dropped my shoulders.

"Didn't Zenny bring a mountain of books for you to read?" Nora's face changed to one of confusion.

"She likes all those mushy romantic books. There's nothing exciting about them." *I'm five, I need stimulus! I have so much energy all the time now. I guess I forgot how much energy kids have, or am I an anomaly?*

"Did you finish any of them?" Nora raised an eyebrow at me.

"I couldn't. They were almost as bad as the geography books you made me read." I shuddered at the memory of those texts.

"You're going to learn geography one way or another." She put her hand on my shoulder. "Now, about that outfit you're wearing."

I looked down at myself. *I don't see anything wrong with it. It's a little on the small side, but it isn't that bad.* "What?"

"Aren't you cold?" She looked worried.

Should I be? "No."

"It looks like your fur will keep you quite warm this ice season." Nora laughed.

That's right, next week will be the start of the ice season. Once the green moon reaches its new moon phase. The red moon's new moon phase was yesterday. Including today, we have seven more days left of the wind season. Each year starts at the beginning of the water season and ends on the last day of the ice season. Each season is sixteen weeks long, leaving five hundred twelve days a year. The yellow moon is always full and has nothing to do with the calendar. Even though there are so many days a year, the days are shorter. I still can't believe I was so bored that I counted how long a day was. Without a clock, I can only guess that each day is about the equivalent of twenty hours in my old world.

"Is it that cold?" *Now that I think about it, I've never been cold in this life.*

"It's cold enough for everyone else to have already put a second blanket on their beds and wear an extra layer of clothes." Nora guided me back to my room. "Go and brush all your fur. It's sticking up all over the place. I'll get Salien after breakfast."

"So what do you want me to do with all of my shed fur?" *I started shedding two days ago. All the hair that I've shed has been shorter than what I'm currently sporting.*

"I don't know. Throw it out the window," she responded uncertainly. "How much are you shedding?"

"Not much, but it might be more later," I said nonchalantly as I kept walking to my room.

"I have got to find Phannidoritthin's books on beastkin. I found all the other races, but not those," Nora whispered as she turned away and headed for the kitchen.

I wonder what she had to do to get all those books. I know she got them after they found Phan's body bled dry and heavily tortured in one of the city's wells three days after the demon attack. Good riddance.

The whole situation of the attack hasn't sat well with me. Nora has also been running around town much more than before.

I returned to my room, gave myself my usual morning brush and did everything I could to quell the bursting need to burn some energy. After tossing the fur that collected on my brush out the window, I headed for breakfast before anyone else. The meal was uneventful and, with the chores divided up amongst us kids, we all went our separate ways. I went to the kitchen with Melody and assisted with the dishes.

After we finished the dishes, Melody left to go shopping for more food, and I went back to my room to wait for Salien, as Nora wanted. I didn't have to wait long for footsteps to head down the hall.

"Come in." I didn't wait for them to knock on the door before granting them entrance.

"You already know when I'm here?" A soft voice preceded the short human woman who entered my room followed by Nora. Salien had long brownish-red hair, braided in an intricate pattern. Her face was cute and looked more at home on someone much younger. She was shorter than Eleanah but carried herself with an unparalleled level of confidence. Her white robe went all the way to her feet and was spotless and unadorned. She was carrying a small leather satchel with a strap over her shoulder. "I see you've taken the liberty of removing your brace."

"I did, and I even walked all morning without any pain," I said, grinning. *You're going to give me a clean bill of health and I'll finally get to go for a run.*

"If you'll allow me, I want to inspect your leg closely," Salien said as she stopped in front of me.

"Please do." I held up the leg as I leaned back.

Once I gave permission, my new doctor went to work.

She has been much easier to work with than Phan. She always asks for permission first. At first, it did seem like she was afraid of me, but she's been unwilling to touch me without my consent. I wish she had been our doctor and not Phan to begin with.

Salien moved her fingers around, feeling my leg bones silently and gingerly. "Please let me know the moment you feel any pain." She placed her fingers around the location of the break and looked at me. I nodded my head. She squeezed her fingers, slowly increasing the strength she was using. There was never any pain, no matter how hard she squeezed. *Is she that weak?* She relented after spending some time trying to crush my bone. She stood up and pinched my leg.

"Ow, why did you do that?" I asked as I pulled my leg back to safety.

"I was making sure you weren't playing the tough girl act so you wouldn't have to wear your brace anymore. Nora told me about your little deal." Salien smiled and gave me a quick wink before she turned to Nora. "She's all healed up." She backed away from me and towards my desk, then pulled a small book out of her satchel and a pen with a bottle of ink.

As she prepared her writing instrument, I turned my attention to Nora. "Ha, told you so." I pointed to Nora in victory. "That means I'm owed a run to the south gate." I stood up to move towards the door.

"You were right."

You sound happy to be wrong.

Salien spoke as she wrote: "Three days to heal a cracked finger bone, four days to heal blisters from burns, two days for gashes on the arms and two weeks to heal a cleanly broken bone." Even though she whispered, my hearing was more than sharp enough to catch what she said. Salien looked and smiled at me. "It sounds like you've been itching to run for a while. Have fun, but please do me a favor and don't hurt yourself. While you're a sweet little girl and I've enjoyed our time together, you should try to avoid needing my services." She turned to Nora. "Thank you again for helping me learn my way around town. Most people don't show such compassion to someone who moves to a new town. Especially after that demon attack."

"Were you taking notes on how long it took me to heal?" I turned to the doctor. "Why?" *That's a little creepy.*

"Those with a recovery aptitude are of particular interest to me." She answered with her nose still pointed at her book. "By the way, if you're interested, your recovery is on par with an average adult who has the recovery aptitude."

Nora stepped forward. "How much do you know about the recovery aptitude?"

Salien looked up from her notes and regarded us. "It's a side project of mine to research it. I hope that by studying those who naturally heal from injuries that have proven fatal to others, I can use what I learn to save those previously thought beyond saving."

That's a noble sentiment, but I don't know what you hope to learn.

"So, what have you learned so far?" Nora asked with enthusiasm in her voice. *I would never have guessed she was curious about this.*

"Much less than I would have hoped for, honestly." Salien's voice clearly emphasized her lack of success. "Mainly that the speed those with a recovery aptitude heal increases the more they are injured and as they age."

"So you're saying that if I break another bone like that, it will take less than two weeks to heal?" I asked.

"That's correct." Salien looked at me curiously.

"But that doesn't give you permission to keep getting hurt like that!" Nora rounded on me quickly.

"You don't have to tell me twice." I shuddered at the memory of the pain I was in when I received my injuries. *I don't want to do that again.*

"Go for your run." Nora motioned to the door. "I want to talk with Salien for a little longer. Just come back right after."

"I will." I gave a thumbs-up as I took off for the front door.

I saw Anna heading for the front door too. She turned to me as I arrived at the door at the same time as her. "I take it this means you have a clean report of health?" Anna smiled at me.

"Yes. Now, I have some long overdue running to attend to." I almost took off running but stopped and turned to Anna. "But what are you going out for?"

"It's getting cold and I need some new socks," Anna said with a slight twinkle in her eye.

"I need some new clothes too, but I don't have any money." *I'm down to just three outfits left. Three outfits I'm growing out of.*

I watched as Anna's eyes grew slowly. "If you go with me, I can buy them for you."

Is that such a good idea? "I don't know. I need to find some place to work if I'm going to pay you back." I waved my hand, ready to dismiss the idea of shopping with her again.

"You don't have to pay me back." She grabbed my hand. "We never got you anything for your birthday, and I don't want to miss this chance to go shopping with you again." Her eyes were practically begging me to go with her. "Besides, we can celebrate your full recovery while we're out too."

"This run is my celebration. But I guess since you're offering..." *I might regret this later.* "After my run, I'll catch up with you," I relented.

"Do you know where the market is? How to get there from here?" She released my hand and stood in the doorway.

I raised my hand with one finger up. "Ah, no." I dropped my hand and let my ears and tail drop too.

She giggled. "I'll wait right here for you to get back and then we can go together." She stood to the side of the door. "Go on, the sooner you get back, the sooner we can go shopping!" She grabbed me and pushed me out the door.

With a sigh, I walked down to the street. There were a good number of people out and about. *I guess even though a demon carved a path of destruction through the city, life goes on. People need to eat, and to eat, you need food, and to get food, you need money. Everything always returns to money.* I turned to the south and plotted my course through the crowd, then took off. *I really missed the feeling of the wind through my fur. It's sad. I don't feel like I'm as fast as I was. I guess sitting still for two weeks will cause some regression. It's just like riding a bike. Oh, something smells really good. I'm almost at the gate. The smell's getting stronger. I must be getting closer.*

Suddenly, someone stepped in front of me, and I didn't have the time to maneuver away. I ran headlong into that person's legs, taking them down with my momentum. The two of us lay on the ground, groaning in discomfort. *Nothing feels hurt. Good, I don't have to explain how I hurt myself again.*

I looked at the person whose legs I was sitting on. A male elf wearing a gray gambeson tunic with long sleeves sat there, staring at me. His face looked like he had gone one too many rounds in a boxing match and hadn't healed quite right. A few scars were visible on his face, with two continuing down into his armor.

"Sorry." I scrambled off him. "I was distracted. I didn't mean to run into you."

The elven man collected himself once I got off his legs. "I know I've gotten old, but I never thought that a beastkin child could bring me down." His voice was mirthful. "Don't worry, kid, I've been through more than a few battles. You didn't do any lasting damage." He looked down at me. *He's tall. Taller than Nora, even.* "You surprised me though. Care to explain how a beastkin came to live here in Aquittemia?"

"It's a long story." I quickly took a couple of steps away from him.

"Alright, keep your secrets." He stood up straight. "You can go back to playing. Although, based on your breathing, you should take it a little easier."

He turned to leave. Only then did I notice the great sword on his back. I also took notice of my breathing. *I am breathing pretty hard. Maybe I'll take a small break once I get to the gate. It isn't far now.* I used a much more controlled pace to finish the first half of my run.

Everyone has done a good job of repairing most of the damage from the demon. Most of the buildings were either repaired or torn down the rest of the way to make room for a new structure. The road had been repaved, with people traveling on it like nothing had ever happened, and the crater that the demon had died in was nowhere to be found.

I, on the other hand, felt a tightness in my chest as I got closer to the gate. I could no longer run because of my nerves.

38

NEW EMPLOYMENT OPPORTUNITY

The smell that distracted me earlier had disappeared. But as I slowed to a walking pace as I got closer to the gate; I could sense a faint smell of something even better than before. *Usually this town stinks. What's up with these smells?* People were filing in from the gate while some were leaving, but two of them—one male and one female—caught my attention. They wore rugged leather and heavy cloaks and were working together to pull a cart, which was where the wonderful smell was coming from.

The man had short golden hair and green eyes. The woman he was with had wavy brown hair and the same green eyes. His skin was dark, while hers was lighter but tanned slightly as though she'd had constant exposure to the outdoors. The man had a square face that was stuck in a constant scowl. *It might have something to do with the limp in his left leg.* Her face was ordinary, with some wrinkles of age, but she stood a couple of inches taller than the man. Both looked tired and dirty.

I really want to know what's in that cart that smells so good. I stopped and stood still once I noticed that they were pulling their cart in my direction. Not wanting to bring more attention to myself than I already normally did, I stood to the side so I wouldn't stop them but could still see what was in the cart as they went by.

As they got closer, the smell got stronger, and I could feel my mouth watering. *There must be meat in there. It's making me hungry even though I just ate breakfast.* As they passed me, they both looked at me with apprehension.

"Is that a beastkin?" the man whispered to the woman.

"It is, and she's been watching us since the gate," the woman replied in an equally hushed tone.

"She's had a hungry look on her face for a while now. Do you think she'll try to steal from us?" The man reached into his cloak at his waist.

Oh, I didn't think about that. I guess I was a little too obvious. Time to go. I ran down a side street.

"She heard you!" the woman yelled at the man as she slapped him upside the head.

"Good, one less thief to worry about," I barely heard the man say as I ran down the road.

I should explain that I'm not a thief, just a little curious. I turned back to see them continuing down the road. Their cart's contents were covered, so I couldn't see what was in it. I ran ahead of them and stopped some distance away. I made sure they could see me clearly.

They stopped. "What do you want?" the man spat in a slightly nasal voice.

"To talk." I held up my hands defensively. "Something in your cart smells wonderful. I was wondering what's in there."

"None of your business." The man lowered his hand to his waist again.

Is that a weapon he's reaching for? "I'm not going to steal from you. I'm just curious. That's all." I started taking a few steps back.

"Stop it, you idiot." The woman grabbed his arm before he got his weapon. "Can't you see that she's just a child? Your paranoia will send you to an early grave." She sighed heavily. "You said you wanted to talk? What's your name?"

"Lucia. What are yours?" I still didn't relax.

"My name is Marigold, and this is my husband, Zane." She motioned to the man. "We're trappers by trade, but we're skilled at hunting as well."

"I'm an orphan." I smiled. "Are you looking to take on an apprentice?" *If I can learn how to hunt, I can feed myself for a fraction of the cost. It's a job I was literally born for. Why didn't I think of it before?*

The two humans stared at me with their mouths wide open. I waved my hand, noticing their eyes weren't following its movements. "Are you okay?"

Zane was the first to recover by shaking his head back and forth quickly. "Let me get this straight." He paused for a moment. "You don't want to steal from us, but you want us to teach you our trade?"

I nodded.

"Why?"

"I don't know what you know about beastkin, but I can only eat meat. As it turns out, meat is expensive." I took a few cautious steps towards the two. "I don't really want to spend fifteen years in the military."

"What makes you think you'll be worth teaching?" *Zane really doesn't like me, does he?* "Can you even keep up with us?" He grinned at me.

A sudden slap on the back of his head destroyed that smile. "Are you crazy? She's a beastkin. That little girl is likely faster than you with your failing leg." Marigold pointed to me. "She even heard us whispering in the middle of the street. That means her hearing is superior to yours. She can likely teach *you* how to hunt, you insufferable idiot."

He whirled on her. "I wouldn't have my leg messed up if you'd gotten out of the way of that boar, old woman."

She got up in his face. "If you had killed it in the first shot, that wouldn't have been necessary!"

I put my hands on my ears. "As much as I don't want to interrupt this lovers' quarrel, Marigold is right. My hearing is quite sensitive and your shouting is starting to hurt. Besides, can't this wait until you're not in the middle of the street?"

Zane just grunted. "She's right. We'll continue this later." Marigold begrudgingly nodded. "Where do you live? What was your name again?"

"Lucia, and I live at Nora's orphanage." I released my ears.

"We'll think about it. If you'll be there after we're done with our trading, we'll give you our decision." Marigold grabbed half of the cart. "Come on, we have to get this meat and fur delivered," she said to her husband.

Zane wordlessly grabbed ahold of the cart and moved forward.

I left the couple to head back home. I still ran since I'd had time to recover, just at a slower pace. Taking my time and not running into anyone again, I made it back home.

Anna was waiting at the front door for me. I told her to wait for me to use the bathroom first, then we could go. She bounced up and down with excitement.

As I entered the orphanage, I could hear someone talking with Nora in her room. I stalked to her door and concentrated on listening in on the conversation. *She's been doing a lot of things in private lately. What's this all about?*

"You were right, Nora," I heard a mirthful voice on the other side of the door say. *That voice sounds like someone I've heard before.* "Something is going on. Several people have gone missing."

"Is there any commonality between the missing?" *That's Nora's voice.*

"Yes. They've all been intellectuals that studied magic. I know your friend Phan was among those that they found dead. Unfortunately, there have been other cases like this across the kingdoms." *That voice has to belong to a man. But why does it sound so familiar?*

"I'm going to outlive almost everyone that I know, but seeing him killed so brutally hurts. You would think with as many deaths as I've seen, I'd handle this better. But I stopped being a knight to get away from all that death." *Is Nora not doing well emotionally? She's put up a brave face for us kids and we're none the wiser.*

"It's always worse when it's a close friend. But Midas was able to find out that it was a cult that worships the demon king. They think that if they bring him to our realm, he'll grant them some boon." *So, Midas is still alive and well. I wonder if I could meet him. Also, this guy talking to Nora knows where he is.*

"But do we know why they summoned a demon here? I'm afraid that they knew that most of the mercenary companies left to deal with the goblins and then struck. What was their goal?" Nora's voice shook slightly.

"There was a similar attack in the Osarin kingdom. Lemming learned that they were attempting to create something known as a 'blood anchor,'" the male voice said hesitantly.

"So there was an attack on the elven kingdom too. Then it might not be too much of a stretch to say that each of the kingdoms was attacked similarly," Nora mused.

"Possibly. Lemming could learn only a minimal amount about blood anchors. But the most important detail is that it requires a large number of people to die in a concentrated location. Here are her notes on the matter." *Were there enough people killed to create this blood anchor?*

"It looks like they were unsuccessful here. There weren't enough casualties. Don't tell Lucia about this. She's blaming herself for what happened. She doesn't need to know that she almost assisted in summoning the demon lord."

Too late for that. I really messed up.

"What are you doing?" Anna asked.

"Shh!" I turned to Anna and put a finger to my lips to get her to be quiet. The next thing I heard was the door opening behind me. *Well, I guess I've been caught red-handed.* I turned slowly and looked up at Nora. "This is exactly what it looks like."

Nora sighed and pinched the bridge of her nose. "How much did you hear?"

"A great deal about blood anchors, a bit about a demon lord and something about the end of the world. Nothing important." I gave an innocent smile.

"You and your sense of humor." Nora looked defeated.

"When did we talk about the end of the world?" the voice she was talking to asked from behind her. He walked past Nora and looked at me. *That's why he sounded familiar.* The man I'd run into earlier was now standing in front of me. "I think your long story just got much shorter, didn't it, kid?" He grinned as he looked at me.

"A bit." I wrapped my tail around my waist.

Nora and Anna both looked at us.

Anna spoke first. "You know him?"

"We had a small run-in with each other by the south gate." I tried to wave the minor detail away with my hand.

"I believe the words you're looking for are that you ran into me."

He sold me out. Rude!

Panic filled Nora's face. "Are you okay? Is anything hurt?" She kneeled and inspected me.

"I'm fine. I didn't hurt anything." I tried to push her away.

"I'm more at fault, anyway." The elf interrupted Nora's fretting. "I wasn't paying attention. I saw her at the last second, but I didn't expect her to be able to knock me down. Do you want to fill me in on how a beastkin came to live here?"

I crossed my arms and pouted. "Not really." *You aren't important enough to know about me.*

"Allen rescued her from orcs. She's like Midas." Nora stood up and rubbed a finger on her temple.

THE BIG BAD WOLF

Hey, isn't that supposed to be a secret? Anna's right there.

"Oh, really?" He looked down at me with a look that sent shivers down my spine. I backed up slowly.

"What is that supposed to mean? Who's Midas?" Anna looked around at everyone.

"That means you both were in the same mercenary company," I thought out loud, ignoring Anna.

Nora turned to the other elf and smiled. "That's correct. Yougnmor and I served in Excelsior together. It's been twenty-seven years since we last saw one another. It's been nice to see you again."

"It is, but I know you just lost a friend. I'm sorry to give you this news. I have felt The Call." His face was hard.

The Call? I looked at Anna and saw that she looked sad. I turned to Nora and found her crying. "What's The Call?" I asked.

Anna ran up to me and grabbed me. "I'll tell you later," she whispered in my ear. She hurried me to the bathroom. I used it quickly and quietly, feeling the tension from Anna.

As we were leaving the orphanage, I saw Nora crying into Yougnmor's chest. *Apparently, this call thing is a serious subject.*

On the way to the market, Anna let out a heavy sigh. "Elves are very different from humans. The average human lives for about forty-five to sixty-five years. Elves live for about one hundred fifty to two hundred fifty years. They also don't physically age beyond twenty. They mature at the same rate as humans, but their natural attunement to magic allows for this eternal youth."

Wow, elves can live a long time. "But what does this have to do with The Call?" I asked.

"Because elves don't physically age, it's hard to know how long they have yet to live. It's funny to see a two-hundred-year-old elf standing next to a thirty-year-old elf and not be able to tell which is older." Anna giggled. "The only way an elf will know they are going to die of old age is by The Call. One year before they pass, the elf will feel an indescribable feeling, and they instinctively know that their time in this world is almost up."

I stopped in my tracks, knowing how insensitive I was, but asked, "Aren't you an elf?" I looked at her ears. "Does that mean you'll feel it, too?"

"I'm a half-elf." Her face darkened. "My mother was an elf, and my father was human. Most of the time, when a child is born through such a coupling, it is a human or elven child. In rare cases, a half-elf is born."

I hugged her. "I'm sorry, I didn't know."

"It's okay. If no one tells you, how will you ever know?" Anna's voice sounded a little choked up. "Half-elves are infertile and will only live as long as a human. But I won't physically age like an elf. I also won't feel The Call, so I'll never have the time to make my peace. Because I'm a half-elf, my parents gave me to the orphanage. My mother couldn't stand the sight of me."

I grimaced. "Both you and Oscar had similar situations. Being abandoned by your parents. It's really sad." *How could parents just do that to their children?* "I'm beginning to think that having dead parents might be a good reason to be at an orphanage." A giggle sputtered out of Anna. "Is it normal for parents to send their children to an orphanage?"

"It's uncommon. But there's no law against it." Anna collected herself enough to continue our trip to the market. "The kingdom gladly takes in children from those who find themselves unable or unwilling to provide for them. The only stipulation is that if they want to have another child, they must adopt the child back. If not, then they must place the newborn child in the care of the government too."

Anna's somber mood pulled a one-eighty once we arrived at the market. I figured out that I'd had a bit of sensory overload the last time I went shopping with her. Forcing her to allow me to take frequent breaks gave me the chance to calm down, and we got me a few more clothes to wear. We saved a little money on tailoring because we could wait a few days. All the clothes Anna bought for me were going to be extra-large on me now so that I had room to grow into them, though Anna didn't like that because she said baggy clothes made me look dull. She, of course, got the socks that she needed.

We set off for home after we made our purchases. *I'll have to have Anna tell me where to pick up all my clothes in two days.* Anna was in such a cheerful mood that she skipped home.

"Why are you so grumpy? We were having so much fun shopping." Anna skipped circles around me.

"You were having fun. I was trying very hard to ignore the hundreds of conversations going on around me." I was keeping up with her skipping even though I hunched my shoulders and stomped through the street. "Do you know what it's like to be surrounded by people all shouting like that?"

"I know your ears are sensitive. Is that why you needed all those breaks?" She transitioned to walking normally next to me.

"Yes. Also because everything stinks." *I nearly dry-heaved at some of the smells.* "And don't get me started with that tanner we walked by."

"I know it stinks." She had a thoughtful look on her face. "I can't imagine what it would be like for you."

"Yet you still walked me by it," I growled at her.

"But the shop across the way makes the best, most comfortable socks around." She hugged her prize from the trip. Then a look of sadness tried to invade her face. "Oh, sorry, you don't know what it's like."

"Nope, I have all-natural socks and leg warmers. I'm okay with that." I smirked. "Besides, what I save from not buying socks and shoes is spent on tailoring my skirts to accommodate my fifth appendage. Why does it cost so much? They aren't even doing that much."

"They're taking time away from making new clothes that they can sell to adjust some that are already done." Anna's tone made it sound like she was stating the obvious. "Besides, are you going to do it?" She poked a finger at my chest.

13 PITCH BLACK CATS

"No." I lowered my head in defeat. "I would likely tear it apart first."

"And that's why I didn't let you touch the silks." She laughed, and I growled.

We arrived back home just before lunch. Nora arrived at the table last. She looked like she had been crying, but had washed her face up to make it less obvious. *It's a difficult time for her. I guess we should think of something to cheer her up.* I had some wonderful lamb while everyone else had extra sides with their steaks.

After lunch, Nora called out to me from the front door. When I arrived at the front door, Zane and Marigold greeted me.

I had to explain myself to Nora and our little meeting in the street this morning. The couple had agreed that they would take me on as an apprentice, but it would have to wait until the water season. Most of the animals they trapped hibernated during the ice season. Nora and I negotiated my pay to be three coins a day with the bonus that if the traps were good, I could take one small animal home to eat. *They don't make nearly as much money as Tobey. Besides, I'm more interested in the free meat.*

They talked to Nora about what I was going to learn and that they wouldn't teach me to hunt until I was ten years old. I would learn basic outdoor survival skills and how to field dress what I trapped and killed. Zane still hadn't warmed up to me, but he was courteous to Nora. I made sure that if at any time I wanted to cancel the apprenticeship, I could. That, in turn, gave them the power to end it as well, so long as they had a good reason. After we all agreed on the details, the couple said their goodbyes and returned home. Nora had me go practice my handwriting.

EPILOGUE: GLOWBUGS

I lay down on the grass in the middle of the courtyard and stared up at the clear sky. Three moons hung in the air. The yellow moon was full as usual, while the red and green moons were practically gone. That meant tomorrow the wind season would end and the ice season would begin. Despite the changing temperatures, I never felt even a chill. *My fur coat is really doing its job.*

Dozens of flickering lights fluttered above me. Each light danced around the others as they pulsed at regular intervals.

The sound of a door opening and closing disrupted my beautiful silence. Footsteps approached me. Whoever was walking towards me wasn't trying to be stealthy, but they weren't rushing either. When the footsteps stopped, I heard the person lay down on the ground next to me.

"Enjoying the show?" Nora whispered.

"Yeah." I turned my head to look at Nora. She was watching the light show. "Are you going to yell at me for staying out after dark again?"

"No." She shook her head. "It isn't every day the glowbugs come out this time of year. It seems we're in for a mild ice season."

EPILOGUE: GLOWBUGS

"Don't say that." I rubbed the thick fur on my arm. "I'm not prepared for mild. All this fur is going to go to waste, if that's the case."

Nora giggled. "Only you would complain about a mild ice season." She rolled onto her side to look at me. "So, other than the glowbugs, what are you doing out here?"

"Where I'm from, they're called fireflies." I sighed. "It's quiet. During the day, there's so much going on. Too many people are out talking and making too much noise for me to relax properly. There's something that's just so comfortable about sitting outside and looking at the sky." I rolled over to watch a glowbug land on a blade of grass in front of me.

Nora rolled over onto her back. "You said you were human, but, to me, you've been acting nothing like any human I have ever known."

"That's because I'm not a human. I don't know how, but the more I live in this body, the more it feels like it's mine. At first, I kept thinking that I was both a human and an animal." The glowbug flew upwards and I rolled back over to follow it.

"What about now?"

"I'm neither. I am a beastkin. What's a beastkin? I don't know. But you said it's up to me to decide who I am. Sometimes I know I act more like an animal than a person, but I will eventually learn to control everything about myself. There's no sense in trying to fit myself into multiple categories when instead I can be in a category of my own."

"That's incredibly mature of you to say. It's hard to remember that you aren't just the child you appear to be, even though there are times you act like a five-year-old." Nora failed to suppress her giggle.

"Ha, ha." I rolled my eyes before I released a heavy sigh. "You are right, though. Sometimes I feel like I'm not alone in here. It's like the old Lucia is still there. You know what I mean?"

"No, I don't. That's..." Nora paused. "Didn't you say that you could feel your instincts sometimes?"

EPILOGUE: GLOWBUGS

"That's what I thought at first, but now? I'm not so sure. It feels like there's more to them. They helped me when I fought my kidnappers. It feels like there's an intelligence to my instincts that you wouldn't expect." *Oh, that reminds me.* "Did you ever catch Decklin?"

"No," Nora grumbled. "Apparently, a guard at the north gate saw someone fitting his description leaving with a group of people the day the demon attacked. Finding him will be impossible now."

"He had to have planned this all along. He knew they were going to summon a demon and hired two idiots who he knew wouldn't live after they finished their job." I flexed my claws as I raked them into the ground to help me calm down. I closed my eyes and visualized a waterfall. Once the waterfall was flowing, I imagined I was sitting near the base on a patch of ground.

"You're right." Nora sighed. "But finding everyone who is associated with Decklin and the people who wanted to summon a demon to create a blood anchor is beyond me. That's why I gave all the information to someone much more qualified. My job is to take care of you kids and make sure you all are safe." Nora stood up, towering over me. "And, young lady, there is a curfew in effect. I know we're in the courtyard and you can hear everything around you, but it is past your bedtime."

I rolled my eyes before I opened them. "You know I don't need as much sleep."

"It doesn't matter. You need to be inside after dark, there's a curfew." Nora extended a hand to me. "You can run around town all you want while the sun is up. And if you can't sleep, there's a mountain of books you still haven't read."

I grabbed Nora's hand, being careful with my claws so I didn't scratch her. "They're so boring."

"There's the five-year-old you." Nora's smile was too infectious for me to hold back my toothy grin. She pulled me to my feet and wrapped an arm around my shoulder. "We need to think about something you can do while it's dark. How about we get you introduced to the training room? You can work out all that extra energy swinging a sword or clawing the dummies."

"That sounds like it could be fun." *Almost as much fun as going out and learning to hunt with Marigold and Zane.*